Cover photograph by David Vine
Cover design by Karen Salsgiver

Ceramics on the cover include works by
(in alphabetical order):
Deborah Ackerman, Sheila Amos, Gene Buckley,
Ron Gilbert, Andrea Henry, Walter Hyleck,
Jay Lindsay, Warren MacKenzie, Polly Myhrum,
Don Reitz, Kyllikki Salmenhaara, and Toshiko Takaezu.

a potter's
handbook
Ceramics

Holt, Rinehart and Winston
New York   Chicago   San Francisco   Atlanta
Dallas   Montreal   Toronto   London   Sydney

Glenn C.
Nelson

a potter's
handbook
fourth edition

Ceramics

Editor   Rita Gilbert
Picture Editor   Joan Curtis
Manuscript Editor   Polly Myhrum
Project Assistants   Susan Adams, Barbara Curialle
Production Manager   Robert de Villeneuve
Manufacturing Manager   Thomas Oborski
Text Designer   Marlene Rothkin Vine
Layout Designer   Karen Salsgiver

Library of Congress Cataloging in Publication Data

Nelson, Glenn C.
   Ceramics.

   Bibliography: p. 326
   Includes index.
   1. Ceramics.   I. Title.
TP807.N363   1978   738.1'4   77-24224
ISBN: 0-03-022725-9 College Softcover Edition
ISBN: 0-03-042826-2 General Book Hardcover Edition

Composition and camera work by York Graphic Services, Inc., Pennsylvania
Color separations by Triggs Color Printing Corporation, New York
Cover separation and printing by Lehigh Press Lithographers, New Jersey
Printing and binding by R.R. Donnelley & Sons Company
8 9 0 1 2   3 9   9 8 7 6 5 4 3 2 1

iv

Preface

The contemporary ceramist occupies a unique position in today's world. An unbroken line of tradition joins the 20th-century potter with counterparts of perhaps 12,000 years ago. And, while modern technology has done much to increase both convenience and versatility, many of the same simple forming and decorating methods that were practiced by primitive artisans are still followed today.

There is little doubt that pottery developed independently in many sections of the world. The cordlike markings found on some early pots have led to the belief that baskets lined with clay initially were used to hold small seeds. The accidental burning of a basket, and thus the firing of the clay lining, resulted in the first pot. It is fortunate that fired clay becomes nearly indestructible. Only pottery remains, stone tools, and occasional artifacts of bone tell the story of ancient peoples. Moreover, primitive burial sites reveal not only the ingenuity of early potters but their artistry as well. From the very beginning craftsmen took an interest in decoration and design, even though their products might have urgently functional purposes. This concern strikes a responsive note in today's artist.

In this fourth edition of *Ceramics* I have attempted to show the continuity of the craft from its origins to the present. Rather than isolating historical works in a special section, I have included with the explanation of each forming and decorating technique examples of the best work from different eras. The ancestors of today's low-fire lusters can be found in 15th- and 16th-century majolica ware, the precursors of contemporary sculptures in figural ceramics of prehistoric times.

Ceramics is intended as a basic how-to manual for the beginning and intermediate potter, as well as a reference source for the more sophisticated craftsman. It begins with a discussion of clays—their origin, composition, and types. Following this, two full chapters cover, respectively, handbuilding and wheel techniques, with step-by-step photos to illustrate each process.

A survey chapter of decorating and glazing techniques shows the complete range of possibilities, from simple dip-glazing to complex figural work combining many methods. The next chapter introduces concepts of design in both functional and decorative wares, with a final section on the unique needs of architectural ceramics. After this come two detailed chapters on glaze formulation and glaze calculations and chemicals. Because the ultimate firing is so crucial to any ceramic work, I have devoted an extensive chapter to kilns, kiln materials, kiln construction, and the various processes for oxidation, reduction, salt-glaze, and raku firings.

The book concludes with an analysis of the role played by the professional potter—whether in the classroom, the studio, or industry—and a chapter on studio equipment, from basic tools through wheels, kilns, clay mixers, and specialized heavy machinery. There are also a bibliography and glossary of ceramic terms.

Readers familiar with previous editions of *Ceramics* will find a great many changes in this version. Recognizing that a pot reproduced in black and white remains a gray pot, we have included nearly three times as many full-color plates as in the last edition. Moreover, these color images are printed directly on the page with the text. Thus, one can read about a particular technique and see a color reproduction of its expression at the same time. In all, there are 460 black-and-white photographs and drawings, plus more than 60 color plates.

The art and technology of ceramics have changed enormously in the past decade. To keep pace with these developments, I have provided much new material on low-fire glazes, lusters, decals, handbuilding methods, sculpture, raku, simple firing arrangements, and a number of specialized techniques that potters may find interesting for experimentation. To support this discussion, the appendix lists new glaze and body recipes. All methods are illustrated with examples of the best work by contemporary potters from around the world.

Ceramics *is* an ancient craft. Simple coiling is done in the 1970s much the way it was thousands of years ago. But at the same time, many of the techniques now in common use would nonplus the potter of even a century past. I would hope that this edition of *Ceramics* will demonstrate that this age-old medium remains one of the most vital and challenging for the artist.

Acknowledgments

Illustrations of contemporary ceramics provide the focal point of this new edition. Many potters have kindly allowed their work to be reproduced, and I am indebted to them for their very real contributions.

Securing photographs from abroad presents considerable problems. I am especially appreciative of the assistance given by Gordon Barnes of the Canadian Guild of Potters, Sandra Dunn of the Ontario Crafts Council, Janet Mansfield of the Potters' Society of Australia, Hildegard Storr-Britz from the Rhineland pottery town of Höhr-Grenzhausen, J. W. N. van Achterberg of the Dutch Ceramic Society, Stig Lindberg of the Gustavsberg Studios in Sweden, Ebbe Simonsen of Bing and Grøndahl, Giovanni Biffi of the State School of Ceramics in Faenza, and the potters Jan de Rooden of Holland, Bill Read of England, Nino Caruso of Italy, and Hiroaki Morino of Japan. The museums, both in the United States and abroad, whose collections illustrate the text have been very cooperative in providing photographs and the permission to reproduce them.

The challenges of the professional potter are of interest to many students. Most helpful in this regard were the illustrations provided by Peter

A. Slusarski, as well as the production photographs from Bennington Potters, Pacific Stoneware, Inc., Syracuse China, Ceramica Revelli, Bing and Grøndahl of Copenhagen, and Mikasa of Japan. Manufacturers of ceramic equipment have likewise been generous in providing material.

I must express my particular thanks to Neil Moss of El Camino College, Miron E. Webster of Northern Arizona University, and Elizabeth Nields of Hofstra University—potters and teachers—who read the entire manuscript for this edition and offered much constructive criticism.

I have been indeed fortunate in that the art staff at Holt, Rinehart and Winston responsible for this edition includes several people with special knowledge of ceramics. My editor, Rita Gilbert, oversaw the entire project and coordinated the efforts of all the others. Much of the chore of securing photographs and permissions was eased by picture editor Joan Curtis. Polly Myhrum—a rare combination of talented potter and trained editor—brought order to the seeming chaos that at first characterizes any book. Susan Adams and Barbara Curialle kept track of the thousand minute production details. The elegant, fresh design is the work of Marlene Rothkin Vine, and Karen Salsgiver created a page-by-page layout marked by style and editorial judgment. My thanks must also go to Robert de Villeneuve and Thomas Oborski, who masterminded the exciting four-color production.

My final, and most important, debt of gratitude is owed to my wife Edith, who has seen me through three increasingly complicated editions of *Ceramics*. As she has shared the work, the worry, the endless correspondence, the constant corrections so must she also share my pleasure in the publication of this book.

Garrison, New York   G. C. N.
January 1978

Contents

a potter's
handbook
Ceramics

1
Clay
and Clay
Bodies

Clay is the very common but unique material that makes ceramics possible. It should not be confused with soil—a combination of clay, sand, humus (partially decayed vegetable matter), and various other minerals. Compared with other materials in the earth, soil forms an extremely thin outermost layer—varying from several inches to a foot thick. There are, of course, large areas without soil, such as most desert and mountain regions. Between the soil proper and the rocky core of the earth rests a thicker layer of subsoil composed of clay mixed with sand and gravelly mineral deposits. Within this layer large beds of clay are found. In order to better explain the variety and nature of clay types, a brief description of the formation of this layer of subsoil is necessary.

Formation of Clay

As the earth cooled very slowly from its fiery origins, a rocky outer crust hardened, while internal pressures and volcanic eruptions pushed up mountainous areas. Gradually, water vapor formed, and an atmosphere was created. The resulting rains and winds caused erosion, while extremes of heat and freezing temperatures led to expansion and contraction of the earth's surface. These combined forces fractured and crumbled the exposed rock. The initial composition of this rock varied greatly from place to place, so that the process of erosion had different effects and occurred in different manners over the surface of the earth. For the formation of clay beds, the two most important forces were the melting and movement of the ice cover during the glacial ages and the organic acids released by the decay of vegetation.

Clay derives from the disintegration of granite and other feldspathic rocks which, as they decompose, deposit alumina and silica particles. The most valuable clays for the potter consist mainly of the mineral kaolinite, which has an ideal formula of $Al_2O_3 \cdot 2SiO_2 \cdot 2H_2O$. Kaolinite particles are

1. Mary Frank, U.S.A.
Untitled (head in two parts).
1975. Stoneware,
11 × 20 × 15″ (27.5 × 50 × 37.5 cm).
Courtesy Zabriskie Gallery, New York.

shaped like very thin plates less than 2 microns in size (1 micron is 0.001 millimeter or 0.00004 inch). Fine grains of sand are huge in comparison—0.02 inch in diameter. Unlike the granular structure of sand, kaolinite particles are flat and cling together like a deck of wet playing cards. These particles slide and support one another in both wet and dry states, giving clay its most valuable quality, *plasticity*. The sculpture seen in Figure 1 illustrates how a very thin slab of clay can maintain its shape when soft and be modeled and pressed into a strong, durable form when fired.

Most clay found in the earth does not contain sufficient amounts of kaolinite to make it plastic, and nearly all clay has some impurities. These impurities and variations of the basic formula account for the different characteristics of the numerous clay types.

Clay Types

As they are mined, clays can be classified as either residual or sedimentary. *Residual* clays have remained more or less at the site of the decomposed rock. They are less plastic than sedimentary clays, and because they have been subject to fewer erosive forces, their particle size is much larger. *Sedimentary* clays are those that, by the action of wind or running water, have been transported far from the site of the parent rock. This action had considerable effect on the mixture and breakdown of the minerals, and therefore the particles are very fine and the clay more plastic.

Kaolin

Kaolin is a very pure form of clay that is white in color and *vitrifies* (becomes nonporous and glasslike) only at very high temperatures. For these reasons, kaolin is seldom used alone but makes an important ingredient in all high-fire whiteware and porcelain bodies. Kaolin also provides a source of alumina and silica for glazes.

The wide variety of kaolin types available illustrates the difficulty of classifying clays. In the United States the major commercial deposits are in the Southeast. North Carolina produces a residual-type kaolin with many coarse rock particles, while the deposits in South Carolina and Georgia are of the sedimentary type. Florida deposits are even more plastic and are often termed ball kaolin or EPK (Edgar Plastic Kaolin from Edgar, Florida). No kaolin is truly plastic in comparison with ball clay.

English kaolin beds are among the largest in the world. They are mined by hydraulic methods and employ a complicated system of separating out the finer particles in huge settling tanks. Clays from the various mines are blended to produce kaolin of several consistent types. The fineness of particle size makes these clays suitable for casting or throwing bodies. The type called *grolleg* is the best kaolin addition for a plastic porcelain throwing body.

Ball Clay

Ball clay is chemically similar to kaolin after firing. In its unfired state, however, the color ranges from a light tan to a dark gray because of the organic material present. Although weathered from a granite type of rock much like that which produced kaolin, the ball clay particles were deposited in swampy areas. Organic acids and gaseous compounds released from decaying vegetation served to break down the clay particles into even finer sizes than those of the sedimentary kaolins.

2. Electron micrograph of Georgia kaolinite (magnified 52,000 times) showing platelike particles. Courtesy Kenneth M. Towe, Smithsonian Institution, Washington, D.C.

3. John Mason, U.S.A.
Firebrick Sculpture.
1974. Firebricks,
$7 \times 16 \times 16'$ (2.1 × 4.8 × 4.8 m).

Ball clay imparts increased plasticity and dry strength when used as a body component. If a clay body contains 10 to 20 percent ball clay, it has greatly improved throwing qualities. Like kaolin, ball clay matures at a high temperature and can serve as a source of alumina and silica in glaze recipes, as well as a binding agent. However, when stored for long periods of time, such glazes tend to form gas that can lead to glaze defects. In this event the glaze can be dried out and reused, or a few drops of formaldehyde can be added to discourage fermentation.

Stoneware Clays

Stoneware clays are of particular interest to the potter because they are generally very plastic and fire in the middle range of temperatures, from about cone 5 to cone 10.* Depending upon the atmospheric conditions of the firing, the color will vary from buff to gray. In the United States stoneware clays occur in scattered deposits from New York and New Jersey westward to Illinois and Missouri, as well as on the Pacific coast. The clays differ in composition. Compared with kaolin they contain many more impurities, such as calcium, feldspar, and iron—all of which lower the maturing temperature and impart color to the clay.

Fireclay

Fireclay is a high-firing clay commonly used for insulating brick, hard firebrick, and kiln furniture (the shelves and posts that hold pots inside a kiln). Its physical characteristics vary. Some fireclays have a fine plastic quality, while others are coarse and granular and more suitable for hand-building than for throwing. Fireclays generally contain some iron but seldom have calcium or feldspar. The more plastic varieties, like some

*See temperature chart in the Appendix giving cone equivalents in degrees Fahrenheit and Centigrade. Cones indicated in text refer to the Orton series. Note that Seger cones have a slightly different range.

stoneware clays, often occur close to coal veins. They can be high in either flint or alumina and therefore have special industrial uses. Fireclays of one type or another are found throughout the United States, absent only from a few mountainous regions and the southeast and northeast coasts. Its availability and plasticity make fireclay a component of stoneware bodies.

Earthenware Clays

Earthenware clays comprise a group of low-firing clays that mature at comparatively low temperatures ranging from cone 08 to cone 02. They contain a relatively high percentage of iron oxide, which serves as a flux (a substance that lowers the maturing temperature of the clay), so that when fired they are rather fragile and quite porous. The iron also gives fired earthenware its deep red-brown color. Unlike stoneware bodies, which are almost completely vitreous, the usual earthenware body, after firing, has a porosity between 5 and 15 percent. Because of the various fluxes it contains, earthenware cannot be made vitreous, for it deforms and often blisters at temperatures above 2100°F (1150°C). All of these factors limit its commercial use to such things as building bricks, flowerpots, and tiles. Many potters, however, have done considerable work in earthenware. Some find its red-brown color attractive; others use it as a base for bright, low-fire glazes.

Earthenware clays of one type or another can be found in every part of the United States, although commercial deposits are abundant in the lower Great Lakes region. Many such clays, available commercially, are of a shale type. Shale deposits are clays laid down in prehistoric lake beds. Time, chemical reactions, and pressure from overlying material have served to cement these clay particles into shale a hard, stratified material halfway between a clay and a rock. Shale clays are mined and ground into a powdered form similar to ordinary clay. The small lumps that remain can be troublesome if not screened out, for, like plaster, they will absorb moisture, expand, and rupture after firing.

Some earthenware clays are of glacial origin and therefore vary greatly in composition. They frequently contain soluble sulfates that are drawn to the surface during drying. When the clay is fired, a whitish film appears on the surface. This defect can be eliminated by an addition to the clay body of 2 percent barium carbonate.

Slip Clay

Slip clays naturally contain sufficient fluxes to function as glazes without further addition. Although white and even blue slip clays exist, the most common are tan, brick red, or brown-black. Most slip clays fire in a middle range from cone 6 to cone 10. The best-known commercial slip clay is Albany, mined in pits near Albany, New York. There are many small deposits of glacial clays scattered throughout the northern United States that will make satisfactory slip glazes with little or no addition. Slip glazes are easy to apply; they usually have a long firing range and few surface defects. (By contrast, casting slips are special bodies compounded for such production methods as jiggering and casting; see Chap. 9, pp. 271–277.)

Bentonite

Bentonite is an unusual clay. In small amounts it functions as a plasticizer. Deposits are found in most of the western mountain states, the Dakotas, and in several Gulf states. It has the finest particle size of any clay known.

4. Ritual bull and attendants, from Menika, Cyprus. 700–500 B.C. Terra cotta. Cyprus Museum, Nicosia.

Bentonite was formed in prehistoric ages from the airborne dust of volcanic eruptions. Compared to kaolin, it is slightly higher in silica and lower in alumina, with a small amount of iron. A nonclay glaze may include up to 3 percent bentonite for an adhesive without noticeably changing the glaze. When used in nonplastic (short) clays, one part bentonite is equal to five parts ball clay. The body should be mixed dry, since bentonite becomes quite gummy when mixed alone with water.

Clay Bodies

An earthenware, stoneware, or porcelain body that is completely satisfactory for the potter seldom occurs in nature. The clay may not be plastic enough, may have an unattractive color, or may not fire at the desired temperature. Even clays from the same bed will vary slightly in chemical and physical qualities. Thus, it is usually necessary to mix clays in order to achieve a workable body.

In making up a clay body, you will generally begin with a clay that is available at a reasonable price and has no major faults, such as an excessive amount of sand or grit. No clay should be considered unless it is moderately plastic. The plasticity can be improved by additions of ball clay or bentonite. In rare cases, a clay may be so fine that it will not dry easily without cracking. In this event, you can add a less plastic clay—silica sand or a fine *grog* (crushed, fired clay)—to *open up* the clay body and make it more porous so it will dry uniformly. This treatment is often necessary to make an extremely fine or *fat* clay throw and stand up better. Some potters add coarse grog to a clay body for the rough, textured effects it creates.

Occasionally, a clay will lack sufficient fluxes to fire hard enough at the desired temperature. When this occurs, inexpensive materials containing fluxes—such as feldspar, talc, dolomite, nepheline syenite, or bone ash—are

5. Colima-style figures, from western Mexico. 200 B.C.–A.D. 500. Terra cotta, height of human figure 10½″ (26.3 cm). American Museum of Natural History, New York.

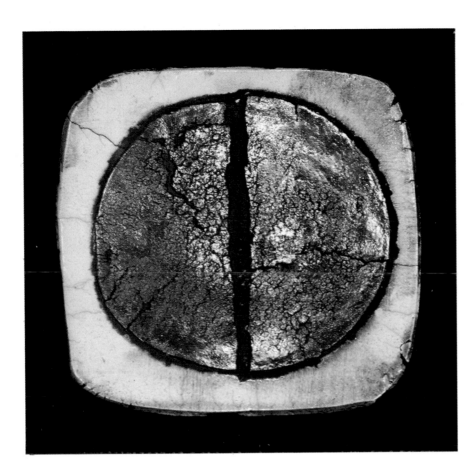

usually added. If the color is not important, you can use iron oxide. In some cases a small amount of lower-firing clay can be added, which has the advantage of not cutting down on plasticity. If, on the other hand, there is too large a proportion of fluxes and the clay body deforms at a relatively low temperature, you must either begin again with a different clay or add clays that are higher in alumina or in silica and alumina. Either a Florida kaolin or a plastic fireclay of high maturity will work for this purpose.

Raku Bodies The composition of raku bodies must be quite different from those for normal firing, because of the raku firing process. The ware is placed in a hot kiln, and, when the glaze becomes molten, it is removed and cooled very quickly. In order to withstand these radical temperature changes, the ware must be thick-walled. The body is generally a stoneware clay containing at least 20 percent grog. Raku pottery remains rather porous after the final glaze firing. (See Chap. 8, pp. 239–241, for firing techniques, and the Appendix for a raku body formula.)

Earthenware Bodies Earthenware bodies are characterized by their deep reddish brown color (caused by the high iron content) and a high porosity that results from their lower firing range. These qualities make earthenware popular with sculptors and handbuilders. White earthenware clay rarely occurs in nature. Low-fire white bodies contain large amounts of talc along with kaolin and feldspar to reduce their firing temperatures to between cone 08 and cone 04. The bright and even color of these bodies provides a good base for high-contrast, low-fire decorative effects, such as decals, lusters, and bright, primary colors. Because of the rising cost of fuel, many ceramists are also adapting traditional stoneware and porcelain techniques to low-fire bodies.

Stoneware Bodies Chemically, there is little difference between a stoneware and a porcelain body, except for the presence of small quantities of iron and other impurities that color the stoneware and reduce its firing range to between cone 6 and cone 10. However, stoneware bodies are generally much more plastic than porcelain and are better suited for throwing and hand-building techniques. Many hand potters are attracted to stoneware for the range of color that can be obtained in a gas kiln under reducing conditions, from a very light buff to tan to a dark brown. Most stoneware bodies contain grog to make the clay stronger and more versatile in its plastic state.

China Bodies Bone china resembles porcelain, except that bone ash has been added to the body as a flux to increase translucency and to reduce the temperature needed for maturity to about cone 6. Like porcelain, bone china is very hard, white, and translucent when thin. Its greatest faults are a tendency to warp in firing and the lack of sufficient plasticity for throwing.

left: 8. Tea jar, Shigaraki ware, from Japan. 19th century. Stoneware, height 3½″ (8.8 cm). Metropolitan Museum of Art, New York (Macy Collection, gift of Mrs. V. Everit Macy, 1923). Coarse particles in the clay body create a rough texture.

below: 9. Tea caddy, from Meissen, Germany. 1713–20. Hard-paste porcelain, height 4¾″ (12 cm). Metropolitan Museum of Art, New York (gift of Mrs. George B. McClellan, 1942).

10. Jan de Rooden, Holland.
Pressure. 1971. Stoneware, width 20″ (50 cm).
Collection J. W. M. van Achterbergh.
The insert of soft, folded clay
contrasts with the stony quality
of the slab and creates a sense of
two heavy masses squeezing together.

The term chinaware is used rather loosely to designate a white body usually fired between cones 4 and 8. Some types, such as restaurant china, are very hard and durable. However, they should not be confused with the even harder and more translucent porcelain bodies fired at cone 10 to cone 16.

Porcelain Bodies The highest-firing category of ceramic wares, porcelain bodies are characterized by a smooth texture, uniform white color, and the ability to accept fine detail. They are relatively nonplastic and fire, between cone 8 and cone 12, to an extremely hard, vitreous ware. These qualities make porcelain ideal for commercial products shaped mechanically by casting or jiggering (see Chap. 9). However, many hand potters have become interested in exploiting these same effects, and therefore porcelain bodies with greater plasticity and slightly lower maturing temperatures (cone 6 to cone 8) have been developed. Porcelain bodies are compounded principally from kaolin, feldspar, and flint. For increased plasticity, some ball clay is generally added, resulting in a higher shrinkage rate. In a throwing body, the ball clay may be as much as 25 percent of the body. (See Appendix for suggested clay bodies.)

11. Peter Voulkos, U.S.A.
Monumental stoneware bottle.
A thin colemanite wash
reveals the rich texture and color
of the stoneware clay.

Special Clay Bodies

Sculpture Bodies Problems often arise in constructing large, thick-walled sculptural forms in clay. The most serious of these are a tendency for vertical walls or horizontal spans to sag and the danger that thick areas will crack during drying. The addition of grog to a sculpture body will help the clay to "stand up" or support itself without collapsing. If grog is wedged into the clay in amounts of 20 to 30 percent of the body, it will reduce shrinkage strains placed upon thicknesses of clay. In drying, the clay pulls away slightly from the grog. This opens air channels, causes a more even exposure of the clay to the air, and lessens the danger of cracks occurring.

Another possible addition to the sculpture body is fiberglass, which is actually glass in fibrous form. Shredded fiberglass can be wedged into the clay to increase its plastic strength. When slabs of unusual stability are needed, some potters sandwich a mesh of fiberglass between layers of clay. Since fiberglass consists mainly of silica, it melts into the body during firing.

Ovenware and Flameware Bodies Most earthenware and stoneware can be heated to 400°F in an oven, provided the walls and bottom are of uniform thickness and that the glaze, if any, coats both inside and outside. This helps the pot to heat and cool evenly. Another general precaution with ovenware is to place it in a cool oven and let it heat up slowly; once it is hot, never expose it to rapid cooling.

A ceramic body can be formulated to control the effects of quartz inversion (see p. 13) and make it more resistant to heat shock. The body should be stoneware or fireclay and should first be tested to determine its chemical composition. Depending upon the alumina-silica ratio and fluxes present, a 15 to 20 percent addition of spodumene, wollastonite, or petalite will reduce the possibility of cracking. (Because of the difficulty in obtaining petalite, 3 parts spodumene and 1 part feldspar can be substituted for 4 parts petalite.) A combination of pyrophyllite and talc to replace part of the feldspar in the body will also cut down on thermal expansion.

A direct flameware body is similar to ovenware except that the petalite may comprise as much as 50 percent of the body, the balance being ball clay, stoneware, or fireclay. A small amount of feldspar will combine with any free silica that may remain. Firing temperatures should be to cone 10 or above, but the body should retain a porosity of 3 to 4 percent.

Colorants Depending upon firing conditions, most earthenware and stoneware bodies range in color from a light tan through buff and orange-red to a deep reddish brown. The warm, earthy tones result from the different amounts of iron oxide present in the clay. These hues can be made darker by adding either red or black iron oxide and/or manganese dioxide. If the colorants are finely ground, they will create an even tone; colorants with a coarse particle size yield a more speckled effect. Always make tests when adding colorants, for too much iron oxide will lower the melting temperature of the body, and a large quantity of red iron will cause the clay to stain whatever comes in contact with it during the forming process.

Pure white bodies are characteristic of porcelain in the high firing range and white earthenware in the lower temperatures. It is possible to add oxides

below: 12. Fragments of fiberglass cut and placed on clay prior to wedging. This increases the clay's strength.

right: 13. Stig Lindberg, Sweden. Coffee pot, saucepan, skillets, casserole, and teapot. Flameproof ovenware. Designed for Aktiebologet Gustavsberg Fabriker, Sweden.

to these bodies to produce green, blue, yellow, or even lavender clays. The oxides should be added to clay in its dry state, and the mixture sieved before adding water. See Chapter 4, pp. 104–108, for decorating techniques with colored clays and the Appendix for colorants and their properties.

Tests for Clay Bodies

Before a new clay or clay body is purchased or used, a few simple tests should be made to determine its various characteristics.

Plasticity

Plasticity is essential to any clay body. A standard, simple test for plasticity is to loop a pencil-size roll of clay around your finger. If the coil cracks excessively, the clay is probably not very plastic. The ultimate test, however, is to work with the clay to determine if it throws without sagging and joins without cracking. In comparing bodies, make sure that all samples have been aged for equal lengths of time. Three weeks in a plastic state is usually adequate for a clay to improve appreciably. In this time the finest particles become thoroughly moist, making possible the slight chemical breakdown caused by the organic matter contained in all clays. (According to legend, ancient Chinese potters prepared huge quantities of clay that were stored in pits and covered with moist straw. Each generation of potters used the clay prepared by the previous one.)

Wedging, a process by which the clay is kneaded by hand to remove air pockets, has considerable effect in increasing plasticity. In a coarse clay, the realignment of particles by wedging can also prove beneficial (see p. 16).

Water of plasticity refers to the amount of water need to bring a dry, powdered clay into a plastic state. The finer the particle size, the more plastic a clay will be and the more water it will absorb.

Porosity

The porosity of a fired clay body is directly related to the hardness and vitrification of the clay. To make a porosity test, weigh an unglazed fired clay sample. After an overnight soak in water, wipe the sample clean of surface water, and weigh it a second time. The percentage gain in weight will be the porosity of the clay body.

Most bodies used by the hand potter can be fired with a variation of at least 50°F (10°C) from the optimum firing temperature without proving unsuitable. As a general rule, fired clay bodies fall within the following porosity ranges: earthenware, 4 to 10 percent; stoneware, 1 to 6 percent; porcelain, 0 to 3 percent. A higher firing will reduce the porosity, but normally a specific firing temperature will have been chosen. Adjustments in the flux ratio will affect the firing temperature and relative porosity.

Shrinkage

Shrinkage of the clay body occurs first as the clay form dries in the air and then again as the form is bisque and glaze fired. The more plastic clays will always shrink the most. The test for shrinkage is quite simple.

- First, roll out a plastic clay slab, and either cut or mark it to a measure.
- When the slab is totally dry, take a second measurement.
- Make a final measurement after firing.

Clay shrinkage rates generally range from 5 to 12 percent in the drying stage, with an additional 8 to 12 percent shrinkage during firings. Thus, you can expect a total shrinkage of at least 13 percent and an extreme of 24 percent, with a median of 15 to 20 percent between the wet clay and the final glazed ware. These normal shrinkage rates apply to plastic throwing clays. Special whiteware bodies using spodumene in place of feldspar and only small amounts of clay have a greatly reduced shrinkage and can even be compounded to develop a slight expansion in firing. Wollastonite as a replacement for silica and flux in a body will also decrease firing shrinkage.

Quartz Inversion

A major problem in the successful compounding of ceramic bodies is quartz inversion. During the firing of a ceramic body, silica (quartz) changes its crystalline structure several times. This is especially true of free silica that is not in a chemical bond with other body components. The most pronounced change occurs when the firing temperature reaches 1063°F (575°C). At this point the quartz crystals change from alpha to beta quartz, with a resultant expansion. At about 1850°F (1010°C) tough, interlocking mullite crystals composed of alumina and silica begin to form, and this chemical combination gives the fired body its strength. In the cooling process the situation is reversed. When the kiln temperature drops to 1063°F, the free silica in the body contracts. Quartz inversion is one of the reasons why a slow cycle of firing and cooling is essential. If a ceramic piece is heated or cooled too quickly, or if the distribution of heat is uneven, the piece will crack. Special precautions are required for ovenware, which must be able to withstand, with minimal thermal expansion, the heat to which it will be exposed in use.

Clay Prospecting and Preparation

There are few sections of the United States in which a suitable pottery clay cannot be found. Digging and preparing your own clay is seldom an economic proposition, but it can be rewarding in other ways. If you are teaching in a summer camp, for example, a hike can easily be turned into a prospecting trip. For the few hundred pounds of clay you may want to obtain, you must depend upon the accidents of nature to reveal the clay bed. A river bank, a road cut, or even a building excavation will often expose a deep bed of clay that is free of surface contamination. If the clay contains too much sand or gravel it may not be worth the trouble. A few tree roots will

14. Digging for clay in the hills at Mashiko, Japan.

13

15. Kaolin mining
at Sandersville, Georgia.
Courtesy Cyprus Mines Corporation,
Los Angeles.

not disqualify a clay, but any admixture of surface soil or humus will make it unusable.

On the first prospecting trip take samples of a few pounds of clay from several locations. Dry the samples, pound them into a coarse powder, and then soak them in water. Passing the resultant clay slip (liquid clay) through a 30-mesh sieve is usually sufficient to remove coarse impurities. If the clay proves too sandy, let the heavier particles settle for a few minutes after stirring, and then pour off the thinner slip. Pour this slip into drying bats until a wedging consistency is reached, and then test for plasticity, porosity, and shrinkage.

In most localities, surface clay is likely to be of an earthenware type. The samples should also be tested as possible slip glazes. It is surprising how many pockets of glacial clay work nicely as glazes, either alone or with a small amount of flux added. In some areas, the river-bank clay may be of a stoneware or fireclay type. All in all, clay prospecting can be profitable, but it is mostly fun. In this day of the super-processed item, starting out from "scratch" gives a rare feeling of satisfaction.

The commercial mining of clay is worth mentioning briefly, even though the production of clay for the potter represents only a very small fraction of the clay mining business. Millions of tons of clay are mined each year for a great variety of industrial purposes—building bricks, refractory liners for steel furnaces, insulating materials, and bathroom fixtures. Especially fine kaolin clays are used for coating printing papers, while other clays serve as extenders or fillers in paint and insecticides.

Depending upon how close to the earth's surface a clay is located, there are basically three different methods for mining clay. High-iron-content clays, primarily for tiles and bricks, occur close to the surface and are usually extracted with a power shovel. Impurities are sieved out after drying and a coarse grinding. Shale clays, found at deeper levels, require blasting techniques, followed by grinding and sieving. Fireclay is often close to coal beds and is mined either in an open pit or in a traditional shaft. The coarsely ground particles are mixed with water, causing the larger particles to settle. After drying, a fine dust is produced by *air-floating*—the separation of particles by air pressure.

2
Handbuilding Techniques

Handbuilding with clay is one of the oldest craft activities known. The techniques are followed today in almost the same manner as they were ten or twelve thousand years ago. It is likely that small figurines and animals were modeled long before the first pots were made. Few of these unfired figures have survived, but some have been found in Middle Eastern burial mounds. They were probably used as fetishes and in connection with hunting, planting, and harvesting ceremonies.

Throughout the history of ceramics, handbuilding techniques have been used to make both functional and sculptural forms. In skilled hands pinching and coiling produce remarkably symmetrical pots. Even after the introduction of the potter's wheel, many cultures continued to prefer the flexibility of these hand methods.

Preparation of Clay

If a coil of moist clay cracks excessively when wound around the finger, it probably is not suitable for forming. Often, sand will cause this cracking; it can be removed by adding water to the body to make a slip and allowing the sand to settle out. But this procedure may require more effort than it is worth. If the base clay has possibilities but is only moderately plastic, an addition of 20 percent ball clay or 5 percent bentonite will improve the body. Some bodies contain up to 40 percent ball clay, but because ball clay absorbs a large quantity of water, the shrinkage rate increases.

It is essential that even a satisfactory body be aged for at least three weeks in a plastic state. Aging allows the microscopic particles to become completely wet, causing them to cling together. If clay is aged for several months, a slight chemical breakdown occurs much like the original formation process. Even a nonplastic casting slip will become suitable for throwing if it is aged long enough. A small amount of clay can be aged in a plastic bag or plastic garbage can. For larger quantities an old refrigerator, a plastic-lined box, or a concrete vault can be used.

Wedging

Wedging is an important process in clay preparation. The clay is kneaded to force out air bubbles, to align coarse particles, and to develop a homogeneous consistency. Start with a 5- to 10-pound ball of clay; the larger the clay mass, the greater the physical strength required. The clay should be softer than desired for forming, because some moisture is lost in the wedging process. A plaster wedging table provides an absorbent surface and should be at a convenient height. (Scrape the plaster surface often to prevent the clay particles from clogging the plaster and making the clay stick.)

Wedge the clay mass with firm pressure from the heel of your hand to compress the clay. A rocking motion with a slight twist keeps the clay from flattening on the table. This pressing, rocking, and twisting will create a corkscrew effect, bringing all portions of the clay into contact with the surface and bursting trapped air bubbles. A comfortable and effective wedging rhythm will evolve only after practice. Beginning students tend to flatten and fold the clay, thus adding rather than removing air pockets.

A wire strung from a post at the rear of the table to a front corner will help to cut the mass of well-wedged clay into smaller pieces. The wire also aids in mixing a stiff mass of clay with a softer body. Cut both bodies into thin slices and throw them onto the table, alternating soft and hard pieces. Repeat this cutting and throwing operation several times, then wedge the clay in the usual manner to obtain a uniform consistency.

16. Votive figure, from Syria. 1400 B.C. Terra cotta. Metropolitan Museum of Art, New York (gift of George D. Pratt, 1933).

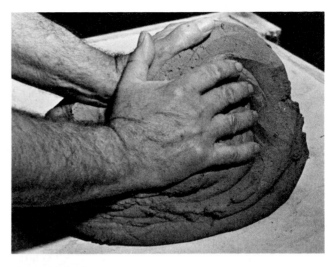

above and right: 17, 18. In wedging, the plastic clay is kneaded with the heel of the hand in a rocking, spiral motion.

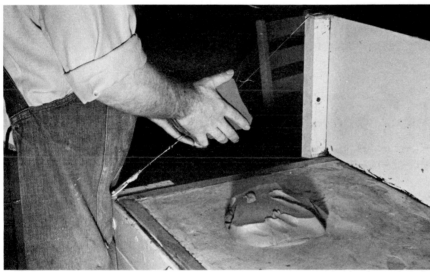

19. Wedging table with wire for cutting clay.

20. Well-wedged mass of clay cut in half (*left*), and improperly wedged clay showing air pockets (*right*).

21. Small standing figure. Archaic Style, 700–500 B.C. Terra cotta. Cyprus Museum, Nicosia.

Depending upon the type of work, it may be necessary to wedge *grog* into the clay body. Grog (fired clay crushed to fine particles) helps plastic clay to "stand up," prevents sagging, and lessens the chances of thick walls cracking. For throwing and for delicate sculptural work a minimum of fine grog is necessary; for large sculptural pieces as much as 20 to 30 percent of medium or coarse grog (mesh sizes 12 to 8) will be needed.

Grog should be wedged into the body in small quantities. Dust thin layers of the type needed onto the surface, and wedge until it is evenly distributed through the body. Then continue adding until the body seems right.

Unusual effects are achieved by adding colored grog to a contrasting clay body. You can make grog by forcing plastic clay of the desired color through a coarse screen. The stringlike particles are allowed to dry and are fired to the glaze temperature of the body. Pound the fired pieces with a mallet, and put them through a sieve to obtain the proper grog size.

Fiberglass is another material added to a clay body to lend greater strength. Since fiberglass is actually silica in another form, it fuses into the body during firing. Strands cut into 1-inch segments can be wedged into a plastic mass of clay in the same manner as grog (Fig. 12). Fiberglass cloth in an open mesh size can be rolled between two slabs to create a thicker slab with greater tensile strength.

Pinching

Pinching requires only properly conditioned, plastic clay and your fingers. Small sculptural pieces can be pinched from one large mass of clay or built up from many units. Remarkably expressive forms can be made with this simple handbuilding method, provided certain basic guidelines are kept in mind. Small cracks that appear during pinching can be smoothed over, but large cracks are likely to reappear during drying and firing. If the clay becomes too dry and cracks excessively, it is best to moisten it, wedge, and begin again. Also important to pinching (and most handbuilding methods) is gentle, even pressure to manipulate the clay.

A pinch pot is a good beginning project for students; making a simple bowl shape will help familiarize you with the qualities of clay. Start with a

right: **22. Tim Storey,** Canada. *Definitive Dragon.* Porcelain with sprigged and stamped decoration colored with slips and stains, salt-glazed to cone 10, low-fire metallic lusters; length 14″ (35 cm).

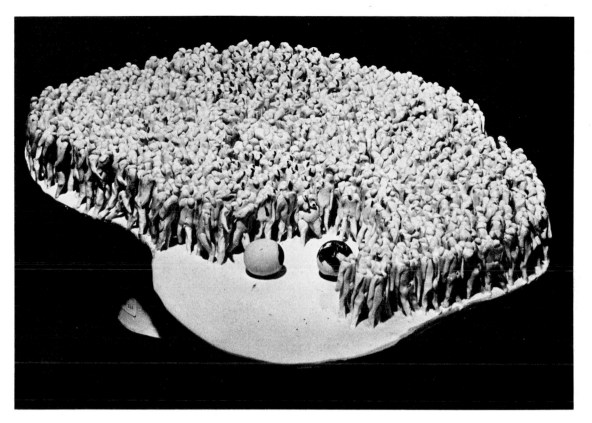

23. Britt Ingrid Persson, Sweden. *Spectacle.* 1969.
A complex of pinched figures surround two giant eggs.

24–27. Steps in the process of pinching a bowl.

24. Make a depression in the
center of a ball of clay.

25. Thin the walls with even, gentle
pressure between the thumb and fingers.

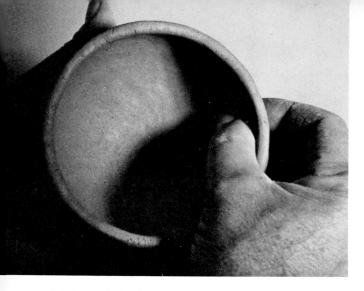

26. Smooth the interior with the thumb to heal cracks.

27. A coil can be joined to the bottom to serve as a foot.

small ball of wedged clay, the size of a tennis ball or slightly larger. Make a depression in the center with your thumbs. Then, holding the ball in one hand, squeeze the clay between the thumb and forefinger of the other hand. More pressure from the inside will make a wider bowl shape, while more pressure with the forefinger against the thumb will result in a taller form.

When the walls are of uniform thickness, the rim can be cut or smoothed with a piece of leather. Once this basic form is established, there are many decorative possibilities—pinched additions, incised lines, or a foot. The foot can be a simple coil joined to the bottom or it can be individually modeled pieces added to make tripod feet. Historically, cooking vessels had tripod feet to elevate them above hot coals.

28. Cooking pot in the shape of a tortoise. American Indian, from Arkansas. 1200–1600. Museum of the American Indian, New York.

29. Sten Lykke Madsen for
Bing and Grøndahl Porcelain, Ltd.,
Copenhagen.
Whimsical bird.
Stoneware with brush decoration,
height 19″ (49 cm).

Modeling

Modeling directly in clay preserves the texture and the feeling of immediacy created by the tool and hands manipulating plastic clay. The use of plaster as a mold material results in a bland, more uniform surface. However, since time immemorial sculptors have modeled solid clay studies, made plaster casts, and created a finished product in stone or metal. Usually, the final piece does not resemble the original clay sketch, which would have been too difficult to fire. Solid masses of clay are apt to explode in the kiln.

Traditional Modeling Method

Over the years sculptors developed methods of modeling that permitted the original study to become the permanent record. If the study is on a small scale and the clay walls are less than 1 inch thick, firing will not present a problem. For larger pieces, it is necessary to hollow out the excess clay inside. While the clay is still fairly plastic, cut the piece in half with a fine wire. With a wire looping tool trim the walls to a thickness of ½ to 1 inch. When both halves have been trimmed, score the cut edges and coat them with slip. Press the two sections together, and touch up any surface defects with your fingers or a tool.

left: 30. Cast of the Ife terra cotta head called *Lajuwa,* from Nigeria. c. 1200–1300. American Museum of Natural History, New York. This head, typical of the golden age of Benin art, was made from thick coils and partial molds, modeled and incised when leather hard.

below: 31. Giovanni Bologna, Italy. Sketch. c. 1564–66. Terra cotta, height 13″ (32.5 cm). Victoria & Albert Museum, London (Crown Copyright). This figure seems to be emerging from the mound of clay supporting the left arm.

32. Peter Fortune, U.S.A.
Mat Boys. 1976.
Low-fire body with bright
polychrome glaze,
height 14″ (35 cm).

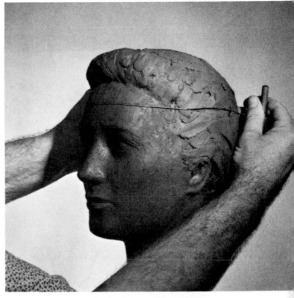

33–35. Hollowing a solidly
modeled head.

top right: 33. The top of the head
is cut with a wire.

above right: 34. Both halves are trimmed
to a thickness of ½ to 1 inch.

right: 35. The edges are scored and coated
with slip and then joined.

Sculpture should dry under plastic and be exposed to air slowly. This will ensure an even drying of the thick areas. The kiln firing should also proceed slowly. It is common practice to leave the kiln on low heat with the door ajar for at least 12 hours before the actual firing begins.

The illustrations show the great range of effects possible with modeling techniques: smooth, soft surfaces burnished with wooden tools, hard-edged lines and plastic additions, to very rough surfaces and incised lines. Expressively modeled clay needs no further embellishment; however, brightly colored glaze will lend more naturalistic effects.

left: 36. Agostino di Duccio, Italy. *Madonna and Child.* c. 1470. Terra cotta. Galleria Nazionale, Perugia. The delicate modeling of features contrasts with the rougher treatment of costume.

below: 37. Detail of the *Apollo of Veii,* Etruscan. c. 500 B.C. Terra cotta, lifesize. Villa Giulia National Museum, Rome. Because this figure was originally an ornament for a temple, the features are sharply defined so as to be clearly distinguishable.

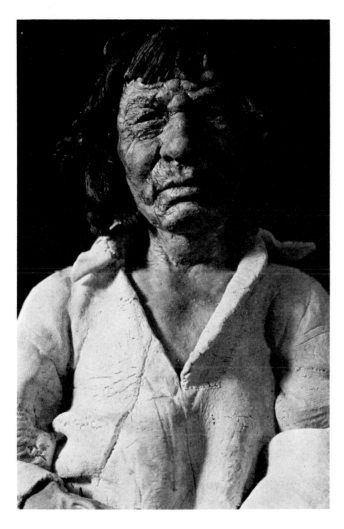

left: **38. Joe Fafard,** Canada.
Cree Man, detail. 1975.
Low-fire talc body, stained
and detailed with acrylic paint.

above: **39. David Gilhooly,** Canada.
Mao Tse Toad. 1976.
Polychrome glazes with luster,
height 26″ (65 cm).
Courtesy Hansen Fuller Gallery, San Francisco.

Hollow Tube

More complicated figurative pieces can also be cut apart, hollowed out, and then joined, but problems are apt to arise from the joining of too many parts. It is simpler to construct the different parts from hollow sections and then join them together. The figure study in Figure 40 was made by a modified tube and slab method. Clay slabs rolled out to a thickness of about ½ inch were wrapped around wooden dowels to form tubes 12 to 16 inches long. The torso was made from another slab joined to make a larger tube. When the individual sections had set up enough to support themselves, they were joined together. The clay must be plastic enough during the joining process so that the joins can be smoothed over. Modeled additions to the tube structure helped to flesh out the figure. Finally, the study was finished with a scraper tool to create a uniform surface texture.

Sagging during firing is always a problem with sculptural projections that lack support. Heads especially are apt to tilt when the weight of the head puts pressure on the forward thrust of the neck. Clay tube supports should be made for the projections when both are leather hard, so that they will shrink at the same rate during both drying and firing. Small holes in several places will allow moisture and combustion gases to escape during firing.

above left: 40. Traditional figure study
constructed of joined clay tubes,
a slab torso, and modeled additions;
height 27″ (67.5 cm).

above: 41. Temple figure (Mercury?).
c. 400 B.C. Roman-Etruscan showing
strong Greek influence.
Terra cotta, originally covered with slip.
Villa Giulia National Museum, Rome.

left: 42. Seated figure of Yen-Lo Wang (Yama),
President of the 5th Court of Hades,
Chinese. Ming Dynasty, 16th century.
Stoneware with green, yellow,
and amber glazes; height 33″ (82.5 cm).
Royal Ontario Museum, Toronto.
An exterior support was needed for the foot.

left: 43. Figure of horse from a tomb.
Chinese, Wei Period, A.D. c. 250.
Terra cotta, length 20″ (50 cm).
Museum of Far Eastern Antiquities, Stockholm.

below: 44. Jerry Rothman, U.S.A.
Opel in the Sky.
Stoneware, built and fired
on stainless steel armature;
length of mule 6′8″ (2 m),
width of hoop 10′ (3 m).

Often, complicated sculptural forms will need some kind of interior support in addition to the exterior support to prevent sagging during drying and firing. Clay partitions that shrink with the form in drying and firing are the most practical solution, provided ample air passages are left. Metal rods and wires can be used temporarily, but these must be removed before major shrinkage occurs to avoid cracking the piece. Jerry Rothman, a sculptor who works in very large scale, has been experimenting with clay bodies that have the unusual potential of zero shrinkage, combined with a stainless-steel armature. The leaping mule in Figure 44 is 6 feet 8 inches long, the hoop is 10 feet wide. The form is supported by a welded armature of stainless steel bars and mesh. Its base is stabilized by concrete weights.

above: 45. Zuñi potter, New Mexico.
Coils are added with a pinching motion
to make a rough curve,
then smoothed and finished with a tool.

right: 46. Bowl with pouring spout
and vulture head.
Veracruz, Mexico. A.D. c. 500.
Earthenware with slip decoration,
diameter 12¾″ (31.88 cm).
Metropolitan Museum of Art,
New York
(Michael C. Rockefeller Memorial
Collection of Primitive Art).

Coiling

Coiling is done by rolling out coils or ropes of clay. Often these coils are joined to a flat or rounded base and gradually shaped to build up the desired form. The coils should be pressed together firmly and the join marks smoothed on the inside with a vertical wiping motion. Unless the piece is purely decorative, you should probably join the coils outside as well. If a more refined form is desired, however, the surface can be finished with a wooden tool or metal scraper when the clay has begun to dry. Coils can also be added to the rims of thrown forms, provided the clay has set up enough so that it will not sag. When joining coils to a leather hard surface, be sure to score and slip the edge before adding the coils.

below: 47. A rope of clay is rolled out to the desired thickness.

below: 48. Laying the first coil on the slab base.

above: 49. Joining the coils with a wiping motion.

below: 50. Using a wooden tool to join the coils.

above: **51. Sandra J. Blain,** U.S.A.
Coil/Wheel Planter. 1976.
Stoneware with oxides
wedged into the clay,
Albany slip glazes fired to cone 9;
height 24″ (60 cm).
The coiled shape with impressed
designs has been joined
to a wheel-thrown foot.

right: **52.** *Pithos* with applied
rope decoration. From Knossos, Crete.
c. 1450–1400 B.C.
Height 4′ (1.15 cm).
British Museum, London.

Thick coil and paddle The size of many ancient pots amazes the modern potter. Intended for the storage of olive oil and wine, some of the Cretan jars are as tall as a person, with a nearly symmetrical swelling form (Fig. 52). These were doubtless made with the thick coil method. Thick coils are joined, then thinned and shaped by beating a paddle against a rounded wooden anvil held inside. Wrapping the paddle with cord or covering it with fabric will reduce the tendency of clay to stick to its surface. When constructing a large, vertical piece, you should begin with a form that is taller and narrower than you want it ultimately to be, because paddling will stretch the clay. The vibration of this forming method causes a tendency for the clay to settle. Burning a crumpled newspaper inside the pot will dry the clay sufficiently so that more coils can be added without collapsing the structure or making it sag unduly.

left: 53. Laying thick coils on a slab base.

below: 54. A curved block of wood and a paddle shape the form.

above: 55. The walls have been thinned and shaped.

right: 56. After the pot has been smoothed with a scraper tool. coils are added to the rim to complete the form.

57. Bruno La Verdiere, U.S.A.
Arch. 1975.
Clay with sawdust and grog,
coil-built; 7'3" × 4' (2.18 × 1.2 m).

Coil construction is the basic technique for much sculpture, especially when used in combination with pinching and slabs. Bruno La Verdiere is a sculptor who works with coils to create works on a very large scale. The arch illustrated in Figure 57 is about 7 feet tall and depends upon internal ribs of clay for support.

Problems in Coil Construction Problems that arise in coil construction can often be attributed to one or more of the following:

- coils that are too thick or thin for the size of the piece
- clay that is either too soft and sticky or too stiff to join properly
- coils added so rapidly that the lower walls sag and thicken
- a form that is too horizontal or has too flat a curve. The wet clay cannot support too wide a shape and may also sag during firing.

Slab Construction

Slabs are sheets or slices of clay that are rolled out, often with a rolling pin, to the desired thickness and wrapped, folded, or cut and joined together. The illustrations show the great variety of forms possible with slab techniques. Although beginning students tend to make slabs into square or rectangular boxlike shapes, there is just as much potential for round, oval, or flaring

right: **58. Dieter Crumbiegel,** Germany. Bottle. Slab form with textured design and overlapping glazes, fired to cone 12; width 12″ (30 cm).

below left: **59.** *Haniwa* warrior, Tochigi Prefecture, Japan. 3rd–6th century. Terra cotta with slip, height 22⅞″ (57.25 cm). Metropolitan Museum of Art, New York (Michael C. Rockefeller Memorial Collection of Primitive Art. gift of Mrs. John D. Rockefeller, III).

below right: **60. Georget Cournoyer,** Canada. *Knapsack.* Stoneware with mat white glaze fired to cone 10, 15 × 13 × 9″ (37.5 × 32.5 × 23.5 cm).

above: 61. Johnny Rolf, Holland. *Flowering Torso.*
Stoneware slab vase with pinched additions,
opaque glaze and colored stains;
height 20″ (50 cm). The delicacy
of the form is enhanced by the
vertical streaks of color
and the petal shapes on the rim.

below: 62. Ruth Duckworth, U.S.A. Sculpture.
Porcelain slabs, height 21″ (52.5 cm).
Porcelain can be rolled into extremely thin slabs.

vertical shapes. When used in combination with modeled, coiled, or thrown sections, slab construction has many more possibilities.

To make a number of slabs it is best to start with a large block of wedged clay and cut off thin square sections with a wire. Roll these out on a piece of canvas or a sanded table top. Rolling the clay out diagonally will preserve the squared form, and turning the slab after two or three strokes of the rolling pin will keep the piece an even thickness. Fabric or such flat objects as leaves and dried flowers placed between the slab and rolling pin will produce interesting textures. Those working extensively with slabs might want to purchase a commercially manufactured slab roller (Fig. 71). This machine consists of two rollers in an etching press arrangement that compress the clay between two pieces of canvas.

If the slabs are draped over a mold, they should be plastic; if formed into a vertical shape, the pieces should be allowed to dry sufficiently so that they

63. John Mason, U.S.A. Plaque. Stoneware with impressed shapes in high relief and low-fire glazes, width 15½″ (38.75 cm).

64. A clay slab is rolled out with a rolling pin.

65. Making a tall vase by pinching the seam of a rectangular slab set on end.

66. When the side and bottom seams are sealed, the top is joined.

above left: 67. A square box should
have edges beveled
at a 45-degree angle.
The edges are scored,
and slip is applied.
Reinforcing the interior seam
with a coil of clay will prevent
the edges from cracking as they dry.

above right: 68.
Open mesh cloth will create
a relief pattern on a slab.
All edges should be scored, coated
with slip, and pressed together firmly.

can support themselves. Do not allow them to dry too much, however, for
they may crack as they are folded. As in other techniques, the edges that are
joined should be scored and coated with slip to prevent them from coming
apart during the drying process. Sharp angles and joints should be reinforced with a coil of moist clay on the interior seam. Horizontal spans may
need to be reinforced with interior clay partitions to support the slab and
prevent it from sagging.

Clay slabs can be smoothed and manipulated to create endless surface
textures and sculptural effects. Some potters choose to fold and shape the
plastic slabs just enough to suggest a form, but leave the method undis-
guised. Marilyn Levine, on the other hand, is a master of detail in the
construction of objects in clay that resemble leather.

The stoneware body Levine uses includes 1½ percent nylon fiber. The
body is mixed in a dough mixer and then run through a slab roller until the
fibers are properly aligned. The slabs are then covered with a layer of plastic
to prevent drying and are cut with scissors to conform to a paper pattern.

69. Mary Frank, U.S.A. *Untitled* (*Lovers*). 1975. Terra cotta with impressed designs,
fired to cone 6; length 5'2" (1.55 m). Courtesy Zabriskie Gallery, New York.

70. Marilyn Levine, U.S.A. *Trent's Jacket.* 1976.
Stoneware slabs, with wood and metal hooks; length of jacket 18″ (45 cm).

71–76. Stages in the construction of Marilyn Levine's *Brown Suitcase Without Handle* (Fig. 77).

71. A slab roller produces thin, uniform pieces of clay.

72. Cutting a slab to the pattern size.

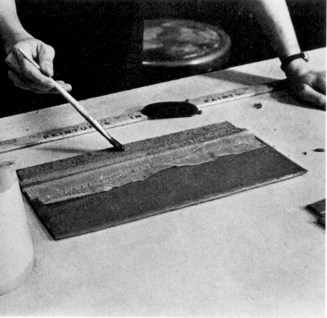

above: 73. The plastic is peeled back and the slab coated with an engobe.

above right: 74. Interior clay partitions are needed to support the lid.

above right: 75. The lid is lowered carefully into place.

right: 76. Applying low-firing lusters to simulate the metallic hardware.

The clay is coated with colored engobes, and textures are imparted by pressing various materials into the slab. A roulette wheel is used to imitate the stitching common on leather articles. The sections, still covered with plastic, are joined and held together with masking tape while drying. Interior clay partitions are then constructed in an irregular grid pattern. These will support the lid and prevent it from collapsing. Details such as buckles and rivets are cut from the plastic-covered slab and joined to the clay while it is still damp. The suitcase cover is then placed over the base, and the entire piece is covered with more plastic and dried very slowly. The glaze firing is to cone 7, after which the "metallic" sections are coated with lusters before a second firing at a lower temperature.

Jane Peiser is a potter who uses slabs to create a totally different effect. The technique is called millefiore and consists of joining pieces of colored clay inside a mold. Thus the slabs serve as a decorative as well as structural element. Pieces and slabs of clay are arranged in a loaf form to create a

77. Marilyn Levine, U.S.A.
Brown Suitcase Without Handle.
Stoneware slabs reinforced with nylon fibers,
engobe, iron stain, and lusters;
length 27½″ (68.75 cm).

design—in this case, a fanciful figure of a woman. The loaf is then cut into thin sections and rolled out, which joins the individual segments, at the same time stretching and elongating the design. The resultant slabs are taped together inside a plaster mold, in a shape that will allow the piece to shrink without damage. After the piece has been assembled, the inside surface is covered with coils to reinforce the structure and prevent the sections from shrinking apart. When the pot has shrunk from the sides of the mold, it is removed, covered with plastic, and uncovered for only about an hour every day. This final drying may take a week or longer, but is essential for a work composed of so many different pieces. For more details about the decoration and glazing process, see Chapter 4 and Figure 296.

78. Jane Peiser, U.S.A.
Millefiore planter.
Segments of colored porcelain,
salt-glazed to cone 10,
overglazes fired to cone 017.

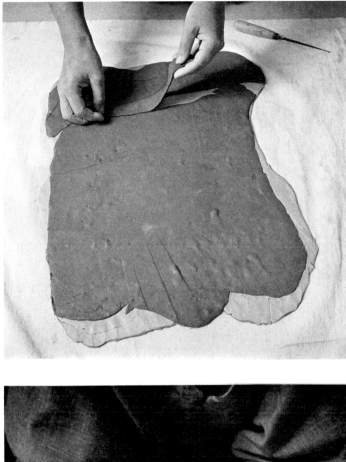

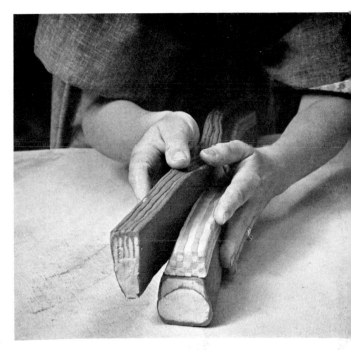

79–84. **Jane Peiser** demonstrating the millefiore construction process.

left: 79. Joining together two thin slabs of contrasting colors.

below: 80. Placing the different segments of the design together.

above: 81. The design is built up in a long loaf shape.

right: 82. The completed clay loaf with figure and surrounding background.

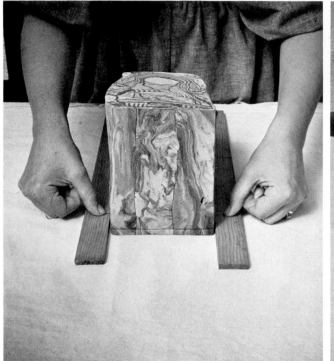

83. The loaf is set on end,
and thin slabs are cut with a wire.

84. The sections are rolled out,
elongating the design and thinning the slabs.

Problems in Slab Construction Practices that may cause problems in slab construction are:

- joining slabs that are too moist, so that they sag.
- joining sections of different moisture content. These will crack apart when drying.
- allowing assembled constructions to dry too rapidly or unevenly. This will also cause cracking.
- providing insufficient interior support of horizontal sections, which causes sagging.

Combined Techniques

Once the basic handbuilding methods have been mastered and you are familiar with the possibilities of each, it will become clear that many forms can be constructed only by combining the different techniques. Pinched and modeled shapes often require coiled accents. Slabs and coils reinforce each other structurally as well as aesthetically. Each method has structural advantages and limitations. If pinching a lump of clay does not produce the desired form, then perhaps a coil should be added to the rim, or a slab joined to the coil. You will discover by experimentation how far plastic clay can be stretched and manipulated. Overly thin walls will sag, and walls that are too thick are likely to explode in the kiln. The illustrations show the freedom of design that is possible when handbuilding techniques are combined imaginatively to create both functional and sculptural forms.

above: **85. James F. McKinnell,** U.S.A.
Baroque fruit bowl.
Stoneware, coil, and slab construction,
opaque glaze with detailed accents in lusters;
diameter 16″ (40 cm).

left: **86. Hans de Jong,** Holland. Slab form.
Stoneware with incised decoration
and mottled brown glaze, height 16″ (40 cm).
Groninger Museum, Groningen, Holland.

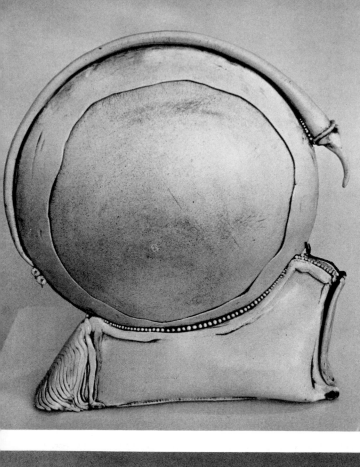

left: 87. **Marion Peters Angelica,** U.S.A. *Task Thirteen.*
Porcelain with details highlighted
by stains and glaze, height 18″ (45 cm).
Slabs and coils can be joined in a multitude of ways.

above: 88. Composite vase, from Cyprus. c. 2100–2000 B.C.
Polished red earthenware, height 25″ (62.5 cm).
Cyprus Museum, Nicosia.
This vase probably was made by a combination
of pinching, coil, and slab techniques.

left: 89. **David Gilhooly,** Canada.
Posing on the Steps of the T. Jefferson Memorial. 1976.
Frog fantasy executed with handbuilding techniques
and glazed in green and white, 17 × 13″ (42.5 × 32.5 cm).
Courtesy Hansen Fuller Gallery, San Francisco.

above: 90. **Paul A. Dresang,** U.S.A.
Tennis Shoes.
Porcelain slabs and coils,
length of each shoe 6″ (15 cm).

right: 91. **Leoni Alfonso,** Italy.
Sculpture. Low-fire body
with white majolica glaze,
12 × 14 × 4¾″ (30 × 35 × 12 cm).
Faenza Istituto d'Arte, Faenza.

Molds

Hump and Press Molds

Many ancient pots were made with a mold of some sort. The mold can be almost any rounded shape, and the technique will produce a finished pot in practically a single step. For a *hump mold,* a slab of clay is draped over a form—a stone, gourd, kitchen bowl, beach ball, or a plaster form made for the purpose. The slab is pressed to conform to the mold, and the excess is trimmed away. Strips of wet newspaper, paper towelling, or plastic will prevent the clay from sticking to the form. After drying slightly—enough to maintain the shape without distorting—remove the mold. If left on the form too long, the contracting clay will crack.

left: 92. Rounded beach stones make excellent hump molds.

below left: 93. Drape a slab of clay over the mold, and use even pressure to make it conform to the shape.

below: 94. Moist paper towels separate the clay from the mold.

95. Tripod feet
can be added to a form
when it has set up.

above: **96. William Daley,** U.S.A. Planter.
Stoneware formed over styrofoam,
unglazed and reduction-fired; height 30″ (75 cm).

97. Peter Travis, Australia.
Spheres. High-fired earthenware
formed in a mold, with textures
emphasized by slips and oxides.

A form can also be covered with coils of plastic clay. The coils should be smoothed together with a tool or the fingers so they will not crack apart when drying. Coils and slabs can be joined over a preexisting shape, provided the seams are well sealed. This will create alternating smooth and rough textures.

Large abstract shapes can be made by placing slabs in a canvas sling extended between the backs of two weighted chairs. Another possibility is a completely round, closed form that results from joining plastic slabs around a heavy balloon. When the clay is leather hard, the balloon should be punctured to permit the clay to contract. The rubber will burn out during the firing. However, the firing should proceed slowly, for this will allow the moisture to escape through the puncture hole instead of turning to steam and causing the pot to explode.

Press molding consists of shaping slabs and coils of plastic clay in a concave form—the inside of a bowl or plate, or a plaster mold. The procedure is the same as for hump molds, except that the slabs or coils are pressed into a form rather than draped over it. In this method the smoothing and joining of coils and slabs is done on the inside surface, and the design will appear on the exterior. With hump molds, join marks are smoothed on the exterior, so that any design will be seen on the inside surface.

Rounded forms can be constructed by joining two semicircular sections press molded in a bowl shape. Both halves must have a similar moisture content. The edges should be scored and coated with slip. Once joined, the piece should dry very slowly to prevent cracking along the seam.

Slip Casting

Another possibility for handbuilding with molds is casting. Although casting is primarily a commercial production technique, some studio potters are

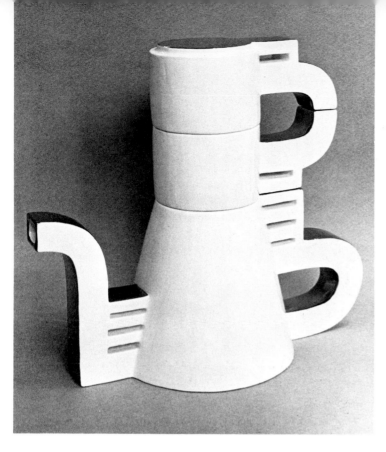

98. Anne Currier, U.S.A.
Teapot with Two Cups. 1975.
Slip-cast earthenware with
slab-built handles and spout,
luster glaze; height 9″ (22.5 cm).

interested in the clean lines and smooth surfaces possible with this technique. However, the process is complicated, and is outlined only briefly here. Slip casting consists of pouring slip, or clay in a liquid form, into a plaster mold. Depending upon the complexity of the piece, the plaster mold may consist of one to five or more parts. In order for the slip clay to dry and shrink away from the plaster mold, it is important that the form be of a smooth texture and the surface even, without crevices and undercuts.

99. Britt Ingrid Persson, Sweden.
Identifications.
Slip-cast stoneware
with white glaze.

100. Charles Lakofsky, U.S.A.
Container. Porcelain slip-cast jar
with lid cast from summer squash,
yellow stain over opaque glaze;
height 8″ (20 cm).

When the plaster mold sections have dried, they are scraped clean and clamped together for the casting. Slip is poured into the mold. Plaster draws the moisture from the slip and causes the clay surface in contact with the plaster to harden or "set up." The excess slip is poured or drained from the mold, and the piece is allowed to dry further. The mold is removed when the piece is leather hard, and then the surface is scraped or sanded to remove the join marks of the mold sections. (See Chap. 9, pp. 267–276, for more information about slip casting.)

Styrofoam as a Model Material

Nino Caruso, an Italian potter known for his architectural modular reliefs, has developed a casting method that uses styrofoam as a model material. The styrofoam has a very dense consistency but is still lightweight and

left: 101. *The Three Graces,*
Meissen, from Germany. c. 1790.
Bisqued porcelain, modeled
in the Neoclassical tradition.
Victoria & Albert Museum, London
(Crown Copyright).
The join marks of the various
cast sections are still visible.

below: 102. Nino Caruso, Italy.
Modular Sculpture, detail.
Slip-cast fireclay with white glaze,
fired to cone 10; each module
approximately 20 × 16 × 14″
(50 × 40 × 35 cm).

103–108. Nino Caruso using styrofoam as a model material.

103. The design is drawn on a block of styrofoam.

104. A taut, hot wire cuts out the design.

convenient to handle. A design is drawn on a block of styrofoam and then cut with a taut, hot wire. The wire is placed in an arrangement like a band saw, but the wire makes a sharper cut and leaves a smoother surface than a saw blade.

The various segments of the pattern are joined with cement to make the model. This is then coated with shellac to fill all the air pockets and repel the plaster. This model serves as the form for making the plaster mold. In Figure 105 plaster is poured to form one side of the mold. The dark section is the original model, the lighter parts are styrofoam pieces acting as retaining walls for the plaster. Figure 106 shows the original model and the four plaster mold sections needed to make the final casting.

When the mold sections have been clamped together, slip is poured in, and after the clay has set up, a plug is pulled from the bottom of the mold to let the excess slip drain out. The mold is opened when the clay is leather hard. The resulting module is hollow and makes the drying and firing process less hazardous. Because of the size of the individual modules and the scale of his projects, Caruso contracts most of his casting to commercial firms (Fig. 442). A completed freestanding wall is illustrated in the section on architectural ceramics in Chapter 5 (Fig. 340).

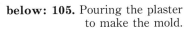

below: 105. Pouring the plaster to make the mold.

right: 106. The original model with the four plaster molds needed to slip-cast the final form.

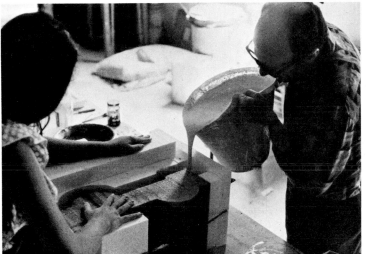

left: 107. Clay slip is poured into the plaster mold clamped together with a vise.

above: 108. After drying, the plaster mold is removed from the clay.

109. Carol Jeanne Abraham, U.S.A.
Covered jar. Thixotropic porcelain,
characterized by a flowing form
and twisted spirals.

Special Handbuilding Techniques
Thixotropic Clay

Thixotropy is the property exhibited by some gels of becoming fluid when
shaken or stirred and setting again to a gel when allowed to stand. In a clay
body this means that the clay becomes fluid when manipulated, then sets up
again when the motion is stopped. This action results from a reduced
attraction between the negatively charged silicate particles and the posi-
tively charged chemical ions in the body. Normally, a clay body is stable
because the charges on the ions are neutralized and cause *flocculation* or
thickening. However, if large ions of sodium, lithium, or potassium are
added, they are not strongly attracted to the negatively charged particles,
and this causes *deflocculation* or thinning.

While a graduate student in ceramics, Carol Jeanne Abraham began a
series of experiments in the particle suspensions of various clay bodies.
Eventually, she compounded a porcelain body with thixotropic properties
(see Appendix for formula). The body is prepared in a slip form and should
be aged for a long time.

Forming the Thixotropic Pot A thixotropic clay body cannot be formed
with the usual handbuilding techniques or throwing. The clay appears to be
firm but becomes increasingly fluid when manipulated. Begin by stretching
and folding the clay until it becomes semifluid. Then gradually work it into
a shape that can be draped over a mold. When it begins to set up again,

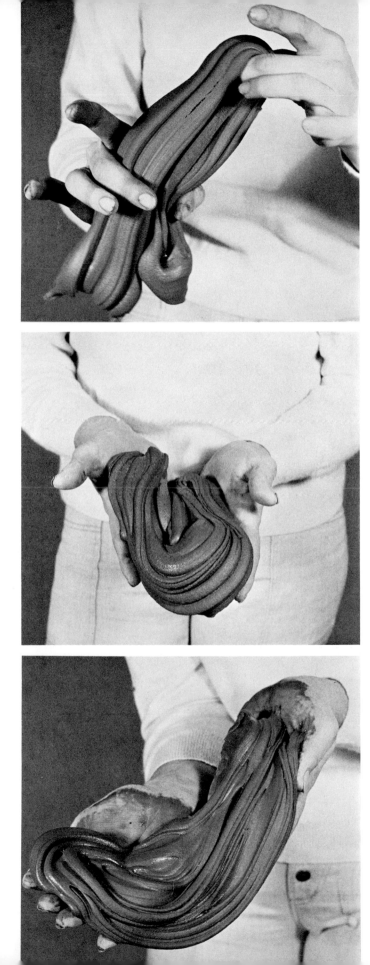

left: 110. Thixotropic clay is wedged
by gently pulling the clay
into ropelike strands.

below left: 111. The strands are then folded.

bottom left: 112. Vibration from the hands
causes the clay to flow into a single mass.

above: 113. With further vibration,
the clay stretches into a convoluted slab.

below: 114. The slab is draped over a mold
and pulled at the edges.

left: 115. When the form has been established, the clay is allowed to set up.

below: 116. A cover is made by inverting the bowl shape, filling it with newspaper, and draping another slab over it. A dusting of alumina prevents the rims from sticking.

plastic additions can be pulled and twisted from the draped clay. Because of shrinkage, the form should be removed from the mold as soon as possible to avoid cracking. However, the surface may appear deceptively dry when the form is still quite plastic.

The technique will require some practice since the clay behaves very differently from other bodies. The effects of fluidity and apparent motion will appeal to many potters, especially those interested in decorative and sculptural forms.

Although Abraham has experimented with joining decorative forms made from a thixotropic body to a regular porcelain body, there are some problems. One is that the thixotropic clay sags. Moreover, the thixotropic body shrinks about 6 percent, while most other bodies shrink about 15 percent. One solution is to bisque-fire the porcelain piece before adding the thixotropic clay, although this will require a great deal of planning during the forming stages, taking into account the different shrinkage rates. Another possibility would be to compound a porcelain body with a lower shrinkage rate, making only one bisque firing necessary.

With such unusual shrinkage rates, a typical porcelain glaze will not be satisfactory for thixotropic clay. A glaze formula suitable for cone 5 and lower is given in the Appendix. This glaze will craze slightly at cone 9.

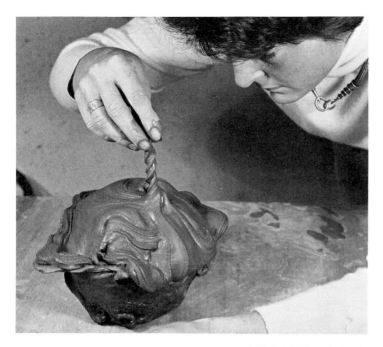

above: 117.
As the form begins to set up,
plastic additions
are pulled and twisted.

right: 118.
Carol Jeanne Abraham, U.S.A.
Mirror frame.
Thixotropic porcelain and feathers,
22″ (55 cm) square.
The baroque quality of this frame
typifies the unique characteristics
of thixotropic clay.

119. Warren Angle, U.S.A.
Dancing Dollup.
Clay and plaster body cast
in nylon form, height 25″ (62.5 cm).

Clay and Plaster Body

Most potters have a natural aversion to pieces of plaster in clay. Plaster fragments from drying bats or molds absorb moisture after firing and expand, erupting through the clay walls, thus producing pits. However, Warren Angle has found a method to actually exploit the qualities of plaster.

Angle developed another unusual clay body suitable for certain hand-building techniques while working on a project involving plaster poured into fabric molds. Because the plaster was fragile, he experimented with adding clay to the mixture to increase its strength. He found that a stoneware body could contain as much as 20 percent plaster. The ingredients are mixed dry, and 50 percent (by weight) water is added. When thoroughly slaked, the plaster-clay slip is workable for about 20 minutes before it begins to harden. This time factor requires that all the mold material be prepared when the mixture is ready to be poured. Nylon stockings and coarsely textured material work well as forms. The fabric will burn out during firing and create relief designs that can be decorated with oxides and glazes. Slip-casting techniques can also be used with this plaster-clay. Twisted and interlocking forms will join and fire successfully, provided the total thickness does not exceed 4 inches.

3
Wheel Techniques

The introduction of the potter's wheel was a technical advance that gave a great impetus to ceramics. Before the development of the wheel, a simple turning device had aided in trimming and refining handbuilt pots. This evolved into a weighted wheel head turning on a peg in the ground. At first, the primitive wheel served only to shape plastic coils and to give a final finish to the lip. This method is still used by many Mexican and American Indian potters. In Figures 121 and 122 a remarkably symmetrical jar is made by rotating a coiled pot on *platos*—one shallow bowl resting on top of another inverted shallow bowl.

Although pots with wheel-turned feet dated as early as 3500 B.C. have been found in Eastern Anatolia and Northern Iran, it was not until about 3000 B.C. that small pots were thrown entirely on the wheel. By this time, improved agricultural methods and more prosperous villages made barter of goods necessary. The crafts of the metalsmith, weaver, miller, and leatherworker, as well as the potter, developed for this market. Often an entire family engaged in pottery making and traded their wares for other goods. The potter's wheel was an essential tool, because it provided a more efficient method of making small and moderate-sized pots. Larger pieces were still coiled or made by a combination of techniques.

Throwing on the Wheel

The overriding advantage of the wheel is that one can make perfectly symmetrical rounded forms in a short time. Most student potters have greater initial success with coiling or slab techniques, but all are eager to try their luck on the potter's wheel. It is fascinating to watch an experienced potter take a ball of plastic clay and produce a form that evolves and changes shape in a seemingly miraculous fashion. However, developing skill at throwing on the wheel demands much practice and an understanding of the proper sequence of operation.

above: 120.
Primitive potter's wheel, from China.
American Museum
of Natural History, New York.

right: 121.
Traditional forming techniques
in the Mexican town
of San Bartolo Coyotepec.
A wet coil is attached
to a pinched form by squeezing
with even pressure while the pot
is rotated slowly on *platos*.

far right: 122.
Once the coil has been joined,
it is thinned and smoothed
with a piece of leather.

123. Cup with turned foot, Tepe Hissar, Iran.
c. 3500 B.C. Pale buff clay unglazed,
with design painted in brown oxide;
height 4⅜″ (11 cm).
Metropolitan Museum of Art, New York
(gift of the Tehran Museum, 1939).

left: 124. Walter Hyleck, U.S.A.
Covered jar. 1976.
Porcelain, clear glaze with accents
of iron, rutile, and cobalt stain;
height 10″ (25 cm).

125. Don Reitz, U.S.A. Platter.
Stoneware, salt-glazed
with color accents resulting
from sprayed rutile, cobalt,
and iron; diameter 22″ (55 cm).

A student should choose a single form, preferably a cylinder, and throw it over and over again. When throwing a different shape each time, the student learns nothing from previous errors and misses the most natural method of developing form and design. It is important to learn how to center the ball of clay and bring it up into a cylinder quickly, before the clay begins to soften and sag from the water. Gradually, the potter gains a sense of how far to push the clay—how thin the walls can be and how wide a curve can open before distorting and collapsing. With practice it will be possible to throw taller and thinner shapes from the same amount of clay. A greater ease and freedom in handling the clay ultimately brings a dynamic quality to throwing.

There is little point for the beginner to make drawings of an ideal pot. Until one gains a feeling for the clay and a knowledge of possible forms, there is likely to be no relationship between the drawing and the pot. The final details should grow out of the actual process of throwing. Plastic clay has a quality all its own and imposes certain restrictions upon the potter. Thus, there are certain forms and decorations that seem natural to clay, expressing a fluidity more difficult to achieve with other media.

Selecting a Wheel

A suitable wheel is even more important for the beginner than for the experienced potter. The potter who throws for many hours every day really needs an electric wheel, but for the beginner a kick wheel is preferable. During the critical moments in throwing one instinctively stops kicking, thus slowing the speed of the wheel. A beginner on a power wheel may actually increase the speed at a moment of crisis, causing centrifugal force to tear the pot apart.

The wheel should have a rigid frame that is free of vibration. Its seat must be comfortable and adjustable for both height and distance from the wheel head. On a foot-powered wheel, kicking should be an easy motion, not tiring or awkward, and the footrest must be in a convenient location. If the student is throwing on an electric wheel, the seat should be adjusted to a comfortable height and brought as close to the wheel head as possible. Before starting the wheel, it is important to understand how to control the speed and operate the wheel without damaging the motor.

On a power wheel the speed control activated by foot or knee must allow easy operation from either a standing or a sitting position. Excessive speed in the wheel is not necessary or even desirable; 80 to 100 r.p.m. is sufficient for centering, and even slower speeds may be desirable for throwing. The most critical factor is the torque transmitted through the reduction gears from the motor. A motor of at least $\frac{1}{3}$ horsepower is essential for potters throwing large pieces, since the pressure needed to center a clay ball of 25 pounds or more may actually stop a $\frac{1}{4}$-horsepower unit.

Preparing to Throw

A pail of water and a few simple tools should be placed in easy reach. These tools are:

- a sponge to apply water and remove excess slip and water from inside the pot, plus a sponge attached to a long dowel
- a small piece of leather to smooth rims and remove finger marks
- a pin (or needle attached to a dowel) to remove uneven rims, pop air bubbles, or gauge the thickness of bottoms
- a fine, double-twisted wire to cut the finished pot off the wheel head

Composition board, plywood, or plaster bats will prevent very soft pots from sagging or distorting when removed from the wheel. They are essential for large pieces and very wide bowl shapes. Some wheel heads are equipped with removable metal pins that can be inserted into corresponding holes in the bats. Otherwise, wooden bats can be attached with clay or plaster bats with slip.

From clay that has been thoroughly wedged (see p. 17), cut pieces that can be held comfortably in one hand. If the clay ball is too small, it will be hard to manipulate; if too large, it will be difficult to center. Pat the pieces into balls, and cover all those you do not intend to use immediately with plastic. Even a slight drying of the surface will lessen the throwing qualities of the clay.

126. The basic tools for throwing: sponge, sponge attached to a stick, piece of leather, needle or pin tool, and wire.

The consistency of the clay is very important when learning to throw. It should be soft enough to be wedged and centered easily, but not too soft to stand up or hold its shape as it is thrown. If a coil of moist clay cracks when wound around the finger, the clay is not suitable for throwing. Clay that is too hard can be very frustrating, for it is difficult to wedge and center. In this case, softer clay should be wedged into it.

Centering

The first step in throwing is *centering* the clay, or forcing it onto the exact center of the wheel head. When a symmetrical mass of clay is turning evenly on a flat surface, it can be controlled and shaped with the hands.

- Press the clay ball down in the center of the wheel head.
- If a plaster bat is attached, moisten it slightly for better adhesion.
- Start the wheel turning.
- Dip your hands in water, and wet the clay.
- With both hands apply pressure downward on the clay to seal it to the wheel, and force it into a rounded beehive form.
- Brace your elbows and arms on your thighs or at your sides to steady your hands.
- Apply a uniform pressure, and do not allow the hands to conform to the movement of the clay, which may be slightly off center. Force any unevenness upward by the pressure of the hands.

Most right-handed people press with the right hand and shape the clay with the left hand. Reverse this position if you find it more comfortable.

Another centering method is to pull the clay first, with the heels and palms of both hands, into a tall cone shape, and then press it back down into a rounded beehive shape. Especially helpful for large masses of clay and clay that is slightly hard, this method gets the clay moving, causing the particles to slide together.

left: 127. Place a ball of plastic clay on a freshly moistened plaster bat.

below: 128. While the wheel is turning, force the clay into the center of the wheel.

129. Brace your elbows,
and apply an even pressure
with your hands and fingers.

130. For larger pieces of clay
or clay that is too hard,
pull the mass with both hands
into a tall cone shape,
then press down into the center.

above left: 131.
When the clay is centered,
make a depression
by pressing both thumbs down
while cupping the clay
with your hands.

above right: 132.
Pull outward with the thumbs
to form the base of the pot.

Throwing Specific Forms

The Cylinder

The cylinder is the basic form from which all other shapes develop. When the initial ball of clay is centered, the clay is *opened up*.

- Cup the clay with both hands, with your thumbs touching at center, and press the thumbs down evenly, creating a small depression.
- Add water or thin slip to both the hands and the pot, or the clay will peel off on the fingers. If slip has accumulated on the hands, strip it onto the clay form, and add water with a sponge rather than by the handful.
- Continue the downward pressure of the thumbs to within about ¾ inch from the wheel head. If necessary, use the pin to gauge the thickness of the bottom. If the bottom is too thick, the pot will be very heavy and may crack; if too thin, it will be difficult to remove from the wheel.
- Encircle the clay with your fingers, and squeeze your thumbs outward against your fingers to form a bowl shape. Be careful to keep the pressure equal with both thumbs.
- Lift your fingers upward while maintaining pressure with your thumbs. This will form a low, thick cylinder.
- To refine the bottom, press the fingertips of the right hand in the center and move them across the bottom, forcing the clay outward. Do this several times. The spiral design created by the fingers can be left or smoothed with a sponge.
- Pull up the walls and make them thinner. The right hand should be on the outside of the pot and the left hand inside. Sit erect with your arms and elbows braced and your thumbs touching for additional support. Pressing the fingers of the right hand against the fingers of the left will pull the clay upward.
- For a small piece three pulls from bottom to top should complete the cylinder.
- If the top is uneven, cut it off with the needle tool.

above: 133. When a low, thick cylinder has been established, press with your fingertips from the outside against the fingers inside the pot.

above right: 134. The walls are thinned by squeezing the clay between the fingers. Near the top, where the walls may be thinner, bracing the inside hand against the outside with the thumb will help to keep a steady pressure.

right: 135. If the rim is uneven, cut it with the needle.

The pressure applied to harder clay or larger pieces often results in deep finger ridges on the sides of the pot. Holding a soft piece of leather or a sponge over the fingertips will eliminate much of this effect. In the initial stages of throwing a large pot or stiff clay, the knuckles of the right hand can be used to apply greater pressure. However, the fingertips are much more sensitive to the movement and moisture content of the clay and should be used for throwing most pots.

above left: 136. For larger pieces, press with the knuckle against the inside hand.

above right: 137. A cross section shows the clay being pulled upward between the knuckle and fingers.

below left: 138. As the walls are thinned, the form grows taller.

below right: 139. In later stages, the walls should be uniformly thick.

The clay should not flare out at the base of the finished cylinder, but must instead be forced into the wall and pulled up. After the first few cylinders are completed, you can cut the pots open with a wire or needle to determine the evenness of the walls. Everyone is eager to make a pot that can be fired, but it is better to continue throwing until you throw a cylinder at least 12 inches high with walls of uniform thickness.

If a pot starts to sag, it is best to roll up the clay, let it dry, rewedge, and begin again. To throw a pot properly takes little time, but much practice is needed to learn the technique. If the beginner spends too much time trying to patch up wobbly pots, the proper sequence that makes throwing relatively easy will never be learned.

right: 140. For a bowl, open the clay leaving a rounded curve for the bottom.

below right: 141. Pull up the walls into a tall, thick-walled bowl shape.

The Bowl

From the basic rounded beehive form any number of shapes can be made. The bowl presents the fewest problems. Bowls should always be thrown on bats, because their wider shape makes them difficult to remove from the wheel. Always open the beehive shape with attention to the inside curve created by the fingers. This curve should be round and continuous, for any flattening will cause the walls to collapse.

- Pull up the clay into a deep thick-walled bowl shape, about twice the height of the planned final form. (The bowl will flatten as it is pulled outward.)
- Leave a rim thick enough for the circumference to expand. Compress the rim occasionally with a leather or with the fingertips to counteract the weakening effect of expansion.
- If necessary, trim the top with a needle, and then smooth it with the leather.
- With the wheel moving very slowly, flare out the high walls to a wide bowl shape. The inside hand should move from the center of the pot out

above left: 142. When the walls
are pulled outward, cut the rim with a needle
to eliminate any unevenness.

left: 143. Finish the rim
with a piece of soft leather.

toward the edges. Try to reach your final shape in a minimum number of pulls so that the clay will not begin to sag.

If you want a taller mixing bowl shape, thin the walls in the same manner as for the cylinder.

Because a large bowl needs support at the base, the throwing pressure should always be light at the point where the clay flares out from the base. A definite rim of some thickness lessens the problems of warping and breaking, allows the bowl to be picked up more easily, and provides a design accent for the bowl shape.

144. Harrison McIntosh, U.S.A.
Bottle. Stoneware with a mat glaze,
iron engobe, and sgraffito design;
height 14″ (35 cm).

The Bottle

In throwing a vase or bottle, one does not make a thick little bottle and then
attempt to thin the walls. Rather, the form begins with a rounded beehive
shape that is opened up to a low, thick cylinder.

- Pull up the thick walls into as tall a cylinder as the clay will allow, at the
  same time keeping the cylinder as narrow as possible.
- Wet the entire arm to prevent any friction from distorting the piece.
- As you throw, remove excess water from the bottom with a sponge

above right: 145.
To throw a bottle form,
first make a tall cylinder.

right: 146.
Hold the form with both hands,
and apply even pressure,
starting at the base
and moving up the side
to make the cylinder
taller and narrower.

attached to a long dowel. (If the base becomes waterlogged, you may
accidentally put your fingers through the bottom.)

- If the body of the pot is to be flared out, make the base of the cylinder
  slightly thicker than usual.
- Expand the shape by applying pressure with the inside fingers against
  the fingers on the outside wall.
- When the shape of the lower section of the pot has been established, neck
  in the upper part. Moisten the clay and your hands. Place your fingers in
  a circular position, and compress the clay in an upward movement.
  Apply a gentle, even pressure. Too great a pressure will cause the clay to
  buckle and fold over on itself. Necking in the top results in a thicker wall,
  which can then be pulled up in the usual manner.
- If the form becomes so reduced that only a single finger can enter the
  neck, at this point hold a wooden tool inside the neck to further refine
  and thin the form.
- Finish the lip with a soft piece of leather after any unevenness is cut
  away with the needle.

147. Applying pressure
with the inside fingers
flares out the base of the cylinder.

148. Necking makes the top
of the cylinder narrower and thinner.
Apply gentle, even pressure
with both hands.

149. Pull up the top section, making the walls thinner
and applying more pressure with the outside fingers
to keep the top narrow. It may be necessary
to repeat the operation several times.

above left: 150.
The process continues
until the desired form evolves.

above right: 151. Finish the lip
with a piece of soft leather.

152. Jan de Rooden, Holland.
Sphere. Stoneware
with a groggy engobe
brushed over for texture,
colored stains, and a thin glaze;
diameter 19″ (47 cm).
This form is thrown
in the same way as a bottle
except that the body
is flared out very wide,
and the neck is closed completely.

153. Cut finished pots from the wheel by drawing a wire underneath.

You should not expect the final bottle or vase to be taller than the original cylinder. Although the necking in of the top section thickens the clay and allows it to be pulled up farther, the inevitable vibration of throwing causes the clay to settle.

Throwing Aids

Most large pots and wide bowls must be thrown on a bat, but many pieces can be thrown conveniently right on the wheel head. These can be cut from the wheel with a wire or string, then lifted off with a slight twisting motion of the first two fingers of both hands. A thicker base and undercut with a

154. Lift the pot off the wheel by holding it with the fingertips at the base where the clay is thickest.

above left: 155. A pointer serves as a guideline when throwing many pots of the same height.

above right: 156. Small pots can be thrown "off the hump." Leave a thick base and undercut to facilitate lifting the pot and to prevent distortion.

wooden tool will provide an easier handle for the fingers and will lessen the tendency of the pot to distort.

A hinged, adjustable pointer is a handy guide for throwing pots of uniform height.

Small pieces such as cups, bowls, or bottles can be thrown "off the hump"—a larger mass of clay. This method is much faster when a great many pots of the same size are being thrown at the same time, for it is easier to center each ball of clay. To remove the thrown form from the larger mass of clay, cut a groove at the bottom, and pull the string through with the wheel revolving slowly.

Problems in Throwing

The following situations and practices may cause difficulty in throwing:

- Clay that is too stiff, too soft, or poorly wedged.
- Opening up the clay before it is properly centered.
- Greater pressure with one thumb than the other when opening the ball, making the walls uneven.
- Applying too much water so that the clay becomes too soft.
- Unsteady pressure from inside the pot, making the pot wobble.
- Pressure from both the inside and the outside fingers, causing a thin spot in the walls.
- Throwing too slowly and overworking the clay, causing the pot to sag.
- Allowing throwing water to collect in the bottom of the pot, making the clay soft and the pot difficult to remove from the wheel. This also creates a tendency for the pot to crack during drying.

Trimming

Trimming removes excess clay from the bottom of a pot, so that it is lighter and less likely to crack. If desired, trimming can give the pot a *foot*—a ridge of clay at the base to serve as a design accent. Some pots can be trimmed during the throwing stage and the mark of the cutting wire left as it is. In Figure 159 the excess clay was pinched into a foot while still plastic.

157. With the wheel revolving slowly, cut the pot from the larger mass of clay with a cord.

below: 158. Cup with handle, from Gournia, Crete. 1600–1500 B.C. (Late Minoan I). Light-colored clay with oxide design, height 3¹³⁄₁₆″ (9.75 cm). Metropolitan Museum of Art, New York (gift of the American Exploration Society, 1907). The photograph shows the wire marks left after the cup was cut from the wheel.

right: 159. Pitcher, English. 14th century. Red ware with slip decoration and pale yellow lead glaze; height 14″ (35 cm). Guildhall Museum, London.

160. James F. McKinnell, U.S.A.
Punch bowl. Stoneware with carved
design, cobalt and iron stains,
and a banded luster glaze;
diameter 16″ (40 cm).
A well-proportioned foot
completes this bowl design.

Most often, trimming or *tooling* is done when the pots have dried to the *leather hard* stage—still moist but dry enough to hold their shape without distorting. If the pot becomes too dry, there is a danger of cracking; if too soft, it will sag. A pot that becomes too dry after throwing can be restored to a leather-hard state by spraying it with a plant mister both inside and out. This should be done several times to ensure an even absorption of water. A plaster bat will absorb the excess moisture and prevent the bottom from becoming too soft. A pot that has become completely dry, however, should be discarded; it will take less time to throw a new one than to reclaim the old.

If thrown on bats, pots should be cut through at the bottom with a wire to allow the clay to contract evenly. Plates, platters, and wide bowls should be inverted on a wooden bat after they have stiffened slightly to allow the thicker bottom to dry. This will also prevent the rims from drying too quickly, and thus reduce the chances of warping and cracking.

When the pot is leather hard, observe its inside shape and judge its thickness to determine how much clay needs to be removed. If you are unsure, insert a pin.

■ Place the pot upside down on the wheel, and center it. A tall vase or bottle can be placed inside a wide-mouthed glass or ceramic jar or a plaster chuck that has been centered and secured to the wheel.

■ Press a roll of clay around the circumference, and attach the pot (or the supporting jar) securely to the wheel. Avoid using random lumps of clay, for these place a strain on the rim and cause cracks.

■ With the wheel turning at a moderate speed, apply the trimming tool to the pot and shape the bottom.

■ Begin by reducing the diameter of the base, where most of the clay tends to be. Trimming will help to control a foot that is too wide.

In trimming, try to maintain the same fluid motion as you did in throwing, so that the foot seems like a natural extension of the pot. Remember that the inside curve of the foot should repeat the exterior. It is interesting to note that while Japanese potters throw with the wheel turning in a clockwise direction, they trim pots turning in a counterclockwise motion. This makes the trimming marks blend into the throwing rings without changing the surface texture.

above left: 161. Place tall vases or bottles in a plaster chuck; the narrow neck cannot support the weight of the pot.

above right: 162. Secure the pot in the chuck or supporting jar, and then begin the trimming process.

below left: 163. Excess clay is first trimmed from the diameter of the base.

below right: 164. Then, the center portion of the foot is cut away.

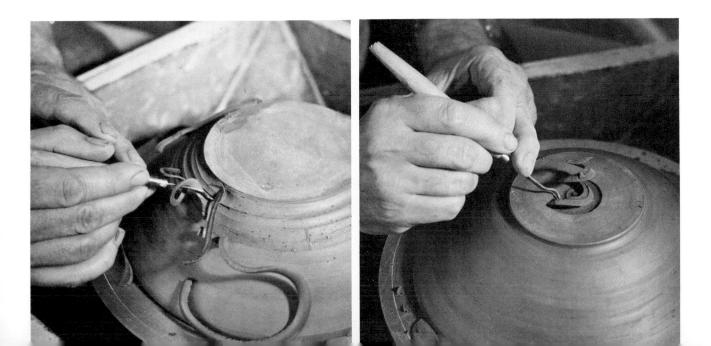

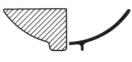

165. Different kinds of feet
appropriate to a vertical cup shape
and a shallow bowl form
are shown in sections.

166. Hispano-Moresque platter,
bottom view.
From Manises, Spain. 1468–79.
Earthenware with luster decoration,
diameter 17½″ (43.75 cm).
Victoria & Albert Museum, London
(Crown Copyright).

Although the height and contour of a foot depend on the overall design, the base edge should have a slight bevel to make it less susceptible to chipping. An outward taper of the foot will give the pot both an actual and a visual stability. Especially wide shapes such as platters may need a second foot to support the large expanse of clay and prevent sagging. Tall pedestal-type feet can be thrown separately, tooled, and then joined to bowl or cup shapes when the clay is leather hard. Handbuilt feet can also be applied to the tooled bottom at the leather-hard stage. More information about the design of a foot will be given in Chapter 5.

After firing, sand the bottoms of tooled pots to remove any roughness and prevent scratching of furniture. In some cases it may be desirable to glue a felt pad to the bottom of the pot.

167. Lucie Rie. England. Footed bowl.
Porcelain with brown-black glaze, sgraffito design,
and unglazed foot; diameter 10″ (25 cm).

below: 168. Luke Lindoe, Canada. Footed bowl.
Stoneware with incised decoration
and reduction-fired crackle glaze,
height 9″ (22 cm).
Part of the foot can be cut out
to provide a design accent.

right: 169. Stem cup. Chinese
(Hsüan-Tê period). 1426–1435.
Porcelain with fish design in copper-red,
height 3⅝″ (8.5 cm).
Victoria & Albert Museum, London
(Crown Copyright).
A pedestal foot is usually thrown separately.

170. Tripod jars, Mexico.
Earthenware, heights $7\frac{3}{8}$″ (18.5 cm)
and $5\frac{1}{2}$″ (13.7 cm).
Metropolitan Museum of Art, New York
(The Michael C. Rockefeller Memorial
Collection of Primitive Art).
Fanciful handbuilt shapes
are another possibility for feet.

Appendages

Handles

Handles are joined to a form after it has been trimmed and while it is still leather hard. Any appendage attached to a thrown pot should be of the same moisture content, so that in drying the two parts will shrink at the same rate. This makes the join stronger, less apt to separate and crack. A pulled handle is made in the following way:

- Wedge clay that is slightly stiffer than throwing consistency, and roll it into a thick taper.
- Hold the butt end in the left hand, wet the right hand, and pull the clay in a swift, downward motion.
- Pull the clay three or four times, wetting the hand each time and turning the mass of clay.
- Apply even pressure that is lighter toward the end of the elongated strip.
- If the thickness varies, cut off the uneven part, because it will weaken the handle.
- Pressure with the thumb against the fingers during the pulling motion will result in a more comfortable handle.
- Score and apply slip to the two points of attachment on the pot.

below left: 171. Pulling a handle
from a butt of clay,
impressing with the thumb.

below right: 172. Handles can also
be pulled directly on the pot
if the taper of clay
is first attached well
with score marks and slip.

173. Kenneth Green, U.S.A. Basket.
Stoneware with dolomite glaze
fired to cone 9, height 10″ (25 cm).
A pulled handle can be decorative
as well as functional.

174. Wanda Garnsey, Australia.
Wine decanters.
The white bottles are porcelain
with a dolomite glaze,
the black is stoneware
with a black slip;
all are reduction-fired to cone 8.
These handbuilt handles complement
the symmetry of the thrown forms.

Appendages **83**

175. Angelo Garzio, U.S.A.
Traveling coffee mugs.
Stoneware with mat iron red
and yellow glazes, reduction-fired
to cone 9; height 5″ (12.5 cm).
The handles on these mugs
were pulled on the pot.

■ Pinch or cut the butt end of the handle and press it firmly against the upper section of the pot, smoothing the clay to strengthen the join.
■ Correct the curve, and fasten the bottom of the handle to the score marks.

Handles for cups and other small objects can be made by attaching the thicker end of the handle to the upper score mark and pulling the handle directly on the pot. The handles in Figure 175 were joined in this manner with small knobs of clay placed on the upper ridge for a thumb rest. Decorative handles made of coils or slabs of clay are also possible.

Whichever method is used, after the joining is completed the ware should be placed in a damp room or covered with plastic to allow a slow and even drying. This will prevent the small diameter of the handle from drying and contracting faster than the body of the pot, causing cracks to develop.

The beginner may have to pull many handles in order to achieve one that looks and fits well on a pot. At first it may help to let the handle dry slightly after pulling. The joining process is easier if the surface of the handle is not wet with slip.

When you need a high, rising handle, as for a teapot, you may prefer to purchase a readymade one of cane. In this event, attach a ring of clay to two sides to later accept the handle. The rings should be joined, with scoring and slip, in the usual manner. You can also use a conventional pulled handle on a teapot.

Spouts

Pitcher spouts are made just after the pot has been thrown, while the clay is still soft.

■ Place the thumb and index finger against the rim to act as a support.
■ Form the spout with a wiping motion of the other hand.
■ Keep the width of the spout in proportion to the size of the pitcher.
■ If the wiping motion is continuous and the edge sharp, the pitcher will not drip.

left: **176. Bill Read,** England.
Fluted tea pot.
Stoneware with talc glaze
reduction-fired to cone 8.
The shape and incised decoration
of this teapot
are enhanced by the bamboo handle.

below left: 177. Making a pitcher spout
with a wiping motion of one finger
on the soft rim supported by
the fingers of the other hand.

below: 178. Polly Myhrum, U.S.A.
Pitchers. Stoneware with mat glaze
fired to cone 6 in electric kiln;
heights 6½″ (16.25 cm) and
3½″ (9 cm).

above: 180. English Staffordshire jug.
Mid-18th century. Red earthenware
with white slip decoration and clear glaze,
height 9½″ (23.75 cm).
Victoria & Albert Museum, London
(Crown Copyright).
This spout is made from a separate slab of clay
joined when the pot is leather hard.

below: 181. Throw a teapot spout
in a cone shape with a wide base
and a slight flare to the rim.

179. Etruscan oïnochoe with trefoil spout,
found in Chiusi, Italy.
Low-fired black ware with incised decoration.
Art Institute of Chicago
(gift of D. P. Armour and C. L. Hutchinson).

182. Geoffrey Whiting, England.
Teapot. Stoneware with red iron glaze
fired in a coal- and wood-burning kiln.

A spout need not be an extension of the rim. In Figure 180 the spout is
formed from a slab of clay that is folded into a V-shape and attached to
the rim.

A teapot spout is thrown at the same time as the pot and the cover, so
that all will shrink at the same rate. This kind of spout is more complicated,
because there are many functional and aesthetic considerations. The spout
must be long enough to reach above the rim of the teapot, or else the pot
cannot be filled to the top. The base must be broad and low on the pot so as
not to become clogged with tea leaves.

- Once the placement has been established, trace the outline of the spout
  on the pot, and score and slip the outline.
- With the fettling knife, make as many strainer holes as the space will
  permit in the portion of the pot wall to be covered by the spout.

left: 183. Cut the base of the spout
to conform to the body of the pot,
trace the outline of the spout on the pot,
and make strainer holes
with the fettling knife.

below: 184. The different parts of a teapot,
tooled and ready to assemble:
the spout, the lid,
the handle, and the pot.

- Wait until the clay has dried to brush away any rough burrs, for otherwise they will stick in the holes.
- Join the spout to the pot while it is still somewhat soft. At this point the base can be pinched into a graceful curve.
- Make the pouring lip sharp in profile to prevent dripping. If the clay is too hard to manipulate, cut a groove in the lip.

Lids

There are many different ways of making covers for pots. However, all are thrown at the same time as the pot and are measured accurately with calipers to ensure a tight fit. A lid should always conform to the shape of the pot and complement its lines. You must be careful when removing a lid from the wheel or bat and during trimming. If the lid is distorted while it is still soft, it will most likely warp as it dries and not fit correctly. It is almost

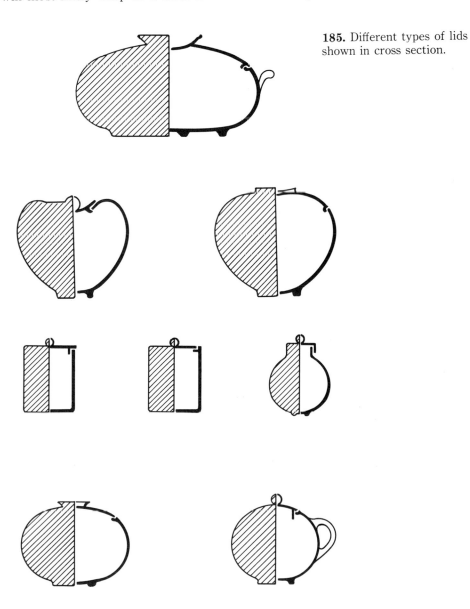

185. Different types of lids shown in cross section.

right: 186. Using calipers to determine the exact measurement for a lid.

below: 187. Angelo Garzio, U.S.A. Casserole. Stoneware with a blue-gray glaze reduction-fired to cone 9, diameter 15″ (37.5 cm). This knob was pulled in a manner similar to the pulling of the handle, and applied when the lid was leather hard.

impossible to make a lid for a pot that is too dry. Because of the different shrinkage rates, the lid will not fit the pot.

One of the simplest types of lid is a flat disk with a knob thrown on top. If small, it can be thrown off the hump, but a wide lid should be thrown on a bat. The vessel must have a depressed inner flange to support the flat lid.

Casseroles or teapots must have an inner flange below the pot rim to hold the lid. This prevents moisture and escaping steam from running down the sides of the pot. In throwing the pot, keep the rim a little thicker than usual. Then, with the finger, depress a portion of the rim to form the inner retaining ring. Finish the rim with a soft leather.

A domed or slightly rounded lid is thrown like a simple bowl. The rim is thick enough to allow an inner retaining ring to fit inside the top of the pot. When leather hard, the lid is inverted and the top tooled. A knob can be thrown on the lid or thrown separately and attached with slip. Knobs can also be made of pulled strips or coils attached to the lid.

Another kind of lid is actually a shallow bowl that conforms to the slightly flared rim of the pot it covers. The knob is thrown on the lid at the same time. Later, the bottom is trimmed of excess clay. This method works especially well when a great number of lids are being thrown, because they can be thrown off the hump, the tooling process is faster, and there is a wider margin of error in the fit.

Once you understand the basics of making a lid, you can explore a great variety of shapes. There are also many possibilities besides thrown clay. For example, corks make very tight-fitting lids and provide an interesting contrast to clay.

188. Angelo Garzio, U.S.A.
Covered jar. Stoneware
with a white mat glaze
over iron stain
and an incised wax-resist design,
height 7″ (17.5 cm).
A lid for a small pot
may not need a knob.

right: 189. Covered jar, Onda ware. Japanese.
White slip with trailed glaze decoration,
done in typical folk-art tradition;
height 24″ (60 cm).

below: 190. Water jar. Japanese, c. 1500.
Coarse stoneware with glaze splashed on,
height 5¾″ (14.5 cm).
Metropolitan Museum of Art, New York
(Rogers Fund, 1917).
The lacquer lid
is an elegant accent for this pot.

left: **191. Harrison McIntosh,** U.S.A.
Covered jar. Stoneware with a mat glaze
over gray and black wax-resist decoration,
fired to cone 5; height 9½″ (23.75 cm).

below: **192. Polly Myhrum,** U.S.A. Covered jars.
Stoneware, brown glaze over white,
blue glaze over white,
both fired to cone 6 in an electric kiln;
heights 8″ (20 cm) and 5″ (12.5 cm).
These lids are shallow bowl shapes
that sit on the flared rim of the jar.

193. James Thornsbury, Canada.
Fantasy Faucet.
Talc body with luster glaze
fired to cone 06; height 4′ (1.2 m).
The sections of this construction
are easily discernible: the tall parts
with deep throwing rings,
the rounded bulbs,
and the faucet handles.
Yet when put together,
they create a unified composition.

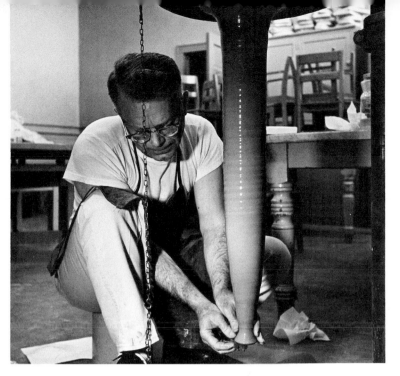

left: 194. Geometric-style funerary vase from Cyprus.
8th century B.C. Earthenware with paneled and banded decoration
of horses, deer, waterbirds, and double axes; height $46\frac{7}{8}''$ (117.5 cm).
Metropolitan Museum of Art, New York
(Cesnola Collection; purchased by subscriptions, 1874–76).

above: 195. The "upside down" wheel for throwing very tall forms
was developed by Sheldon Carey.

below: 196. Covered stem cup with pierced base.
Korean, Old Sill Dynasty, 57 B.C.–A.D. 668.
Gray stoneware, height $9\frac{1}{4}''$ (23.25 cm). Seattle Art Museum
(Eugene Fuller Memorial Collection).

Multiple-Section Forms

There are limits to the potential size of forms thrown from one section of
clay. Most people can comfortably center only about 20 pounds of clay at a
time, and 50 pounds is certainly the maximum. It is foolish to try to stretch
clay beyond its natural capacity. Trying to make walls ever taller always
leads to excessive thinness and may cause the form to flop. A number of
devices have been developed to counteract this problem, including the
"upside-down wheel." The wheel is attached to a heavy shaft so that it can
be raised and reversed after the basic cylinder is begun. This enables the
potter to throw extremely tall cylinders and bottles. An air bubble, however,
is disastrous, for the whole pot will collapse.

Many potters find it more convenient to throw an extremely tall or large
shape in sections. The sections should be allowed to dry to leather hard and
then joined. The Greeks used this method for their funerary vases, which
often stood more than 4 feet tall.

If a smaller pot consists of different angular shapes, it too can be thrown
in multiple sections.

197. Don Reitz, U.S.A.
Five-section form.
Stoneware, unfired;
height 42″ (105 cm).
The photographs that follow
show its construction.

The pot by Don Reitz in Figure 197 is more than 3½ feet tall and consists of five separately thrown sections. The following sequence of photographs illustrates twelve steps in the construction of the form. Some general guidelines will help the beginner attempting a multiple-section pot.

- Make a sketch of the final form, deciding upon the number of pieces, how they will be thrown, and how they will be joined.
- Throw the sections from one clay body, wedge and prepare the pieces at the same time, and cover with plastic all but the one being thrown.
- Throw the pieces in a sequence so they will be of the same consistency as they dry.
- Cover the rims with plastic after they set up to promote an even drying.
- Join the top of one section to the top of another, and bottoms to bottoms to ensure a similar moisture content.
- Score all joints, and thoroughly coat them with slip.
- Make curves round and uniform as in a bridge arch, for any flatness will cause the form to collapse.
- Cover the assembled form with plastic for three or four days. This will equalize the shrinkage of the different parts and prevent cracking.

left: 198. Opening up a large mass of clay.
A wide plywood bat has been attached
to the wheel head with three concentric rings
of clay to allow for the widest possible diameter
of this base section.

above: 199. Smoothing the rim of the bottom section.
The base is thrown upside down in a flat cone shape;
a cone will support the weight of the clay
better than a rounded form.

below: 200. For the largest section
of the form, two 25-pound balls
of wedged clay are compressed together
on a plywood bat.

right: 201. The clay is opened up to the edge of the bat
(so as to conform to the width of the cone shape)
and then thrown into a beehive shape.

202. On a smaller plywood bat,
a short cylinder
(to sit on top of the beehive shape)
is thrown and measured with calipers.

left: 203. The rim of a second, taller cylinder
being measured with calipers
to ensure a close fit
with the rim of the shorter cylinder.

above: 204. When the base section is leather hard,
it is tooled, and the rim is scored
and coated with slip.
A stiff slab of clay cut to fit the hole
is then joined.

205. After the base has become firm, it is inverted and recentered on the wheel head. A thick coil of plastic clay attaches the piece to the wheel and supports it while the other sections are added.

below: 206. The beehive shape is attached to the base section after both have been scored and slipped. The join is reinforced by impressing with the thumb.

right: 207. The shorter cylinder is joined to the rim of the beehive shape. The thumb marks from the previous join have been smoothed over.

above: 208. When the second cylinder
is added, the rim is recentered
and smoothed.

above right: 209. To complete the form,
a collar is joined
to the rim of the cylinder.

right: 210. Finally, to counter the vertical movement
of the vase, appendages of plastic clay
are joined to the neck.
These are attached like handles,
but instead of being pulled
symmetrically, they are modeled
into decorative shapes.

4
Decorating and Glazing

Decoration should complement and not overwhelm a ceramic form. The character and shape of a piece will suggest an appropriate type of decoration. However, there is never only one method suitable for a particular shape. The Italian drug jar (Fig. 211) and the Art Nouveau vase (Fig. 212) are both cylindrical forms, but the very different painted designs create two unique effects.

Decoration

You should decide how you want to decorate a piece during the forming stages, because some types of decoration are undertaken while the clay is still plastic. Often, freely thrown or elaborately handbuilt forms are complete in themselves, and some may need only a coating of a single glaze. Other simpler shapes may benefit from plastic additions or a painted design in slip or underglaze. Planning the decoration and glazes for a form while you are making it will help to create a more unified result.

When faced with the many potential glaze colors, textures, and methods of application, the novice potter often tends to try a little of everything on one pot. The result usually resembles a discarded paint can, devoid of accidental charm. With experience it is possible to use a single stroke of color or a single glaze and produce a free and fluid effect, or to allow a heavy application of glaze to make its own design.

below left: 211. Drug jar, from Caffaggiolo, Italy. Early 16th century. Earthenware with majolica glaze, height 8⅞″ (22.25 cm). Victoria & Albert Museum, London (Crown Copyright).

below right: 212. Georges de Feure, designer; E. Gérard, potter. Art Nouveau vase, produced at Limoges. c. 1898–1904. Porcelain with design in green, lavender, and gray. Metropolitan Museum of Art, New York (Edward C. Moore, Jr., Gift Fund, 1926).

left: **213. Bertil Vallien,** Sweden.
Sculptural form. 1968.
Stoneware with vigorous applied clay additions
that almost obscure the original shape.

below: **214. Ruth Duckworth,** U.S.A. Form.
1976. Stoneware slab construction
with variegated textures,
diameter 25″ (62.5 cm).

below left: **215. Don Schaumburg,** U.S.A. Vase.
Porcelain with trailed slip design and alkaline glaze
fired to cone 9, height 7″ (17.5 cm).

below right: **216. Ogata Kenzan,** Japan. *Bellflowers,*
fan-shape cake tray. Edo Period, 18th century.
Stoneware with enameled decoration on cream-colored glaze,
length of sides 6⅝″ (16.5 cm).
Seattle Art Museum (Eugene Fuller Memorial Collection).
The freely painted design complements the fan shape.

above: 217. **Ken Ferguson,** U.S.A. Vase.
Stoneware, freely thrown with pinched depression,
wood-fired; height 8″ (20 cm).

right: 218. **Ingeborg and Bruno Asshoff,** Germany.
Constructions. Wheel-thrown forms
embellished with slabs and ornament,
white feldspathic glaze;
height of larger piece 20⅜″ (51 cm).

Clay in the Plastic State

Decoration can be incorporated into a form while the clay is still soft. In a wheel-thrown piece, deep throwing rings, pinched depressions, or modeled designs will provide decorative accents. After removal from the wheel, the form can be modeled even more, although you must take care not to stretch the clay too much, or it might collapse.

In the handbuilding process there are many possibilities for decoration. Coils or slabs can be pinched together or modeled into an endless variety of shapes for both functional and decorative purposes.

Colored Clay Bodies   Colored clays offer one of the most basic means of decoration in both throwing and handbuilding. Oxides are added to dry clay ingredients, and then the batch is mixed with water and dried until of wedging consistency. (See the Appendix for amounts of colorants added to bodies.) Some of the possibilities for colored clays include *neriage, millefiore, Egyptian paste,* and *marbling.*

above: 219. **Rolf Overberg,** Germany. *Fruit.* Wheel-thrown and altered spheres
with green and rust ash glazes on a dark manganese body, wood-fired to cone 6; height 6″ (15 cm).
The slabs with type set in relief increase the tactile quality of these objects.

below: 220. **Robert Eckels,** U.S.A. *Dish.* Stoneware slab with coiled additions and mat glaze,
length 12″ (30 cm). The glaze has been wiped off the raised decoration for increased contrast.

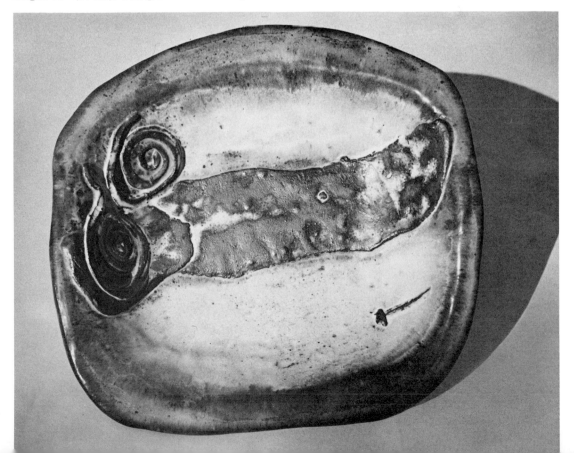

221. Bernard Palissy, France.
Oval platter. Late 16th century.
Polychrome ceramic,
length 20½″ (51.25 cm).
Louvre, Paris.
Plastic decoration can be carried
to amazingly detailed
and fanciful extremes.

Neriage and millefiore utilize colored clays pieced together in molds. In neriage, shaped segments of plastic clay are joined in a concave mold to make a pattern identical on both the interior and exterior surfaces of the pot. The contrasting clay pieces can be strips, coils, or small slabs. They must be joined well and allowed to dry slowly.

Millefiore is a more complicated technique evolved from glass making. The different-colored clays are rolled into slabs, then layered in "loaves" or long rectangles that show the colored design in cross-section. The loaf is sliced through to make a slab, then this slab is joined with other slabs and small pieces of clay in a plaster mold. (See Chap. 2 and Figs. 78–84 for forming techniques.) Needless to say, the decorative possibilities with this technique are great, for the colored clays combined with glazes, lusters, or decals can create an ornate design (Fig. 296).

Egyptian paste is another technique in which both decoration and glazes are combined in a plastic clay. The paste has colorants and glaze-forming materials incorporated into the body in a soluble form. The actual clay content is very low—no more than about 20 percent of the body—with the major portion being nonplastic materials such as flint. As the clay dries, sodium is deposited on the surface and combines with the flint and colorants to create a glaze. Developed by the Egyptians before 3000 B.C., this paste was the earliest form of glaze known. It is most often seen in turquoise-colored beads and small, modeled figurines.

above: **222. Robin Hopper,** Canada. Bowl.
Porcelain with neriage inlay,
diameter 12″ (30 cm).

right: **223.** *Ushabti of King Seti I,*
Egyptian, from Thebes. 1313–1292 B.C.
Alkaline-silica body, height 11¾″ (29.4 cm).
Metropolitan Museum of Art, New York
(Carnavon Collection, gift of Edward S. Harkness, 1926).
Ushabti are small, mummylike tomb figures
that accompanied the dead in the afterlife.

below: **224.** *Hippopotamus,* from the tomb of Senbi
at Meir, Egypt. XII Dynasty (2000–1788 B.C.).
Egyptian faience, height 4⅜″ (11 cm).
Metropolitan Museum of Art, New York
(gift of Edward S. Harkness, 1917).

above left: 225. Clay masses in which pieces of different-colored clays have been joined together. The piece in the foreground has been sliced through crosswise after a minimum of wedging.

above right: 226. Agateware vessel, English, from Staffordshire. Early 18th century. Body composed of different-colored earthenware clays wedged together, height 6⅜″ (15 cm). Victoria & Albert Museum, London (Crown Copyright).

The paste is highly nonplastic and suitable mainly for simple handbuilt forms and beads. Another limitation is that excessive handling will remove the surface coating of sodium. Pieces should be dried and fired on stilts, or, for small objects such as beads, strung on Nichrome wire, because fingerprints on the paste will leave unglazed patches. When completely dry, the finished piece can be once-fired to cone 08 or 07, depending upon the formula. (See Appendix for an Egyptian paste body.)

Marbling, an ancient technique to make clay look like stone, became popular in Europe during the 18th century and was termed *agateware* by the English. Slabs of different-colored clays are placed on top of each other and wedged just enough to remove air pockets. The mass is then thrown in the normal manner, with the layers creating color striations.

Leather-Hard Clay

The term *leather hard* refers to clay that has dried enough to be handled without distorting but contains sufficient moisture to permit joins to be made and slips applied without cracking. Incising, carving, and stamping are most conveniently done at this stage, because the clay cuts cleanly and does not stick to the tool.

Thrown forms that have "set up" can be paddled to flatten the sides. If the walls are very thick, they can be cut with a fettling knife and then carved. Elaborate handles joined to thrown or handbuilt forms can serve as decoration and a design accent.

right: 227. Horst Kerstan, Germany.
Five-sided bottle.
Stoneware with iron glaze
fired to cone 10, height 8″ (20 cm).

below left: 228. Shoji Hamada, Japan. Vase.
c. 1935. Earthenware with faceted sides
and gray-green glaze, height 14⅞″ (37.25 cm).
Victoria & Albert Museum, London
(Crown Copyright).

below right: 229. Pat Probst Gilman, U.S.A.
Dragon vase. Porcelain
with delicately incised lines
and ornate dragon handles.

left: 230. **Johnny Rolf,** Holland. *Dec. 4.* 1972.
Stoneware slab form with incised figures,
background highlighted by colored stains
and a thin glaze coating;
height 20⅜″ (51 cm).

below: 231. **Geoffrey Whiting,** England. Teapot.
Stoneware with white glaze, reduction fired.
The carved lines enhance the graceful shape
of this teapot and complement
the vertical movement established
by the rising handle.

Incising consists of carving lines with a tool into a clay surface. These lines can be deep cuts providing a strong accent or shallow ones following the contour of the pot. Incised lines can also carve out a design that may be glazed later in a contrasting color.

Stamping is one of the oldest decorative techniques for ceramic objects. Many Neolithic pots have impressed designs of weaves, cords, or basket patterns. These devices are still used today to provide interesting textural decoration. Other possibilities for stamps include shells, leaves, pebbles, and an infinite variety of found objects.

left: **232. Shiga Shigeo,** Australia. *Large Pot.*
Stoneware with incised lines and brushed decoration,
height 18" (45 cm).

below left: **233. Penny Smith,** Australia.
Square vase. Stoneware slab
with pinched coil additions,
carved areas, and wire-cut center piece,
dolomite glaze; height 12⅛" (32 cm).

below right: **234. Donald Frith,** U.S.A.
Bottle. Porcelain with
delicately carved floral pattern.

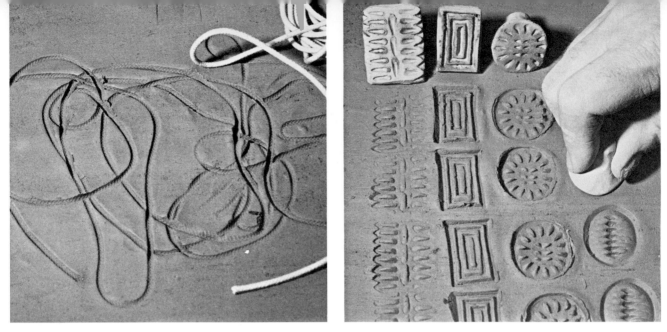

left: 235. Pressing rope into a slab of clay to create an abstract design.
right: 236. Bisqued clay stamps produce relief patterns.

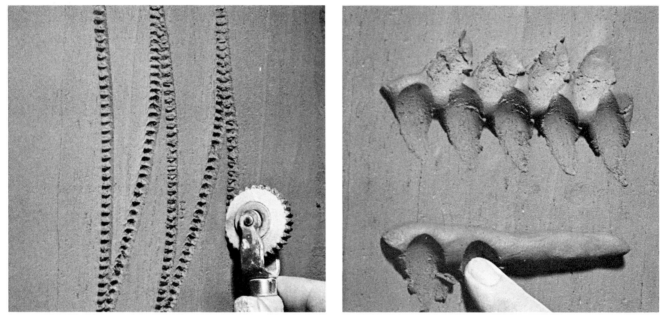

left: 237. Impressed decoration applied with a serrated-edged wheel.
right: 238. Coils of clay joined to a slab and pressed with the fingertips to create a raised design.

Potters also carve stamps out of clay and bisque-fire them for increased durability and to prevent their sticking to wet clay. Stamps should be applied with a fair amount of pressure to make a clear impression. If you are stamping a vertical wall, support the wall with your hand to determine the proper pressure needed. The moisture content of the clay is important. If it is too dry, the clay may crack; if too wet, the stamp may stick.

Rolled stamp decoration has the advantage of greater speed in application but generally produces a less complex design. Applied clay pressed with a finger or a stamp will create a raised pattern and a more ornate, textured design effect.

above: 239. Neolithic pot,
found in the Thames near Mortlake.
Terra cotta with weave imprint,
height 5¼″ (13 cm). British Museum, London.

right: 240. Jug (Bellarmine),
German, from Frecken. Early 17th century.
Stoneware with impressed decoration
and mottled brown salt glaze, height 7¼″ (15.9 cm).
Metropolitan Museum of Art, New York (Rogers Fund, 1917).

below: 241. Ting ware bowl, China. Sung Dynasty, c. 1111–1125.
Porcelain with impressed decoration
showing through a semitranslucent body,
silver band on rim; diameter 7⅞″ (19.75 cm).
Victoria & Albert Museum, London (Crown Copyright).

above: 242. Small balls of clay stamped with a bottle cap for a relief pattern.

right: 243. Hans de Jong, Holland. Vase. Stoneware with incised and stamped decoration, beige glaze with gray-blue and green recesses; height 8″ (20 cm).

below left: 244. Applying bands of slip to a leather-hard vase.

below right: 245. Sgraffito designs are scratched through slip.

Slip decoration can be applied to leather-hard clay in many ways. Slip is clay in liquid suspension. For decorative purposes oxides are added to produce colors. Slip can be brushed over the entire surface of a pot, painted on in designs, or applied in bands. Once the coating has dried, you can scratch lines through to the clay beneath. This is called *sgraffito*. The incising should not be done when the slip is completely dry, because it might flake off. On the other hand, if the slip is too wet, the design will smudge. Do not brush away the rough edges until the slip has dried completely, because this, too, will smudge the design.

right: **246.** Jug, from Gastrica, Cyprus. 7th century B.C. Earthenware with red and black slip decoration, height 13″ (32.5 cm). Victoria & Albert Museum, London (Crown Copyright).

below: **247.**
Harrison McIntosh, U.S.A. Plate. Stoneware with sgraffito design through beige glaze to reveal dark engobe.

248. Vase, French, from Sevres. c. 1785.
Porcelain with sprigged decoration
and blue-and-white glaze,
height 16″ (40 cm).
Victoria & Albert Museum, London
(Crown Copyright).

Sprigging consists of applying relief designs with slip onto a leather-hard surface. Perhaps the best-known examples of sprig designs are the Wedgwood cameos and vases. Sprigs can be formed individually of leather-hard clay, but generally they are made in plaster or bisqued clay molds. First, plastic clay is pressed into the mold. When it begins to dry and shrink away from the form, it is removed, scored and slipped, then pressed onto the pot's surface. If a sprig is too large, it is apt to shrink away from the pot. It is better to build up designs from smaller units.

Slip trailing is the application of slip with a syringe. The line created by this method is very flexible and shows a slight relief effect. The three examples illustrated here demonstrate the great variety possible with the slip-trailed line—a fluid design that blends with the glaze, a raised geometric pattern on terra sigillata ware, and a highly ornate design of lines and dots.

A variation of slip trailing is *combed* or *feathered* slipware, a technique popular in Europe, especially England, from the 15th through the 18th centuries. The procedure is unusual and can be applied only to wide, shallow shapes. In this method slip is trailed in parallel lines across the entire surface. Then, the piece is lifted a few inches off the table and dropped. The impact flattens the lines, causing them almost to touch each other. A feather or comb brushed gently across the surface at right angles to the lines creates a delicate pattern. If you wish, you can use the slip trailing technique on a clay slab, and later drape the slab over a mold for shaping.

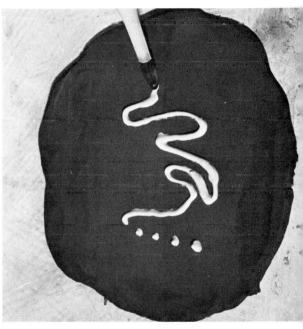

249. *Boney Chicken,*
English. 17th century.
Earthenware dish with trailed slip design
over a glaze,
diameter 7″ (17.5 cm).

above: 250. Applying slip with a syringe
to make a thick raised line.

left: 251. Tom Kerrigan, U.S.A.
Repeated Fours. Lidded container
of burnished earthenware
with designs in terra sigillata,
reduction-fired; height 14½″ (36.25 cm).

left: 252. **Thomas Toft,** England, Staffordshire. Dish. 17th century. Trailed slip design on earthenware. Metropolitan Museum of Art, New York (Rogers Fund, 1924).

below: 253. Platter, English, from Staffordshire. 18th century. Red earthenware with combed white slip decoration, length 20½″ (51.25 cm). Victoria & Albert Museum, London (Crown Copyright).

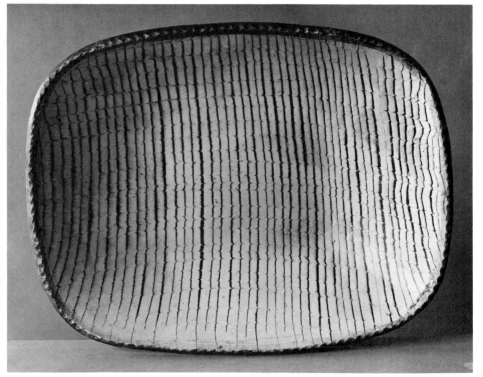

Inlay Decoration   The early and widespread use of incised lines and slip decoration eventually led to a combination of these techniques. One of the simplest methods is to apply a light-colored slip to incised lines in a darker clay body. After the slip has dried slightly, the surface is wiped clean with a scraper, further defining the color contrast. The bowl in Figure 255 has horizontal lines that were incised while it was on the wheel. These were filled with a dark engobe, and the piece was covered with a gray mat glaze.

254. Scraping incised lines to reveal the slip inlay.

255. Harrison McIntosh, U.S.A. Bowl. Stoneware with black engobe in incised lines
and mat gray glaze, fired to cone 5; diameter 4½″ (11.25 cm).

256. Bowl, Korean.
Koryo Dynasty, 14th century.
Porcelain with inlaid
floral decoration and celadon glaze,
diameter 7¾″ (19.4 cm).
Seattle Art Museum
(Eugene Fuller Memorial Collection).

Mishima is an inlay technique of Korean origin. In this method incised lines are filled with clay of a contrasting color. When partially dry the surface is scraped flush. A contemporary example of mishima is seen in the shallow dish called *Garden of Delight* (Fig. 257). Here pieces of different-colored clay were pressed into the surface of the dish, making a surrealistic pictorial composition. The incised details and overlapping clay units were accentuated by acrylic and oil paints.

Clay in the Dry State

When a clay body has dried completely it is known as *greenware*. Decorative possibilities become more limited because of the fragility of clay in this state. The moisture content of soft or leather-hard clay makes it apt to distort, but generally it can be pressed back into its original shape. Greenware is likely to crack and break when knocked or held by the rim. Provided the ware is handled gently, however, there are some decorating techniques possible on dry clay bodies.

Engobes and oxides can be brushed onto dry clay to create colored designs and patterns. An *engobe* is a slip that has a reduced clay content to lessen contraction problems. Usually, half the clay is replaced by feldspar, silica, and a flux, and a small percentage of such plasticizers as bentonite or macaloid can also be added. Coloring oxides and stains are also painted on raw clay, but too thick an application will flake off or cause poor glaze adhesion. A small amount of flux or feldspar added to the colorant and water mixture will help seal the color to the body and make it less susceptible to flaking during the glaze firing.

257. Jack Sures, Canada.
Garden of Delight.
Earthenware with inlaid clay
and acrylic and oil paints,
diameter 22″ (55 cm).

Wax-resist decoration is generally used in conjunction with coloring oxides. The wax may be hot paraffin or beeswax thinned with turpentine; a more convenient water-soluble wax emulsion can be applied cold. The hot preparation makes a cleaner definition and is less apt to pick up specks of color. Be careful not to overheat the wax, because the mixture can ignite. A brushed wax design repels the applied stain, making the stain the background color. Lines incised through a band or panel of wax will absorb the stain or glaze application and produce a decoration of contrasting color.

Glazes with a high clay content, such as the Bristol type, can be applied to dry ware and fired only once. The ware must be of a uniform thickness and the glaze applied quickly to prevent excessive absorption, which will result in cracks. This procedure is most successful on tiles.

258. Applying colored oxides over a wax-resist design.

Bisqued Clay

After a clay body has been bisque fired, the major decorative techniques are associated with glazes and their methods of application. However, a few techniques can be used for underglazing or even to replace a glaze.

Engobes can be applied to bisqued ware to create a rough texture or to alter the color of the body. The engobes must contain sufficient fluxes to fuse with the body, but they should not be so fluid that they create a glossy surface. The dark engobe on the vase in Figure 260 has been wiped off in most areas, leaving a dry textured surface.

Coloring oxides or underglazes are sometimes used as brush decoration, bands of color, or an overall colorant on a bisqued body or a glazed surface. Groggy, textured clays or incised designs can be coated with an oxide-and-water solution and then the excess wiped off. This technique works well on large sculptural pieces where a glaze application is not necessary. Underglazes—oxides mixed with flux or feldspar—produce more uniform colors and are less likely to cause running than oxides mixed just with water.

259. Paul Soldner, U.S.A. Plate. Slab with white and copper slip, brushwork in copper and iron oxide, low-fired and lightly smoked; 10 × 11″ (25 × 27.5 cm).

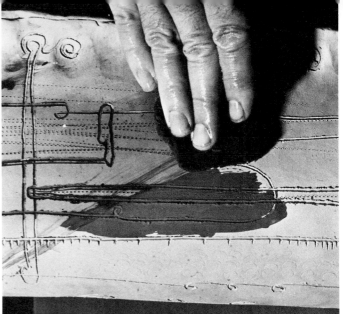

left: 260. **Hans Coper,** England.
Vase, Pilgrim bottle shape. 1958.
Stoneware, assembled from flat bowl shapes
joined to foot and rim,
textured surface with dark engobe accents.
Victoria & Albert Museum, London (Crown Copyright).

above: 261. Coloring oxides
brushed over an incised design
and wiped off with a sponge.

below: 262. **Robert Eckels,** U.S.A. Plate/ashtray.
Stoneware with oxides brushed on over glaze,
diameter 10″ (25 cm).

below: 263. **Russell Collins,** England. Bread crock.
Stoneware with brushed iron-oxide
decoration and talc-dolomite glaze,
height 15″ (37.5 cm).

264. Victor Brosz, Canada. Vases. Porcelain with decorating-pencil designs under a transparent glaze fired to cone 6; height of tallest vase 6″ (15 cm). Glenbow-Alberta Institute, Calgary, Alberta.

Decorating pencils in a variety of colors are manufactured commercially. These are actually oxides or stains in a pencil form. The potter can draw fine lines not possible with brushes on a bisqued surface. The pencils are most successful on smooth, white clay bodies later to be glazed in a clear or translucent white. The decoration can be very intricate, especially when used under a crackle glaze with portions inked for further contrast.

Wax-resist can be brushed on bisqued ware before glazing. The result is a strong contrasting pattern of surface texture with the smooth glaze color. Often, the wax coating does not resist all the glaze, but this accident can be incorporated into an abstract design.

265. Carl E. Paak, U.S.A. *Tree Scape #2.* Porcelain plate with black decorating-pencil design under clear crackle glaze, fired to cone 7, with some portions inked after firing; diameter 16″ (40 cm).

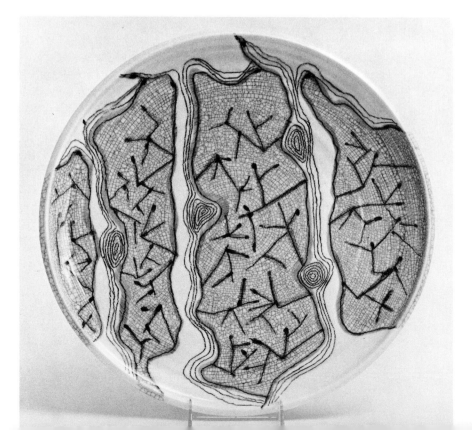

above left: 266.
Luke Lindoe, Canada. Vase.
Dark stoneware body
with wax-resist decoration
and white glaze, height 15″ (37.5 cm).

above right: 267.
Masayuki Imai, Japan. Vase.
Incised lines and wax-resist design
using calligraphic techniques.

right: 268.
Warren MacKenzie, U.S.A. Teapot.
1975. Stoneware with wax-resist
decoration under red kaki glaze,
height 6½″ (16.25 cm).

Glazing

Glazing in the raw clay state has definite advantages. By eliminating the bisque fire, there are savings not only in the labor needed for the extra stacking, unloading, and operation of the kiln but also in the fuel or power needed for the extra firing. A single firing also promotes a better union between the body and the glaze, because the two shrink simultaneously. There are, however, several disadvantages to the combined firing. Because of its fragility, the dry raw-clay vessel may be broken in handling. Expansions caused by the moisture absorbed into the dry clay may cause the vessel to crack. In general, only when the body of a piece is rather thick and uniform can glaze be poured safely. Other pieces should be sprayed, since the glaze, with its troublesome moisture content, can then be applied at a slower rate. One additional precaution must be taken in glazing raw ware: alkaline fluxes must first be fritted. These compounds have a high coefficient of thermal expansion. When they are absorbed into the outer portion of the clay, their expansion and contraction rate during firing and cooling is so great in contrast to the rest of the body that they will cause it to crack.

Glazing in the bisque state is the most common procedure. Normally, bisque ware is fired between cones 010 and 06 (1641°–1830°F, 894°–999°C). At this stage the bisque is hard enough to be handled without mishap yet sufficiently porous to absorb glaze readily. Bisque ware fired at lower temperatures will absorb too much glaze, and the clay structure may break down; if fired too high, it is especially difficult to glaze, for the glaze tends to run off. An exception to the normal bisque firing is high-fire chinaware. Such pieces as thin teacups, which are fragile and likely to warp, are often placed in the kiln with supporting fireclay rings inside their lips, or they are stacked upside down and then fired to their maximum temperature. Later, these chinaware pieces are glazed and fired on their own foot rims at a lower temperature where warpage losses are much less.

How to Glaze

Glazing is a process that can be described only inadequately. Before the actual glazing operation takes place, a few precautions must be taken. If bisque ware is not to be glazed immediately upon its removal from the kiln, it should be stored where dust and soot will not settle on it, or covered with plastic. The bisque ware should not be handled excessively, especially if the hands are oily with perspiration, for this will deter the glaze from adhering properly. All surfaces of the bisque ware should be wiped with a damp sponge or momentarily placed under a water tap to remove dust and loose particles of clay. The moisture added to the bisque ware by this procedure will prevent an excessive amount of glaze from soaking in and thus allow a little more time for glazing. Extra moisture also helps to reduce the number of air pockets and pinholes that form when the glaze dries too quickly on a very porous bisque. The amount of moisture required depends upon the absorbency of the bisque, the thickness of the piece, and the consistency of the glaze. Should the bisque-fire temperature accidentally rise much higher than cone 06, the ware should not be dampened at all.

The glaze must be cleaned completely off the bottom of the pot and 1/4 inch up the side as soon as it is dry enough to handle. Excess glaze will always run, so it is never advisable to allow a heavy layer of glaze to remain near the foot rim. The cleaning operation can be simplified by dipping the bottoms of bisque pots into a shallow pan of hot paraffin before glazing.

269. Norman Schulman,
U.S.A. Vase.
Thrown and slab construction
with brushed glaze decoration.
The brightly colored low-fire
glazes brush on easily.

left: 270. Brushed glazes must be applied evenly with a wide brush.

right: 271. Tongs are used for dip glazing small pieces.

A brushed glaze is easiest for the beginner, although experience is needed to produce an even glaze coating. The technique is best suited for the glossy surface of low-fire glazes. You will need a flat brush, at least 1 inch in width and possibly larger. An oxhair bristle is preferred, for camel hair is much too soft and floppy. Unless a considerable amount of clay is in the glaze, the addition of bentonite or a gum binder is necessary for proper adhesion. You must work rapidly, using a full brush, and cover the piece with a second and third coat before the bottom layer is completely dry, for otherwise blisters will develop. The glaze must be neither too watery nor so thick that it will dry quickly and cause uneven laps and ridges.

Dip glazing is probably the simplest glazing method. After the vessel has been cleaned and moistened with a damp sponge, it is plunged into a large pan of glaze. It should be withdrawn almost immediately and shaken to remove the excess glaze. The object is then placed on a rack to dry, and any finger marks are touched up with a brush. Small-size pots can be dip glazed with metal tongs, which come in several shapes. The slight blemishes in the glaze caused by the pointed tips usually heal in firing. A more uniform surface is produced if the glaze is thin enough to allow dipping two or three times within a few seconds. Interesting patterns and colors evolve when a piece is dipped in two different glazes that overlap.

Pouring requires less glaze than dipping, and the technique can be applied to a greater variety of shapes. For example, the insides of bottles and deep, vaselike forms can be glazed only in this manner.

In the case of a bottle, the glaze is poured through a funnel, and then the vessel is rotated until all its surfaces are covered. The remainder is poured out and the bottle is given a final shake to distribute the glaze evenly and to remove the excess. Glazes that are poured or dipped must be a little thinner in consistency than those that are brushed on. The insides of bowls are glazed by pouring in a portion of the glaze, spreading it by rotating the bowl, and then pouring out the excess. This must be done rather quickly, or an overabundance or uneven amount of glaze will accumulate.

left: 272. Glaze is poured through a funnel to coat the interior of a bottle.

right: 273. Pouring glaze from a pitcher over a large platter, with a tub underneath to catch the excess.

To glaze the exterior of a bottle, grasp it by either the neck or the foot rim, and pour the glaze from a pitcher, allowing the extra to run off into a pan beneath. Finger marks are then touched up with a brush, and the foot rim is cleaned when dry. The outsides of bowls are glazed in the same manner, provided the foot is large enough to grasp. Otherwise the bowl can be placed upside down on wooden dowels extending across a pan. It is better to glaze the interior of a vessel first and the exterior later.

left: 274. The platter is tipped so that the excess glaze will run off into the tub.

right: 275. Dowels support large pieces and bowl shapes for pouring.

above left: **276.** The glaze must be sprayed on in a uniform coating.

above right: **277.**
A properly sprayed glaze develops a soft, woolly surface of even thickness.

Sprayed glazes permit subtle variations of color and control over glaze thickness and coverage. A thin overall glaze coating over delicate designs is most easily applied with the spray method. However, sprayed glazes are more common in commercial ceramics than among studio potters. Dipped and poured glazes are quicker to apply, less wasteful of glaze, and less liable to damage in loading. Another drawback is that brush and wax-resist decoration cannot be applied over a sprayed glaze.

The glaze for spraying should be more fluid than usual and should be run through a fine mesh sieve. Alkaline compounds that tend to settle or become lumpy must be replaced by fritted substitutes. The small electrically powered spray units for paint work well for glazes. Airbrushes, commonly used by graphic artists and for photo touch-ups, can produce overlapping color fields on a much smaller scale. Because many glaze materials are toxic, spraying should be done in a properly ventilated booth.

The insides of deep bowls or closed forms should be glazed before spraying the outsides. To obtain an even layer, spray the glaze slowly at a moderate distance from the pot. Turn the pot as the spraying progresses, building up a soft, "woolly" surface. If the application is too heavy, the glaze will run. When this occurs, the glaze must be scraped off and the pot dried and then reglazed. When the spraying is completed, handle the pot as gently and as little as possible. Dipping the foot in paraffin before spraying will eliminate the need to handle the pot while cleaning off the bottom.

278. If the glaze is sprayed on in too heavy an application, it will run.

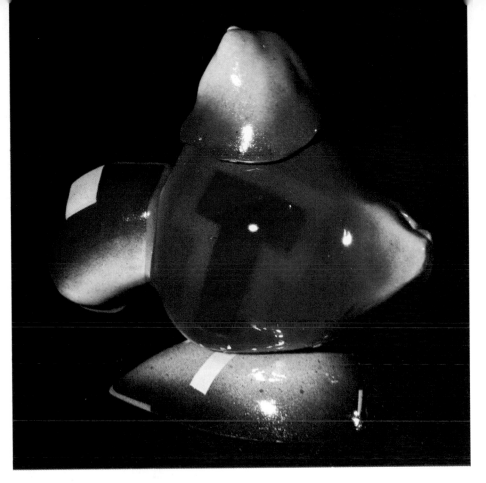

279. Glenn Jampol, U.S.A. Teapot.
Slip-cast porcelain
with a vibrant coloration
developed by numerous firings
of airbrushed overglazes.

280. Mutsuo Yanagihara, Japan.
Cloud and Hemisphere,
form with illusionistic clouds evolving from
glaze applied with an airbrush technique
in shades of blue, white, and gray.

Decoration with Glazes

The manner in which a glaze is applied can become a decorative technique. A single glaze will vary in color if applied in layers of different thicknesses. Several glazes dipped or poured over each other will create contrasting color fields. An interesting design often results from brushing an oxide or second glaze over a dipped or poured surface. If the base glaze is completely dry, however, another glaze applied on top may crack or peel off.

A simple decorating technique consists of wiping away a portion of the glaze. On a textured surface, this will leave glaze in the rougher sections. If the glaze is wiped away from a smooth surface, the slight residue of flux from the glaze may alter the color of the clay body. A variety of textures will also result from the glazes themselves—from a very dry to a smooth mat through a glossy finish.

left: 281. Gene Buckley, U.S.A. Weed vase. Slab with wheel-thrown foot, blue slip in layers with glossy white overglaze; height 15″ (37.5 cm).

below left: 282. Warren MacKenzie, U.S.A. Tea bowl. 1976. Stoneware with a mat white glaze overlaid with an iron-red glaze pattern.

below: 283. Robert Eckels, U.S.A. Bottle. Stoneware with sgraffito and applied decoration, paddled leather hard, with the glaze rubbed off in the center panel for color and textural contrast; height 16″ (40 cm).

284. Hiroaki Morino, Japan. Box.
Slab construction
with red, white, and black glazes
applied in an undulating pattern.

right: **285. Ulrica Hydman-Vallien,** Sweden.
Angel Protection. Figure group
with details brushed in black, red, and brown
over a white glaze; height 14″ (35 cm).

below: **286. Dieter Crumbiegel,** Germany.
Sculptural relief. Stoneware construction
with a variety of mat and glossy ash glazes
in hues of beige, white, blue, and black-brown
fired to cone 11; length 24″ (60 cm).

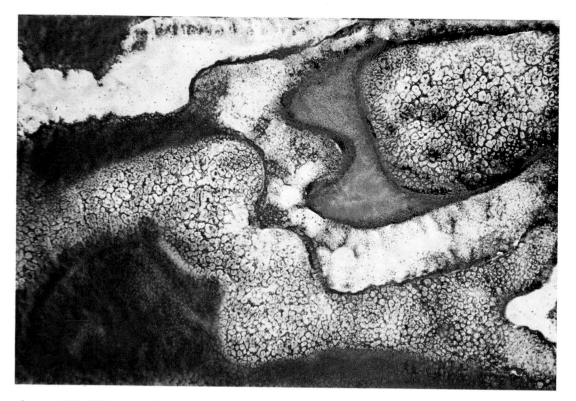

above: 287. Hildegard Storr-Britz, Germany. Wall tile.
Stoneware with rich texture created by a variety of glazes
reduction-fired to cone 8; 12 × 18″ (30 × 45 cm).

right: 288. Angelo Garzio, U.S.A. Casserole.
Stoneware with sgraffito, wax-resist,
and cobalt and iron oxide decoration,
wood-ash glaze fired to cone 9;
diameter 15″ (37.5 cm).

    When a glaze has dried to a firm coating, lines scratched through the
glaze to the body will create a subtle relief pattern. Wax designs can also be
applied to a firm coating of glaze, and lines incised through the wax. These
lines can then be filled in with an oxide stain or a glaze of a different color to
contrast with the body or base glaze. The bowl in Figure 289 has a wax
design painted over the glaze. A cobalt wash is being brushed over the wax.
The waxed areas will be the color of the original glaze, while those covered
with cobalt will be darker.

Glaze-Fired Ware

Until recently, most hand potters were concerned with functional ware decorated with glazes formulated in the studio. Decorating techniques associated with commercially manufactured ceramics (or those that made the ware unsuitable for practical use) were largely neglected. Contemporary potters are now experimenting with low-fire techniques that result in less durable finishes characterized by bright colors and metallic lusters.

One possibility for decoration on glaze-fired ware is the application of acrylic or oil-base paints onto the glazed surface (Fig. 257). Although acrylic paints adhere best to bisqued ware, oil and enamel paints work well on both bisqued and glazed surfaces.

Overglazes, lusters, and decals are fired between cones 020 and 015 (1175°–1479°F, 635°–804°C) in an electric kiln. This extremely low temperature fuses the colors to the previously glazed surface; the finishes would probably burn out above cone 010. Hard, glossy glazes are more reliable bases for these effects than rough or mat surfaces. The application and firing processes are exacting. The work area must be clean and free of any dust, and the ware should be wiped with alcohol to remove dirt and oily fingerprints. Although it is possible to compound overglazes and lusters, the ingredients are expensive and the process time-consuming. You will find it more profitable to choose from the commercially manufactured products.

Overglaze colors contain coloring oxides or stains, a flux, and a binder, such as oil of lavender. They can be purchased in small containers and applied directly from the bottle. Make certain that the vials are fresh, for if the colors are too old, they will become gummy and form a jellylike mass. Follow the manufacturer's instructions carefully, noting which type of medium is recommended for thinning and cleaning purposes.

289. Applying a cobalt stain with a wide brush over a wax design on a glazed surface.

290. Jay Lindsay, U.S.A. Platter. Stoneware with wax-resist and cobalt stain decoration over a white glaze, diameter 16″ (40 cm).

Apply thin coats of color with soft camel-hair or sable brushes. The brushes should be kept very clean and used only for overglazes. Mistakes can be wiped off with a cloth dipped in the proper thinner. A spray gun or airbrush will create subtle modeling details. However, the colors should be thinned to a more fluid consistency, to prevent the spraying mechanism from clogging.

If the design is complicated, do not expect to paint and fire the piece in one operation. First, apply the broad color washes; these can be intensified later if necessary. Then begin painting on the finer details. Many unusual color effects can be achieved by applying different colors over each other.

Most overglaze colors are fired between cones 020 and 015. The temperature is critical and should be controlled to the exact degree stated in manufacturers' instructions. Overfiring will cause the colors to burn out; underfiring will prevent them from developing. Always handle the ware with caution to avoid damaging the fragile surface.

Decals are produced by several commercial firms and are available from many ceramic supply houses. Watermount decals are printed by either a lithographic or a silkscreen process onto a thin paper sheet coated with water-soluble film. Lacquer is then applied over the decal material.

To apply the decal, cut the desired design from the sheet, and soak it in room-temperature water until the paper has become saturated. (If it is left in the water for too long, the adhesive quality will be diminished.) When the backing paper has released, lift the decal from the water, drain it, and slide it from the backing onto the clean, glazed surface. Adjust the position, and pat away the excess water with a cotton pad. If the decal is large, use a squeegee to seal the decal to the surface. It is important to remove all water and air bubbles, or the decal will not adhere properly during the firing. Application on curved surfaces is facilitated by first heating the ware to about 85°F (29°C). This will cause the lacquer backing to stretch and conform to the surface when the decal is pressed onto the form.

Allow the decal to dry completely before firing. Most decals mature between cones 020 and cone 018 and should be fired in an electric kiln.

above: **291. E. C. Le Guay,** decorator. Pitcher, French, from Sevres. 1813. Hard paste with overglaze and gold decoration, height 8⅜" (21 cm). Metropolitan Museum of Art, New York (gift of Mr. and Mrs. D. N. Heineman, 1956).

right: **292.** *Pine, Bamboo, and Flowering Tree.* Kakiemon ware plate, Japanese. Edo Period (early 18th century). Porcelain with gold and enameled decoration, diameter 7⅜" (18.5 cm). Seattle Art Museum (Eugene Fuller Memorial Collection).

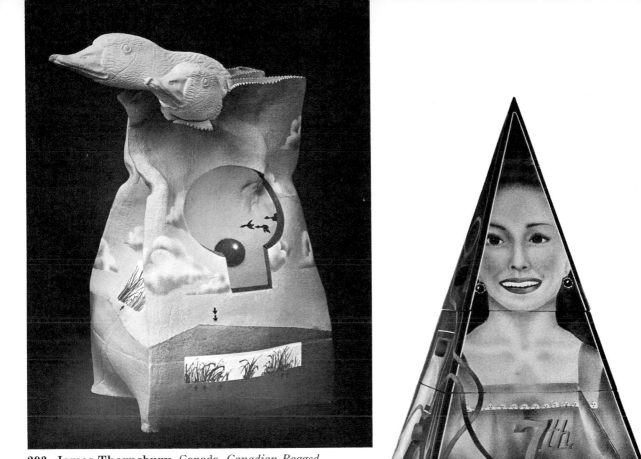

293. James Thornsbury, Canada. *Canadian Bagged.*
Construction in talc body fired to conc 02
with acrylic and enamel paint, height 21″ (52.5 cm).

above: 294. Patti Warshina, U.S.A.
Love It or Leave It.
Porcelain pyramid with airbrushed
overglaze design, height 30″ (75 cm).

left: 295. Paul A. Dresang, U.S.A.
Fat Freddie Frog on a Dirt Bike.
Modeled form raku-fired
with an off-white glaze,
lusters, and decal;
length 24″ (62 cm).

Luster glazes produce metallic, iridescent, and pearlescent colors on glazed surfaces. They are available in a large selection of hues, and in such liquid metal colors as gold, silver, and bronze.

Like overglazes, lusters can be brushed or sprayed onto a glazed surface in thin, even coats. Lusters will become increasingly brilliant with repeated firings; unusual effects result from applying colors over each other.

Firing should proceed slowly, with the kiln door left open in the beginning to allow any toxic fumes to escape. Most lusters mature between cones 020 and 018, although this may vary with the product.

Glaze Defects

Opening the kiln and finding a runny, crawling, or rough glaze is one of the great disappointments faced by the potter. Because glaze chemicals vary slightly in their composition and because potters are always tempted to experiment with new combinations of glazes, the problem of glaze defects is a continuing one.

There are usually several reasons, all logical, why a particular glaze fault occurs, but trying to deduce the cause from one piece may prove quite difficult. When there are a number of pots having the same glaze from a single kiln load or when there are several glazes on a single body, the problem of deduction is much easier. The following section outlines some of the factors that can cause glaze defects. Glaze faults may result not only from the composition of the glaze but from the improper selection or preparation of the clay body, faulty kiln operation, or, as is most frequently the case, lack of skill and care in application.

**below left: 296.
Jane Peiser,** U.S.A. Vase.
Porcelain millefiore slab construction
salt-glazed to cone 10,
with decal and overglazes
fired to cone 017;
height 16″ (40 cm).

**below right: 297.
Nan Bangs McKinnell,** U.S.A. Bowl.
Thrown and altered porcelain
with iridescent pearl luster glaze,
height 3½″ (8.75 cm).

Defects Caused by the Body

- A body that is too porous because of improper wedging, kneading, blunging, or pugging may cause small bubbles, beads, and pinholes to form in the glaze as the body contracts and the gases attempt to escape.
- Excessive water in the body can result in similar conditions.
- A large amount of manganese dioxide used as a colorant in a body or slip may cause blisters to form in both the body and the glaze.
- Soluble sulfates are contained in some clays and come to the surface in drying, forming a whitish scum. Pinholes and bubbles develop as these sulfates react with the glaze to form gases. This condition can be eliminated by adding up to 2 percent barium carbonate to the body. A slight reduction fire at the point when the glaze begins to melt will reduce the sulfates and allow the gas to pass off before the glaze develops a glassy retaining film.
- If the body is underfired in the bisque and therefore very porous, it may absorb too much glaze. Soluble fluxes in the glaze, because of their higher thermal expansion and contraction rates, can cause the body to crack. In any case, a glaze applied to a very absorptive body could have a coarse, or even a sandpaperlike surface.

Defects of Application

- Blisters or pinholes may result if the bisque ware has not been moistened slightly before glazing. The glaze traps air in the body's surface pores.
- Dust or oil on the surface of the bisque ware may cause pinholes, crawling, or a scaly surface in the glaze.
- If the glaze is applied too heavily, it will run and obscure the decoration, perhaps causing the pot to stick to the kiln shelves.
- In addition to flowing excessively, glazes that have been applied too thickly will usually crack in drying. When the piece is fired, these cracks will not heal but will pull farther apart and bead at the edges. If the drying contraction is great enough, the adhesion of the glaze to the body will be weak, causing portions to flake off during the initial water smoking period of the cycle.
- On the other hand, a glaze application that is too thin will result in a poor, dry surface. This is especially true of mat glazes.
- If a second glaze coating is applied over a completely dry first coat, blisters will form. The wetting of the lower glaze layer causes it to expand and pull away from the body.

298. Dick Evans, U.S.A.
Sculptural form.
Porcelain construction fired first
to cone 1, with a white glaze
fired to cone 05,
gold and mother-of-pearl lusters
fired to cone 020;
6 × 20″ (15 × 50 cm).

- If the bisque ware is considerably cooler than the glaze at the time of application, bubbles and blisters may develop later.
- Glazes high in colemanite should be applied immediately after mixing. If they are allowed to set, they thicken from the deflocculating effect of the colemanite. The extra water necessary to restore their consistency causes the glaze to separate and crawl in drying. A type of colemanite called gerstley borate should be used if possible, because it is less apt to settle. The addition of .5 to 1 percent soda ash or 3 percent Veegum T will retard the tendency of colemanite to thicken.
- Bristol glazes require perfect surface application. Because of their viscosity, thin areas will pull apart and crawl when fired.

Defects Originating in Firing

- If freshly glazed ware is placed in the kiln and fired immediately, the hot moisture will loosen the glaze, causing blisters and crawling.
- Too-rapid firing will prevent gases from escaping normally. They will form tiny seeds and bubbles in the glaze. For some especially viscous glazes, a prolonged soaking period is needed to remove these bubbles.
- Excessive reduction will result in black and gray spots on the body and glaze and will produce a dull surface.
- Gas-fired kilns with poor muffles using manufactured gas are troublesome to use with lead glazes. The sulphur content in the combustion gases will dull the glaze surfaces and possibly form blisters and wrinkles.
- Overfiring generally causes glazes to run excessively and clay bodies to distort and crack.

Defects in Glaze Composition

- Glazes that are not adjusted properly to the body are susceptible to stresses that may cause the glaze, and at times even the body, to crack. If the glaze contracts at a slower rate than the body does in cooling, it undergoes compression. This causes the glaze to crack and, in places, to buckle and separate from the body. This defect is commonly known as *shivering.*
- Slightly similar to shivering, and also caused by unequal contraction rates in cooling, is *crazing* of the glaze. When this happens, the glaze contracts at a greater rate than the body, causing numerous cracks to form (see pp. 181–183).
- Glazes that run excessively at normal firing temperatures should be adjusted by the addition of kaolin to increase the refractory quality of the glaze or, if possible, by changing the bases.
- A dull surface will result if the proportion of silica to alumina or barium is too low.
- An excessive amount of tin, rutile, or colored spinels, which are relatively insoluble, will also cause a dull or rough-surfaced glaze.
- Bristol and colemanite glazes not fitted properly to the body will tend to crawl or to crack. This may be due in part to an excess of zinc, usually contained in these glazes. Zinc has a very high contraction rate at greater temperatures.
- Glazes ground too finely—thus releasing soluble salts from the frits, feldspar, and so forth—will develop pinholes and bubbles.
- Glazes that are allowed to stand too long may be affected by the decomposition of carbonates, organic matter in ball clay, or gum binders. Gases thus formed can result in pinholes and bubbles in the final glaze. In some cases, preservatives like formaldehyde will help. If washed, dried, and reground, the same glaze can be used without difficulty.

5
Ceramic Form
and Design

Very often the term design as applied to ceramics is confusing, because it seems to suggest an intellectual process undertaken before and apart from the act of forming a pot. In practice, of course, the acts of forming and designing go together, with one and then the other taking precedence during various stages in the evolution of a form. Nevertheless, it is possible to discuss design separately from other considerations, just as one isolates decoration from form in order to point out its particular characteristics and problems.

The examples of ceramics from the past illustrated throughout this book are unquestionably a source of interest and inspiration for all students, reflecting as they do the efforts of countless generations of potters. There is a danger, however, in uncritically accepting them as models to imitate. When social and economic conditions change, the function of ceramics within a culture also changes. Much of the variety found in historical ceramics is the result of the different needs experienced by the cultures that produced them.

299. Peter Voulkos, U.S.A. Plate. Stoneware with porcelain additions, cobalt, and sandy mat glaze fired to cone 5; diameter 22¼″ (55.5 cm).

In this respect our own era is drastically unlike earlier periods. Technological advances have produced glass, metal, fiber, and plastic containers, completely eliminating the need for many of the standard forms. Never again will it be necessary to make huge earthenware containers, as many ancient civilizations did, since objects like this can be more efficiently supplied by mass-production methods.

The Industrial Revolution, which began to change the basis of pottery making as early as 1750, severed the age-old pattern by which form and design, nurtured by a local market, evolved in the transition from one generation to the next. With no guidance from the past, the contemporary potter is most eclectic, absorbing influences from hither and yon. Many theories have been proposed regarding ceramic design, and they serve a guiding role, much as did the older traditions. But, like all theories, they can become self-defeating if applied in a rigid manner. The only truly reliable standard is the sensitive eye of the designer.

Material and Method

The inherent nature of clay imposes restraint on ceramic design. Clay in either the plastic or the fired state has unique qualities that distinguish pottery from artifacts made of wood, metal, fiber, or glass. It is logical that these characteristics be stressed in the design development. A plate by Peter Voulkos illustrates this approach very well, with its rough, perforated surface evoking the earthy quality of the material (Fig. 299).

While a thrown clay form and a piece of blown glass have much the same effect in terms of expanding volume, attempts to achieve in clay the thinness and translucency of glass would be unsuccessful. Similarly, metal has a strength that permits the construction of apparently fragile and protruding forms that would be impossible in clay.

Lacking both transparency and tensile strength, clay has other qualities that make it a particularly satisfying medium for the designer. One is its plasticity—its ability to respond to the touch of the finger, to be stretched, impressed, incised, and added to with ease. Another is the natural color, rough texture, and "stony" quality of many clays, which are often sufficient decoration. The addition of glazes gives a new dimension of surface effect and color that may rival the attractiveness of the form itself. These two elements, form and surface decoration, must be in harmony in order for a ceramic design to be successful.

Of critical importance to the character of a ceramic piece is the forming method used. Ancient pottery was usually coil constructed, and this technique is still employed today for very large pieces, for groggy clay, or for asymmetrical forms. Not all thrown pieces reveal their origin by finger-impressed throwing rings, but they have in common the tensions of expanding plastic clay and a symmetrical form. This tension in the clay, as it expands and contracts, can sometimes be exploited to good advantage.

Slab constructions, by their angularity, are perhaps easiest to identify. A slip-cast piece, on the other hand, can take almost any form, with the clay often serving as a neutral ground for other decoration. It is desirable that the forming method be revealed in a clear and straightforward manner, both for the integrity of the design and for a logical economy of time and effort. Most often it is pointless to laboriously coil and refine a hand-built form that might more easily be thrown on the wheel.

The plastic quality of clay, which readily permits addition, encourages a combination of construction methods. The contrast of expanding thrown form with angular slab can be a pleasing design element, but the potter must

300. David Shaner, U.S.A.
Bowl. 1976.
Stoneware with thick application of
porcelain slip, wood fired;
diameter 10″ (25 cm).

301. Carlo Zauli, Italy. Sphere.
Stoneware with mat white glaze fired to cone 6, diameter 28″ (70 cm).

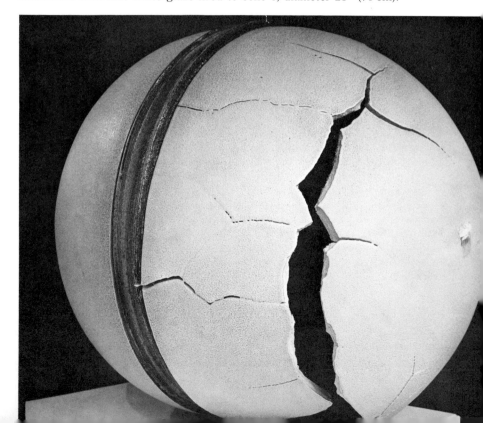

above: 302.
Carol Jeanne Abraham, U.S.A.
Zeitgeist.
Thixotropic porcelain, cotton,
candlewick, and flax;
5′6″ × 3′4″ × 8″ (1.65 × 1 × .2 m).

above right: 303.
Johannes Gebhardt, Germany.
Stoneman. 1972. Stoneware with dark,
mottled glaze; height 12″ (30 cm).

right: 304. Mark Thompson, Australia.
Doll.
Slip-cast with painted features
and feather costume.

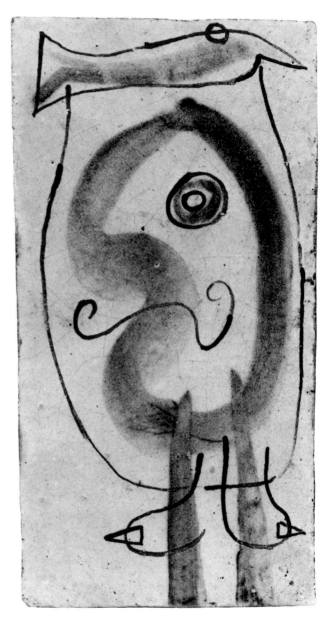

above: **305. Pablo Picasso,** France. *Centaur.* 1950.
Terra cotta, with painted design, height 17″ (42.5 cm).
Courtesy the Arts Council of Great Britain, London.

right: **306. Joan Miró,** Spain,
in collaboration with Joseph Lloret Artigas.
Femme (*Woman*). 1955-56.
Ceramic tile with painted design,
$8\frac{7}{8} \times 4\frac{1}{2}$″ (22.25 × 11.25 cm).
Courtesy Pierre Matisse Gallery, New York.

take care that the two elements of construction are in harmony, and not fighting each other for dominance.

For the beginner, designing in clay presents a special challenge. Not until one understands the material—what it can and cannot do—is there total freedom in exploring form. It is unlikely that the student or layman, lacking an understanding of the nature of clay or a basic grasp of the techniques, will be able to conceive of the ceramic form in a manner that fully exploits the qualities of clay. For this reason it is interesting to study ceramics made by artists who work principally in other media. Picasso, Miró, and Gauguin, among others, all tried their hands at ceramic design. In each case the results are strongly imprinted with the artist's personality and style. There is a tendency to treat the clay as a support, just as one would use a canvas, and yet the clay still asserts itself, lending a unique quality to the design.

Form and Function

The term *function* has many meanings. In narrow definition, *practicality* is one possible meaning. An object is practical if it serves the purpose for which it was intended. A generally accepted idea of contemporary design is that the *form* of an object is largely dictated by its *function*. About this there can be little debate, for if a spout on a pitcher does not pour well or if the handle on a vessel is difficult to hold or is in poor balance, the value of the entire design can be questioned, regardless of how beautiful or unusual the pot may be.

The pitcher illustrated in Figure 308 exemplifies the concept of utilitarian function coupled with a natural use of material. Its sturdy form is stable, the handle is comfortable and well balanced, and the pouring lip, being

right: 308. Angelo Garzio, U.S.A. Pitcher.
Stoneware with ash glaze,
fired in a wood-burning kiln to cone 10;
height 13″ (32.5 cm).

below left: 309. Harrison McIntosh, U.S.A.
Footed bowl. Stoneware with blue and black engobe
and mat white glaze fired to cone 5,
height 11⅛″ (27.75 cm).

below right: 310.
Footed bowl, Iranian, from Tepe Sialk.
c. 3000 B.C. Earthenware with decoration
in brown and black slip, height 6⅝″ (16.75 cm).
Metropolitan Museum of Art, New York
(Rogers Fund, 1957).

sharp, is not likely to drip. The pulled handle, throwing ridges, and fluid movement of rim and spout express the quality of plastic clay. A thin ash glaze reveals rather than disguises the iron-speckled stoneware body.

The same principles could be applied to the two bowls—one contemporary, one historical—reproduced in Figures 309 and 310. Each is a hollow form planted firmly on a stable foot, so that the function of containing something is admirably fulfilled. In both, too, the decoration complements the shape without overwhelming it.

Because of the emphasis on form as a whole, details of foot, spout, and lip are often neglected. The most common design error is to make the base area of a pot too large, thus imparting a heavy and clumsy feeling. Ideally, the

above: 311. Pitcher,
Iranian. c. 1000 B.C.
Earthenware, height 5¼″ (13 cm).
Metropolitan Museum of Art, New York
(Rogers Fund, 1962).

below: 312. Vessel in the shape
of a horned animal, Iranian, from Acdebil.
Early 1st millennium B.C.
Burnished earthenware, height 8¹¹⁄₁₆″ (22 cm).
Metropolitan Museum of Art, New York
(Rogers Fund, 1965).

313. Double-spout vessel, from Peru,
Paracas Necropolis. c. 400 B.C.–A.D. 400.
Earthenware with burnished slip decoration,
height 7¼″ (18 cm).
Metropolitan Museum of Art, New York
(Michael C. Rockefeller Memorial
Collection of Primitive Art).

pot should suggest a form in space, resting lightly on its foot rim. Many primitive pots have their main interest at the foot, with special projections that avoid the flat bottom altogether. We can assume that these containers worked well for the people who used them, which proves that a utilitarian object need not absolutely *look* like a utilitarian object.

It is quite satisfactory for a small, functional pot to have a flat base, showing the slight ridges left by the cutting wire. Generally, however, the center of the base is trimmed out with a looping tool (Fig. 164) in order to lighten this area, as well as to give a feeling of the continuing curve of the form. There are many types of foot rims—low and high, thin and broad, flat and delicate—and the kind that is used should relate to and complement the character of the pot form. The foot rim may be the result of the trimming operation, or, in the case of a high foot, it may be a cylinder thrown separately and joined to the pot with slip. Because the potter's name is usually incised or stamped here, and also because it is an inconspicuous area, most pot lovers look immediately at the foot for what it reveals about the attitude and craft of the potter. Regardless of the type of foot that is used, the base of the pot should be perfectly smooth and have a slight bevel at the edges.

A small pot can have a simple, rounded rim, but a larger piece may appear weak without some accent at the lip. Apart from aesthetic considerations, a slight thickening is desirable to strengthen the rim, to reduce warpage in drying, and, in the case of a very large bowl, to make lifting more convenient. Again, the primitive potter was innovative in design, often turning the spout and/or handle into a design accent, replacing a rim.

We can too easily become creatures of habit and, during a day's throwing, put a similar rim on all our pots. It is far better to analyze the form as it develops and plan the rim to harmonize with the total design. Occasionally, just a finger depression in a flat rim or a simple impression from a roller will add distinction and emphasis.

314. Oribe ware teapot, Japanese.
Momoyama Period (1573–1615).
Stoneware with green and transparent glazes
over brown slip decoration
in a tortoise-shell design,
height 7⅝″ (19.25 cm).
Seattle Art Museum
(Eugene Fuller Memorial Collection).

The teapot offers an unusual challenge to the potter, since it generally consists of four separate parts that must combine to form a unified whole. It is a good project for the student who has mastered basic techniques.

Tea growing in China dates back to about 2700 B.C. So closely is the teapot associated with the Orient, and in particular with the Japanese tea ceremony, that it is almost impossible for the western potter not to be influenced by traditional forms. Nevertheless, as the 17th-century pot in Figure 316 shows, traditional form does not necessarily mean stereotyped form. The teapot in Figure 315 seems so "modern" in its design—with its

below left: **315.** Yung-lo teapot,
Chinese. Ming Dynasty (1403–1424).
Porcelain. National Museum, Taiwan.

below right: **316.** Yi-Hsing teapot
in the shape of a prunus stump,
Chinese. Ming Dynasty (17th century).
Red stoneware, height 4¼″ (10.5 cm).
Seattle Art Museum
(Eugene Fuller Memorial Collection).

317. Nabeshima ware teapot, Japanese. Edo Period (mid-18th century). Porcelain with pale celadon glaze in "plum blossoms and buds" design, height 6″ (15 cm). Seattle Art Museum (gift of Mrs. Charles E. Stuart).

smooth, streamlined forms—that we might easily mistake it for a contemporary Italian design, yet it dates from the 15th century. Possibly the delicate teapot with a long, flowing handle or the squat, homey version seem more to match our idea of what a classic teapot is. All four of the pots illustrated, however, have several things in common: They have well-balanced handles, efficient pouring spouts, and bodies appropriate for holding the tea and retaining heat.

The Japanese tea ceremony, first performed by Zen Buddhist monks as a contemplative pause during their long hours of meditation, is intimately involved with a peculiarly Japanese concept of beauty. From its beginnings about four hundred years ago, the informal partaking of a cup of tea grew gradually into the present ceremony, first among the monks and a few members of the royal family, then among the Samurai warrior class, and finally expanding to include the wealthy merchants. Eventually, all Japanese of culture were expected to understand the Way of Tea, which is essentially a philosophy of aesthetics.

The ceremony is held in a small room or a simple structure in the garden. Except for the tea utensils themselves, plus a flower arrangement or hanging scroll, the room is bare. Of prime importance to the potter is that nearly all the items involved—water jar, tea caddy, washing bowls, flower vase, cake trays, and tea bowls—are ceramic. The spread of the tea ceremony, therefore, focused great attention on pottery.

At first, rare and valuable old Sung bowls were used. By the Momoyama period (1573–1615), however, the tea masters protested that this practice was not in keeping with the Zen philosophy, which stressed the simple and unaffected life. At first they sought the old peasant pottery of Korea and Japan, but later raku ware, with its irregularities from a heavily grogged body, became popular. It is not easy for an experienced potter to consciously affect a primitive style, yet it has been done for several centuries. The secret is to allow the natural qualities of clay and glazes to assert themselves, without forcing the accidental (Fig. 352).

Decoration and Design

In our discussion of form and function, we have occasionally touched upon this question of decoration. This is inevitable, since the two are closely interrelated. Ideally, decoration should be a part of, and inseparable from, the form, such as throwing rings or stamped and applied clay accents, which reveal the plastic nature of clay in a simple, unobtrusive manner. The character of a form largely determines the type of decoration that would be most effective. A set of dinnerware, for example, does not need a strong motif, since it will be covered by food most of the time. Many potters avoid making "sets," because they fear the boredom of doing the same design over and over again. But a set need not have an identical pattern on each piece, as long as the colors and the design are generally harmonious. At the opposite extreme from the purely functional dinnerware is the "plate" used as a ground for a unique design. The plate shape, being a perfect round form and basically flat, makes an ideal surface for free improvisation—whether figural or abstract in nature.

Skill with the brush is rather rare among contemporary Western potters. It is not surprising that those cultures that traditionally have used the brush as a writing medium excel in this type of ceramic decoration. Even to make a simple bold stroke of color or slip across a plate in a way that will produce the effect of careless freedom requires a certain amount of practice.

318. Polly Myhrum, U.S.A. Dinner set. Stoneware with blue underglaze design and white glaze; diameter of dinner plate, 10″ (25 cm); height of candlestick 8″ (20 cm).

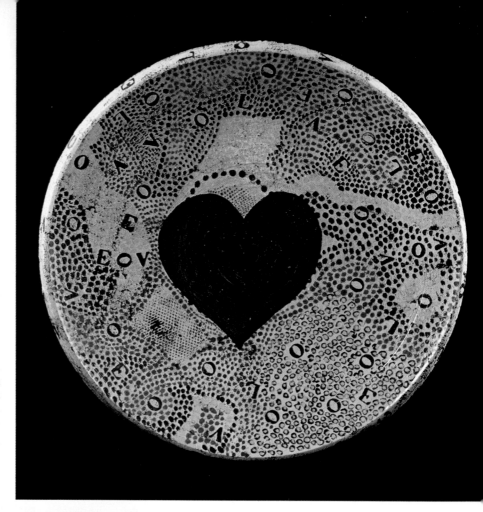

right: **319. Vaea,** U.S.A. *Love Plate.*
Stoneware with brush and stencil
decoration fired to cone 04,
diameter 14″ (35 cm).

below left: 320.
Young Lady and Gentleman,
from Capodimonte, Italy. 1743–59.
Porcelain with overglaze decoration
depicting a farce in
the comic opera tradition.
Filangeri Museum, Naples.

below right: 321.
Alan Watt, Australia.
Sculpture. Porcelain with
elaborate slip-trailed design
over a thin-cut slab structure.

right: **322. Shoji Hamada,** Japan. Dish. Stoneware with pressed border design and trailed glaze decoration.

below: **323. Dick Evans,** U.S.A. *Untitled Form #23A.* White stoneware body with porcelain slip fired to cone 1, white glaze fired to cone 05, and gold and mother-of-pearl lusters fired to cone 020; length 18″ (45 cm).

There is a tendency today among many potters to push clay and decoration to their limits, to use both in the sense of pure form. We see this, for example, in works that utilize clay as a drawing or sculpting medium, especially in cast or slip-trailed works. A relatively new trend in ceramics is the application of exquisite, bright colors on pure geometric form.

Quite different criteria apply to the decoration of functional wares and of the "art pot." Figural ceramics are not new, but the contemporary potter has investigated whole new areas of imagery, whimsy, and social comment. These types of expression call for a different approach to decoration.

left: **324. Victor Cicansky,** Canada.
Moosejaw Woman.
Earthenware with polychrome and luster glazes,
26 × 16 × 16″ (52.5 × 40 × 40 cm).

above: **325. Paul A. Dresang,** U.S.A.
Wonder Master Beater.
Sandy stoneware body with low-fire glazes,
raku-fired and smoked in excelsior;
height 18″ (45 cm).

Aspects of Form and Design

Aside from the dictates of function, and perhaps because of the unique qualities of clay, a tremendous variety of form is feasible in ceramics. The flexibility of techniques—coil, thrown, cast, slab, modeled, or a combination—permits the realization of nearly any conceivable form. A ceramic piece embodies, simultaneously, concepts of negative space and solid form. Because of the nature of the construction and firing processes, we know that every ceramic work, however heavy and solid it may appear, is hollow.

The perfect form, the sphere, when cut in half becomes a hemisphere or bowl, another aesthetically pleasing form. But when we depart from these geometric absolutes, we find that some shapes are much more satisfying than others. This is because of our psychologically influenced perception. The human eye is attracted to a dominant form or color; if we are presented with two centers of interest, the effect is distracting, even psychically disturbing. A desire for order seems basic to human equilibrium.

Geometric shapes—the sphere, the cylinder, the cone, and the cube—have a strength and simplicity that make them complete in themselves. When we begin to stretch and elongate these stable forms, we develop a sense of movement. Interest in a form is proportionate to the length of time needed for one's eye to travel over it, sense the movement of contours, the swelling of volumes, and to enjoy subtle contrasts of color and texture. To sustain our interest, the contour must maintain this flow and progression as the volume contracts or expands.

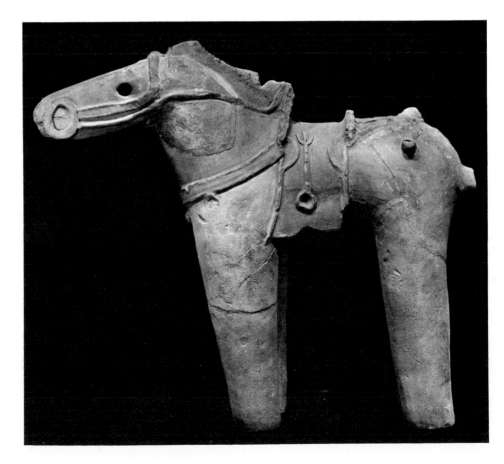

326. *Haniwa* horse, Japanese. Tumulus Period (3rd-6th century). Terra cotta, height 26½″ (66.25 cm). Seattle Art Museum (Eugene Fuller Memorial Collection).

327. Maurice de Coulon, Germany.
Wall relief in two parts.
Textured stoneware glazed blue-green
and metallic brown and gray,
36″ (90 cm) square.

right: 328.
Robert A. Sedestrom, U.S.A.
Box Canyon Suite #5.
Slip-cast porcelain oxidation-fired
to cone 9 with a satin mat glaze
and cobalt and copper, crystalline
glaze in the panel; height 18¾″ (47 cm).

A pot with a base and top that are similar in size or one with the greatest girth in the center is generally unsuccessful, for the equal division that results creates a feeling of monotony and little sense of movement. The most satisfying design is one conceived with a definite zest and sweep. Our senses react more favorably toward forms with unhesitant convictions of roundness or straightness, with no physical ambiguity. This does not rule out subtlety—only indecision.

Contrasts in the character of the form heighten our enjoyment; textural areas serve the same function, as they react against smoothly defined forms or surfaces. Elaborate embellishments and colorful glaze effects are best suited to rather simple shapes, for otherwise the form and decoration compete for attention. For the same reason a brilliant color, which might be overwhelming on a large vase, will be more satisfying on a small piece.

above: 329. **Wayne Higby,** U.S.A. *Canyon Lake* (landscape containers). 1976. Inlaid earthenware slab-construction, raku-fired, height 12″ (30 cm). Collection T. Klein, New York.

below: 330. *The Source,* French, in the manner of Bernard Palissy (c. 1510–90). Lead-glazed earthenware with nude figure modeled in interior, length 7^{15}/₁₆″ (19 cm). Metropolitan Museum of Art, New York (gift of Julia A. Berwind, 1953).

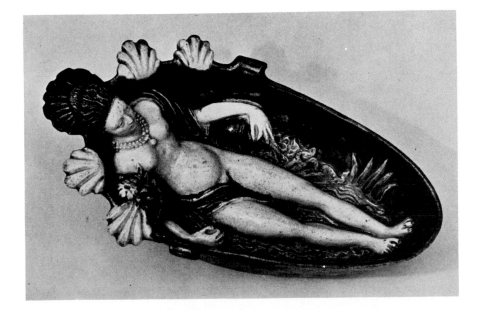

above left: 331. Standing figures,
from Chupicuaro, Mexico. c. 300 B.C.
Modeled terra cotta, heights 6⅛″ (15.5 cm), 4½″ (11.25 cm).
Metropolitan Museum of Art, New York
(Michael C. Rockefeller Memorial Collection
of Primitive Art).

above: 332. *Horseman* (George II?),
from Staffordshire, England. c. 1740.
White stoneware, salt-glazed; height 9¼″ (23 cm).
Victoria & Albert Museum, London (Crown Copyright).

left: 333. Standing figure of a laughing child,
from Veracruz, Mexico. c. 500 B.C.
Terra cotta, height 18¾″ (46.88 cm).
Metropolitan Museum of Art, New York
(Michael C. Rockefeller Memorial Collection
of Primitive Art).

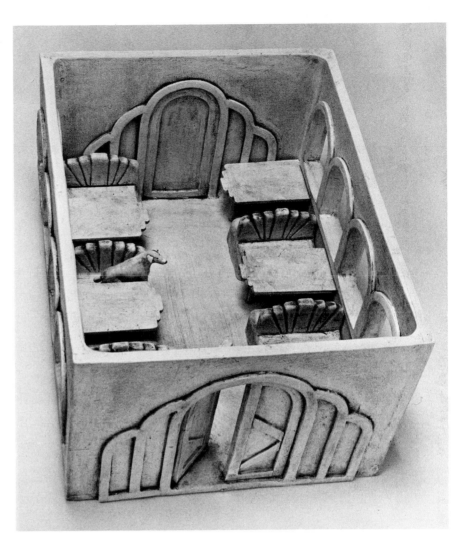

334. David Furman, U.S.A.
Molly at the Art Deco Diner. 1974.
Low-fire clay, 10 × 13 × 7″
(25 × 32.5 × 17.5 cm).

Figural ceramics, as we have noted, were probably the first clay objects made in primitive times. Some early pieces appear to us as crude and roughly formed, yet it would be a mistake to ascribe this to a lack of skill in the sculptor. In all eras figural work has employed a *stylization* of form and feature, which usually involves selecting certain features for emphasis and treating them in a simplified, distorted, or exaggerated way. In other words, representational ceramics are not copying from nature but rather creating a new *design* based on a natural prototype.

One aspect of design that is currently receiving much attention is *scale*, very loosely defined as the size of an object. Actually, scale is a consideration of size in relation to some constant, such as the size we expect something to be. For example, a vase 5 feet tall would be thought of as very large in scale, because we are accustomed to vases being much smaller.

A number of potters today work primarily in miniature, or very small scale. A ceramic building or whole environment reduced to tiny scale creates a special design challenge and evokes a special response in the viewer, because it encourages minute examination and study of all the details. At the opposite extreme, of course, are works designed in very large scale, including architectural ceramics.

Designing for Architecture

Ceramic reliefs or murals provide an exciting, colorful, and durable means of decorating public or private buildings. This is especially true for reception rooms and lobbies, which tend to be bland and boring. Unfortunately, such projects are relatively rare, because of the lack of interest among architects and their patrons.

The ceramic mural can be conceived as the focal point for an interior design or as part of a continuous wall decoration. The modular sections shown in Figure 336 are of stoneware fired to cone 9. Their size allows for dramatic contrasts of form and shadow. Another approach is to slip-cast individual sections in wet sand molds (Fig. 338). This process allows one to develop intricate forms and textures. The stoneware sections shown were stained, glazed, and inserted into a plaster wall, which in turn was textured and enlivened with linear patterns.

Ruth Duckworth's mural *Clouds over Chicago* (Fig. 339) was conceived as a continuous, nonrepetitive composition. It would seem to have been inspired by an aerial photograph. We see a portion of the lake, as well as the winding paths of the Chicago and Des Plaines rivers. The main interest, however, is in the thin, platelike cloud forms that swirl through the mural and finally break up into small textured areas. The individual stoneware panels making up this mural consist of base slabs 2 feet square, with the modeling superimposed. Color washes of copper, iron, and nickel, with glazes of varying gloss or opacity, result in a panorama of muted tones.

left: **337. Giovanni della Robbia,** Italy. *The Nativity.* c. 1500. Terra cotta, polychrome glazed. National Museum, Florence.

above: **338. Stig Lindberg,** Sweden. Sections of a sand-cast mural prior to glazing. Stoneware.

339. Ruth Duckworth, U.S.A. *Clouds over Chicago.* Stoneware mural constructed of slabs, each 24″ (60 cm) square, decorated with washes of iron, copper, and nickel and four glazes; 24′ × 9′7″ (7.2 × 3.2 m). Located in the Dresdner Bank, Board of Trade Building, Chicago.

Designing for Architecture **163**

The buildings of ancient Rome, which were constructed of brick and concrete, have been regarded with awe over the centuries. Naturally, buildings of such size, with their elaborate system of cornices, moldings, and arches, called for surface ornamentation. Surviving examples influenced the Renaissance architects and sculptors. Their work continues to inspire potters to reinterpret the concept of architectural ceramics in modern terms.

Figure 340 shows an exhibit of Nino Caruso's modular ceramic walls in the Piazza dei Consoli at Gubbio. The ornamental details of the windows and doorway arches of the medieval palace make a beautiful backdrop for Caruso's work, and the seeming contrast provides a note of continuity with the past. The Caruso wall is constructed of four units, which can be interchanged to present a variety of textural patterns. Each of the hollow sections was slip-cast from models in styrofoam.

These few examples should readily suggest the great potential for experimentation in architectural ceramics.

340. Nino Caruso, Italy. *Modular Sculpture.* 1970. Slip-cast fireclay with white glaze fired to cone 10, each module 20 × 16 × 14″ (50 × 40 × 35 cm). Installed in Piazza dei Consoli, Gubbio, Italy, 1974.

6
Glaze Formulation and Types

*U*se of a flux to melt silica is essential to both glass making and the glazing of pottery. Glass beads dating from the 4th millennium B.C. have been found in various areas of the Middle East. The initial discovery of this simple process may well have occurred in Egypt, where the first ceramic glazes we know appeared about 3000 B.C. A natural soda carbonate called *natron* occurs in many localities in Egypt's desert climate. When natron was mixed with silica sand, the heat of a hot campfire would have been sufficient to fuse the mixture into glasslike particles.

The first glazes were applied not to pots but to ceramic tiles, which the Egyptians used extensively to decorate their fabulous tombs. The tiles, of a sandy clay mixed with natron, were usually of a turquoise color from the addition of copper and were decorated with cobalt or manganese, which produced a blue or black hue. Termed *Egyptian faience* or Egyptian "paste," this is the material so familiar in colored beads and figurines. It was the precursor of all modern glazes.

A ceramic glaze and its formulation are not as mysterious as they seem to most beginning pottery students. Basically, a glaze is nothing more than a thin, glasslike coating that is fused to a clay surface by the heat of a kiln. While some glaze compositions are quite elaborate and use a variety of chemical compounds, a glaze can be made from only three necessary elements: silica, the glass former; a flux or glass melter; and alumina, the refractory element.

Silica, also called flint, is the essential glaze ingredient. In its pure, crystalline state it is known as quartz. Were it not that the melting point of silica is so high—about 3100°F (1700°C)—this single material would suffice to form a glaze. However, most earthenware clays mature at about 2000°F (1093°C) and will seriously deform if fired higher, while most stoneware and porcelain bodies mature between 2250°F and 2400°F (1238–1315°C). Thus, pure silica cannot be used alone on these bodies.

Flux is a term applied to those compounds that lower the melting point of a glaze. Fortunately, many chemicals with a low melting point will readily combine with silica to form a glassy crystal. Two types of materials are commonly used as fluxes in low-fire glazes: *lead oxides* (lead carbonate, red lead, galena, and litharge) and *alkaline compounds* (borax, colemanite, soda ash, boric acid, and bicarbonate of soda). Although these two categories of low-fire fluxes have comparable fluxing power, their effects on glaze colorants and many of their other qualities are different (see Chap. 7). The chief high-fire fluxes are the alkaline earth compounds that melt at higher temperatures; calcium carbonate (also called whiting), dolomite (containing both calcium and magnesium), and barium carbonate.

A **refractory element** helps to form a stronger glaze that will better withstand the wear of normal use. The glaze produced solely by a mixture of silica and a flux would be soft and rather runny. A third ingredient, alumina, is therefore added to the glaze to make it harder and to prevent excessive running. Silica and alumina unite to form tough, needlelike mullite crystals, creating a bond more resistant to abrasion and shock.

Simple Formulation

In its final composition, then, a glaze includes its three necessary elements: silica, the glass former; a flux, which lowers the fusion point of silica; and alumina to give increased hardness to the glaze and increase viscosity.

It is not economically practical to use refined and pure oxides to make up glazes. The compounds employed by the potter are usually those minerals that are abundant in nature in a relatively pure state. Therefore, a simple, low-fire glaze will consist of:

kaolin $(Al_2O_3 \cdot 2SiO_2 \cdot 2H_2O)$
potash feldspar $(K_2O \cdot Al_2O_3 \cdot 6SiO_2)$
gerstley borate $(2CaO \cdot 3B_2O_3 \cdot 5H_2O)$

The silica content will be provided by both the clay (kaolin) and the feldspar. Alumina is also a constituent of both kaolin and feldspar. Feldspars are minerals that contain alumina, silica, and varying amounts of potash, sodium, and calcium. The predominant flux gives its name to the compound, such as soda feldspar. Potash feldspar, the more common type, is slightly cheaper and fires harder and higher than soda feldspar. Feldspar should be considered only incidentally as a flux in the low-fire range, since it is an important source of silica and alumina. In addition to aiding the fusion of the glaze ingredients, a flux also combines with the silica contained in the clay body of the pot to form a bond uniting the body and the glaze. This union becomes stronger as the temperature increases. Occasionally, a porous clay will absorb so much flux that the glaze will become thin and rough and require adjustments to either the glaze or the body.

Low-Fire Glaze Tests

In order to gain an understanding of the qualities imparted to the glaze by silica, alumina, and the flux, the beginner should make several tests with

341. *Camel.* Chinese, T'ang Dynasty (A.D. 676–908). Glazed terra cotta, height 34¾″ (86.9 cm).
Los Angeles County Museum of Art (William Randolph Hearst Collection).

varying proportions of feldspar, kaolin, and gerstley borate fired to cone 04. Earthenware tiles 2 by 3 inches and 1/4 inch thick make satisfactory tests. These should be bisque fired to about cone 010. The glaze samples should always be fired upright to detect a tendency in the glaze to run. The bottom quarter inch of each tile is left unglazed to catch the drips and evaluate the fluidity of the glaze.

A suggested beginning formula for an 04 glaze test is:

3 parts gerstley borate
3 parts feldspar
4 parts kaolin

Unless the scales are extremely accurate, a total sample of 100 grams is advisable. After weighing, the ingredients are ground in a mortar, and water is added until a creamy consistency is obtained. Modern ceramic materials are finely ground, so only a brief mixing is needed for a small sample. The glaze is brushed on a clean, dust-free tile in several thin coats. Experience is the only guide to the proper thickness of application. Cracks will develop if a layer is too heavy. In succeeding tests the feldspar is left constant, the kaolin decreased by half, the gerstley borate increased by the amount necessary to replace the kaolin. The total number of parts should be kept at 10, so that valid comparisons can be made. This process is repeated until the clay content is reduced to one part. The clay also functions as a binder to hold the nonplastic ingredients together; thus, if no clay is present, methocel or another binder must be added.

The fired samples will show a gradual change from a claylike white coating to one that becomes more fluid and glassy as the increased flux combines with the silica. Finally, a point is reached at which the glaze runs excessively. This tendency can be retarded by substituting additional feld- spar for some gerstley borate. At different firing temperatures the necessary proportions of flux, alumina, and silica will vary. When the temperature exceeds 2050°F (1130°C), the low-fire fluxes in the glaze must be replaced gradually by calcium carbonate (whiting), the principal high-fire flux. At temperatures above 2100°F (1150°C) the lead and alkaline fluxes will tend to run immoderately and are used only in minute quantities. A glaze can have a different crystalline surface structure because of variations in the propor- tion of alumina to silica. A slight excess of alumina produces a mat instead of a glassy finish; either too much or too little silica will result in a rough surface. Silica in its pure form can easily be added to a glaze if this should prove necessary.

After completing successful glaze tests with these three basic ingredi- ents, we can substitute for all or part of the feldspar other materials such as nepheline syenite, spodumene, lepidolite, or Cornwall stone. Further possi- bilities are cryolite, talc, and dolomite, which fire at slightly lower tempera- tures. Although some of these compounds contain silica and alumina, their main purpose is in varying and increasing the proportion of flux. These additions can affect the color and surface quality of the glaze. The principal advantages of having several fluxes in a glaze are the extension of the firing range and the more complete fusion of the chemicals with fewer glaze defects. (See Chap. 7 for more specific details about these materials.)

Barium carbonate additions will produce a mat glaze in cases where increasing the alumina content is not convenient. Zinc oxide can be added to the glaze in small quantities to obtain more fluxing action and reduce surface defects. It is essential that the glaze and the body cool and contract at the same rate after firing. If the body is weak and underfired, a contract- ing glaze may cause it to crack. Uneven contractions are also responsible for crazing. If sufficient tensions exist, the glaze will eventually craze, although this may not occur for days or even years. Expansions resulting from moisture collecting in a porous body may have a similar effect (see Chap. 4, pp. 139–140). On a decorative piece, tiny hairline cracks can add to the interest of the total design. If they are intentional, such effects are called crackle glazes to distinguish them from the unexpected and undesirable crazing.

Elimination of crazing is necessary in all functional ware to prevent seepage of moisture and to avoid odors resulting from trapped food particles. Changes can be made in the clay body to increase or reduce contraction and thereby adjust it to the glaze. The addition of silica to either the body or the glaze is one method used to prevent crazing. In the body the crystal formation developed by excess silica usually increases contraction, but in the glaze's glassy state silica is more likely to produce an expansion. Generally a potter has developed a satisfactory body with desired plasticity, vitrification, and so forth, and for this reason experimental glazes are adjusted to fit the body, rather than the other way around.

Although gerstley borate and colemanite are roughly similar in composition, colemanite has a greater tendency to settle in the glaze, making gerstley borate the preferred flux.

High-Fire Glaze Tests

High-fire glaze tests differ from those in the low-fire range only in the substitution of calcium carbonate ($CaCO_3$), commonly called whiting, for the low-melting lead and alkaline compounds. In this experiment tiles must be made from a stoneware or porcelain body. A good starting formula for a cone 6 to 8 glaze would be:

4 parts kaolin
4 parts potash feldspar
2 parts whiting

This will produce a sample that is white and claylike in character. In succeeding tests the whiting is held constant, the amount of feldspar gradually increased, and the proportion of the more refractory kaolin decreased. As the kaolin is lessened, the test glazes will become smoother and glassier. Depending upon the temperature, a satisfactory glaze should be achieved at the point when the kaolin content is between 10 and 20 percent. Throughout this series of tests we have lowered the fusion point of the glaze by the addition of the active flux, potash, which is contained in the feldspar. Only at higher temperatures can feldspar be considered a flux, since it is also a major source of alumina and silica.

A successful stoneware glaze can be made using only feldspar, kaolin, and whiting. As mentioned earlier, however, it may be desirable to add small amounts of other chemicals to obtain a greater firing range, achieve a better adjustment to the body, provide a more varied color spectrum, and develop a surface free from minor defects. Flint can easily be added to supply silica, if it should be needed.

You should attempt to vary the basic glaze to produce a glossy surface, a mat surface, and one that is fairly opaque (without the use of an opacifier such as tin oxide). Substitutions of some of the feldsparlike materials with different fluxes, such as lepidolite or nepheline syenite, can be tried. Often small amounts of another flux will result in a great improvement in a glaze. Other suggested additions are zinc oxide, talc, and barium carbonate. (See Chap. 7 for more detailed information on these and other chemicals, including colorants that will be used in further tests.)

Glaze Types

At the beginning of this chapter we stressed the simplicity of glaze formulation, and indeed it is so. A functional and attractive glaze can be made from only a few materials. Several glazes, however, use rather uncommon ingredients or require special firing techniques. The glaze recipes in the Appendix will clarify the general descriptions of the glazes that follow.

The glaze types have been grouped into two general categories—low fire and high fire. Low-fire glazes are those that fire generally between cone 020 and cone 04. High-fire glazes mature between cones 6 and 10. Some people identify a third classification—medium-fire glazes which mature between cones 02 and 4. Medium-fire glazes frequently exhibit some qualities of each of the two extremes.

In addition to these temperature categories, there are a number of special glazes formulated to give particular effects. Some of these fire predominantly in either the high or the low range, but others span the entire firing spectrum.

High-Fire Glazes

High-fire glazes generally are compounded to fire in a range from cone 6 to cone 14, or 2250°F to 2500°F (1230–1370°C). At these extreme temperatures, common low-fire fluxes, such as lead and borax, must be replaced with calcium carbonate, which has a higher melting point—about 1500°F (816°C).

Porcelain and stoneware glazes are identical, except in cases where adjustments must be made to accommodate a difference in firing shrinkage. Because feldspar is a major ingredient in such glazes, the term *feldspathic glaze* is often applied to stoneware glazes. Due to the high temperature, the union of glaze and body is quite complete. The interlocking mullite crystals prevent detection of the line of junction that is easily visible between a glassy glaze and a porous earthenware body. Feldspathic glazes are very hard (they cannot be scratched by steel), and they resist most acids, the exceptions being hydrofluoric, phosphoric, and hot sulphuric acids. The surfaces may be either mat or smooth, but they never reveal the high gloss of low-fire glazes.

Medium-Fire Glazes

Glazes firing between cones 02 and 4 contain both high- and low-fire fluxes in order to adjust to these temperature limits. (See Appendix for glaze recipes.) Generally, they combine the smooth, glossy surface and potential for bright colors of lead and alkaline glazes with the more durable heat and shock resistance of higher-firing glazes. There are also many commercially prepared glazes available in the medium-fire range providing a wide spectrum of colors—purples, yellows, reds, and oranges—difficult to achieve in the high-fire glazes and more likely to chip and crack in the lower-fire range. Many hand potters and sculptors are working with glazes in this medium-fire range for the bright designs and details possible with these very stable glazes. Another desirable feature is the energy saving in firing to lower temperatures.

Low-Fire Glazes

Most low-fire glazes can be further subdivided into two distinct groups—alkaline or lead—according to the major flux included in the glaze. Both fire

in the range of cone 016 to cone 02, and both result in smooth, glossy surfaces. They often are characterized by bright, shiny colors.

Alkaline Glazes Alkaline glazes use such fluxes as borax, colemanite, or soda ash, which encourage bright color effects, particularly turquoise-blues. Because of their extreme solubility, alkaline glazes should never be applied to raw ware. When absorbed into the clay, the expansions and contractions that alkaline compounds undergo during firing and cooling will cause the body to crack.

A very soft bisque ware also reacts poorly to an alkaline glaze, for it will absorb a portion of the flux, leaving an incomplete and usually rough-textured glaze after firing. Because of their solubility and tendency to become lumpy in the glaze solution, the alkaline compounds (such as borax) are often fritted into a nonsoluble silicate form. Colemanite gives a milky blue tinge to the glaze, while the lead compounds are completely transparent. Alkaline glazes are generally more successful when used on a body fairly high in silica.

Lead Glazes The most common fluxes for lead glazes are oxides of lead compounds—lead carbonate and red lead. A very active flux that melts at about 950°F (510°C), lead gives glazes a bright and glossy surface.

In general, the lead glaze should be high in alumina and calcium. Additions of zinc, barium, and zirconium will also make the glaze more

342. Peter Voulkos, U.S.A. Platter. Manganese stoneware with white slip, sand engobe, colemanite wash, and low-fire color accents; diameter 18⅝″ (47 cm).

343. Victor Cicansky, Canada. *Pigeon Fancier.*
Earthenware with polychrome glazes, length 21″ (52.5 cm).

successful. Lead has the disadvantage of being very poisonous. It requires careful handling to avoid breathing the dust or getting particles in the mouth. For this reason, lead is often converted into a nontoxic silicate form by fritting. Fritting is a procedure by which a flux and silica are melted and later ground to form a glaze addition that is both nontoxic and insoluble in water. Vessels glazed with lead must never be used to store liquids containing large percentages of acid, such as fruit juices. Copper oxide should never be included as a colorant for glazed ware intended to hold food of any kind, for it increases the poisonous effects of lead.

In spite of their disadvantages, lead glazes do produce uniquely soft and shiny surfaces. They should not be overlooked because of the potential health hazard. Glazes can be tested for lead release. In order to be absolutely certain that the glaze will have no side effects, glaze only the exterior of any pottery that might come into contact with food.

Lead glazes are ideal for low-fire earthenware sculpture. Lead-tin glaze was especially common on Italian and Spanish ware, the tin lending opacity and a whitish color to the glaze.

left: **344.** *Ginevra de' Benci,*
portrait bust attributed to
Leonardo da Vinci (1459–1519).
Glazed terra cotta. Private collection, Rome.

below: **345. Joe Fafard,** Canada. *Jan Wyers.*
Talc body fired to cone 03
with low-fire glazes,
gold and platinum lusters, acrylic paint;
height 14″ (35 cm).

346. Bernard Leach, England. Vase.
Stoneware with combed decoration
and runny ash glaze.

Special Glazes and Effects

Ash Glazes   Ash glazes were probably the first glazes used. At present they have no commercial application, but they are of interest to the studio potter. The ash can derive from any wood, grass, or straw. Depending upon the specific source, the chemical composition can vary considerably: it is generally very high in silica and contains some alumina and calcium; moderate amounts of fluxes, such as potash, soda, and magnesia; plus iron and small quantities of numerous other compounds. Because of the high silica content, ash can seldom be used in low-fire glazes in amounts over 15 to 20 percent. This is not sufficient to make much change in the basic glaze.

A suggested starting point for a stoneware ash-glaze test would be:

40 parts ash
40 parts feldspar
20 parts whiting

Fireplace ashes should be collected in a fairly large quantity and then mixed thoroughly to ensure uniformity. The ash is first run through a coarse sieve to remove unburned particles. It can then be soaked in water that is decanted several times to remove soluble portions. However, many potters prefer to run the dry ash through a fine sieve without washing (taking care not to inhale the fine ash particles), and thus retain the soluble fluxes. The latter procedure will allow a larger percentage of ash to be used in the final glaze. An ash glaze is quite caustic and should not be stirred with the hand.

While wood ash can be incorporated into a glaze and fired in an electric, oil, or gas kiln, an ash glaze can also be the accidental result of a long firing in a wood-burning kiln. Results are not predictable, because much depends upon the placement in the kiln, the path of the flame, and the length of firing. These factors cause the ash to be deposited on the ware in an uneven fashion, much like the effects of salt glazes. The tall bottle in Figure 347 reveals the patterns of salt accumulations and the running of ash, both of which complement the austere form.

Salt Glazes   Salt glazes have enjoyed a revival in recent years after a long period of neglect by the studio potter. From the 12th to the mid-19th century, such glazes were common in Germany, England, and Colonial America. Commercial applications are largely limited to stoneware crocks, glazed sewer pipe, hollow building brick, and similar products.

Salt-glazing is a simple procedure. The ware is fired to its body-maturing temperature, at which time common salt (sodium chloride) is thrown into the firebox or through ports entering the kiln chamber. This sodium combines with the silica in the clay to form a glassy silicate. Since deadly chlorine gas is released at the moment of salting, the studio must be well ventilated. Adding a small amount of borax will reduce the firing temperature but often results in a shiny glaze.

The toxic chlorine and hydrochloric acid fumes have caused potters to search for alternatives to sodium chloride. Of these, sodium bicarbonate seems the most successful. Because of its higher melting point and lower vapor pressure, the sodium bicarbonate should be introduced through a burner or porthole with a blower attachment to ensure its distribution throughout the kiln.

For salt-glazing, the usual stoneware or porcelain body is often satisfactory. However, additions of silica and feldspar may be necessary to obtain a good glaze coating. Under reducing conditions (incomplete combustion to introduce carbon into the kiln atmosphere), buff or red clays will develop a pebbly brown or black glaze. Other colors can be obtained only by using colored slips or body stains. In addition, iridescent effects much like lusters

above: 347.
Peter Rushforth, Australia.
Tall Stoneware Pot.
Stoneware with salt and ash glazes,
height 22¾″ (57 cm).

left: 348. Tom Turner, U.S.A. Jar.
Porcelain with cobalt in the body,
salt-glazed with copper
and stannous chloride.

right: 349. Early American jug
attributed to John Crolius
of New York (1733–1812).
Stoneware with incised decoration
and cobalt oxide accents, salt-glazed;
height 10″ (25 cm).
Metropolitan Museum of Art, New York
(Rogers Fund, 1934).

below: 350. Chris Dell, Canada. *Brinks Bank.*
Porcelain salt-glazed to cone 10
with oxide stains and low-fire lusters
for the metallic parts, length 12″ (30 cm).

can be produced by fuming. The kiln is cooled to a low red heat (about cone 020). With the draft and burner ports open, combinations of stannous chloride, ferric chloride, and bismuth, sodium, or silver nitrates are introduced into the kiln through the burner ports. Unique copper reds are achieved by reducing the ware after copper oxide has been introduced by fuming. Other color oxides can be thrown into the kiln during the salting procedure.

Whatever coloring devices are employed, the glaze will have a mottled and pebbly surface. The salt does not collect on the sharper edges of plastic additions or in incised decoration, so that a natural contrast develops between fully and thinly glazed areas. Because the salt does not reach the insides of closed forms or tall bottles, the insides should be glazed in the normal manner.

The major disadvantage of the salt glaze is that it coats the whole interior of the kiln. This makes the kiln unsuitable for bisque and other types of glaze firing. The firing range of salt glazes is wide, from cones 02 to 12, but the most common firings are between cones 5 and 8. (See Chap. 8, p. 242 for more specifics on the salting technique.)

Raku Glazes Raku glazes are applied to stoneware bodies containing a high proportion of grog, usually 30 percent of the body, in order to withstand the rapid heating and cooling involved in the firing process. (See

351. Wayne Higby, U.S.A.
Calico Canyon Overlook. 1976. Handbuilt container, slab construction with inlays, raku fired with crackle and luster glazes; height 15″ (37.5 cm). Collection Paul M. Ingersoll, Philadelphia.

Chap. 8 for raku firing techniques.) Because the firing temperature may be as low as 1750°F (955°C) or cone 09, the glaze can consist of 80 percent gerstley borate and 20 percent potash feldspar. Low-firing borosilicate frits can also be used and will eliminate the lumpiness resulting from the borax.

The glaze is applied to bisque ware. Because of the low firing temperature, the stoneware body remains underfired, and the glaze is not waterproof. The speed of the firing, the exposure to open flame, and the reducing atmosphere and smoking result in a great variety of unusual and unpredictable glaze effects. Copper oxides tend to develop reds and lusters, red iron oxide often becomes black, and deep crackle patterns occur.

Raku ware is associated with the Japanese tea ceremony which evolved under the influence of Zen Buddhism. Raku tea bowls are usually handbuilt and irregular, allowing the effects of the firing to complete the decorative design. The high grog content and the firing process tend to limit the size and shapes of raku forms, although many contemporary potters have greatly expanded the scope of raku ware.

Reduction Glazes Reduction glazes are those especially compounded to develop their unique color characteristics only if fired in a kiln capable of maintaining a reducing atmosphere during certain portions of the firing cycle. The normal kiln firing is an oxidizing fire. An electric kiln always has an oxidizing fire, since there is nothing in the kiln atmosphere to consume the oxygen that is always present. To reduce the atmosphere in a gas or oil kiln, the draft is cut back to lessen the air intake, resulting in an incomplete combustion that releases carbon into the kiln interior. In a closed blower type kiln with a forced-air system, the air intake is reduced. In a muffle kiln, some of the muffles will have to be removed to allow the combustion gases to enter the kiln chamber.

Carbon has a great affinity for oxygen when heated and will steal it from the iron and copper-coloring oxides in the glaze. It was in this manner that the Chinese produced their famous copper reds (sang-de-bœuf) and celadons. When either copper or iron oxide is deprived of its oxygen, it remains suspended in the glaze as the pure colloidal metal. Thus a normal green copper glaze becomes a beautiful ruby red with occasional blue or purple tints. The iron oxide loses its customary brownish-red tone and takes

352. Choniu, Japan. Tea Bowl.
c. 1760. Raku ware, height 3½″ (8.75 cm).
Metropolitan Museum of Art, New York
(Howard Mansfield Collection;
gift of Howard Mansfield, 1936).

353. Box. Porcelain, handbuilt with slabs, showing the mottled copper-red and green characteristic of a fluid alkaline glaze, reduction-fired to cone 6; height 8″ (20 cm).

on a variety of soft gray-green hues. Because of their likeness to jade, which had religious symbolism for the ancient Chinese, celadons of remarkable quality were developed. In a small muffle kiln, a reduction can occur if pine splinters or moth balls are inserted into the peephole. The usual reduction fire starts with an oxidizing fire, and reduction does not begin until just before the melting of the first elements of the glaze. After the reduction cycle, the firing must return to oxidation in order to develop a surface free from pinholes and other defects (see Chap. 8, pp. 238–239).

Reduction can also affect the color of a stoneware body. Stoneware that is light gray or tan in oxidation becomes darker gray or even brown under reducing conditions. The iron particles contained in most stoneware become darker and melt into the glaze, making it speckled.

A local copper reduction can be achieved by using a small amount (about 0.5 percent) of silicon carbide (carborundum) in the glaze. The effects are slightly different from the standard reduction, for the color is concentrated in little spots around the silicon carbide particles. But this technique has an advantage in that it can be used in an electric kiln, since the heating elements are in no way affected. The firing range of copper-red and celadon reduction glazes is quite wide, ranging from about cone 08 all the way up through the porcelain temperatures.

Mat Glazes Mat glazes generally are formed either by adding an excess of alumina or by substituting barium carbonate for some of the flux in the glaze. Therefore, they are often called *alumina mats* or *barium mats*. A mat glaze should not be confused with a thin, rough, or underfired glaze. It should be smooth to the touch, with neither gloss nor transparency. The mat effects sometimes observed on an underfired glaze are caused by incompletely dissolved particles, whereas a true mat develops a different surface crystalline structure. An unusually long cooling time will encourage the formation of mat textures. One test for a true mat is to cool the glaze quickly to see if it will develop a shine. A mat surface caused by the incomplete fusion of particles will continue to have a mat surface, regardless of the cooling time. It is generally a bit rough to the touch and lacks the smooth-

354. Kim Bruce, Canada.
Casserole. 1976.
Stoneware, reduction-fired
with a gold glaze; diameter 11″ (27.5 cm).

355. Carl E. Paak, U.S.A.
Two Pronged Victory in the Landscape.
Porcelain with underglaze pencil, wash,
and crackle glaze, fired in an electric kiln
to cone 7; height 10″ (25 cm).
After firing, portions of the surface
were brushed with ink.

ness of a true mat. Mats can be calculated for all temperatures, but they are particularly attractive in the low-fire ranges, since typical lead and borax glazes are so shiny that their glare tends to obscure all decoration and form. Mat glazes are related to the crystalline group, because both depend upon the surface structure of the glaze for their effects. Therefore, mats can also be made with iron, zinc, and titanium (rutile) when properly compounded and cooled slowly.

Crackle Glazes   Crackle glazes cannot be characterized by their composition, for they are merely the result of tensions that arise when a glaze and

356. Chien Yao, China.
Tea bowl. Sung Dynasty (A.D. 960–1279).
Stoneware with temmoku glaze,
height 2¹⁵⁄₁₆″ (7.5 cm).
Art Institute of Chicago
(Buckingham Collection).
Temmoku is a high-iron-content mat glaze.
The streaking effect (called hare's fur)
is caused by surface crystals
formed in cooling.

left: 357. Kenneth Green, U.S.A.
Hinged pot with rosewood pin.
Porcelain with dolomite glaze
fired to cone 9, height 4½″ (11.25 cm).

below: 358. Kuan porcelain with celadon glaze.
Chinese, Sung Dynasty (A.D. 960–1279).
"Gall-bladder shape" vase (left),
height 5⅛″ (13 cm);
Lu incense burner (right),
diameter 6⅛″ (15.5 cm).
Cleveland Museum of Art.

a body expand and contract at different rates. In most glazes, except perhaps the mats, a crackle can be produced. The simplest way is to substitute similar-acting fluxes for others having a different contraction rate. The reverse is true if a noncrackling glaze is desired. Sodium has the highest expansion rate, followed by potassium. Calcium has about half the rate of expansion of these, lead and barium follow, with boron and magnesium having the lowest expansion rates of commonly used fluxes.

A crackle is a network of fine cracks in the glaze. It must be used on a light body to be seen properly. To strengthen the effect, a coloring oxide or strong black tea is often applied to the crackled area. In Figure 355, only portions of the clear crackle glaze were inked with a brush, creating a shading effect around the drawn lines. The Chinese were able to achieve, by successive firings, a network of both large and fine crackles, each stained with a different coloring oxide. A crackle glaze is more practical on a vitreous stoneware or porcelain body, because a crackle on a porous earthenware pot will allow liquids to seep through and make it unsatisfactory for holding food.

Crystalline Glazes There are two types of crystalline glazes. The more common, macrocrystalline, has large crystal clusters embedded in or on the surface of the glaze; the second type, called aventurine, has single crystals, often small, suspended in the glaze, which catch and reflect the light. These

359. Marc Hansen, U.S.A. Bottle. Porcelain with large zinc crystals; height 9⅝" (22.57 cm). The alkaline crystalline glaze was fired to cone 10, allowed to cool 100°F, held at that point for 4 hours, and then cooled very slowly.

360. Warren MacKenzie, U.S.A.
Covered jar. 1976.
Stoneware with wax-resist decoration
and crystalline glaze fired to cone 10,
height 11″ (27.5 cm).

are interesting glazes technically, but they must be very carefully related to the pot shape. The jewellike effects seem to float off the surface of all but the most simple and reserved forms.

The crystalline formation is encouraged by additions of zinc and iron or by titanium (rutile). Borax and soda can also be used, preferably in a fritted form, but lead is not advisable. The alumina content must be very low and is in fact absent from some crystalline formulas. The silica content is also lower than in most glazes.

A mat glaze is actually an example of a microscopic aventurine type glaze. Possible firing ranges are wide, and, as with mat formations, the rate of cooling is most important. In order to allow the crystals to develop properly, the temperature of the kiln should be permitted to drop only about 100°F (38°C) after maturity, and it must be held at this level for several hours before slow cooling. Crystalline glazes are quite runny, so a pedestal of insulating brick should be cut to the foot size and placed under the ware. You can also throw a separate foot ring, coat it with kiln wash, and place it under the ware. If fired high, or with an especially heavy glaze application, the piece can be set in a shallow bisque bowl that will collect any excess glaze that might run off the sides.

Luster Glazes Historically, luster glazes consisted of a thin, decorative metallic coating fired over a lead-tin glaze. This coating was a solution of pine resin, bismuth nitrate, and a metallic salt dissolved in oil of lavender. The luster was then fired to a low red heat in a reducing atmosphere sufficient to fuse the metal and burn off the resin, but not to melt the original glaze. This made possible a variety of colors as well as iridescent sheens. The metals employed were lead and zinc acetates; copper, manganese, and cobalt sulfates; uranium nitrate; and even silver and gold compounds. Bismuth generally served as the flux. The luster was rarely an overall coating; rather it was applied in the form of a decorative design. This is especially true in Islamic ceramics, which featured intricate, interlocking decorative motifs because of the religious ban on figural representation.

Whereas the lusters of the Islamic potter contained impurities to soften their brilliance, commercial lusters used today are bright and strident. Their popularity reflects the chrome, stainless steel, and fluorescent lights of much contemporary sculpture. The lusters usually are fired in an electric kiln

left: 361. Wall tile,
Persian, from Kashan.
13th century. Earthenware,
lead-tin glaze with luster decoration;
diameter 5¾″ (14.5 cm).
Metropolitan Museum of Art,
New York
(bequest of Edward C. Moore, 1891).

below: 362.
Keith T. Campbell, Canada.
Lollipop Box.
Porcelain with clear glaze
fired to cone 10, low-firing lusters
in hues of orange, gold, and silver
fired to a low temperature.

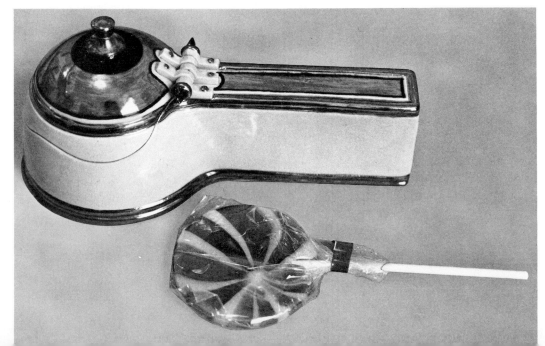

between cone 020 and cone 014 and are available in pearl-like iridescent hues and various colors—turquoise, blue, pink, red, gold, and silver. They can be brushed, sprayed, or drawn with special pens onto nearly any low-fire or stoneware glaze. (See Chap. 4, pp. 135–138, for decorating techniques.)

Frit Glazes Frit glazes may be little different chemically from the two low-fire types described earlier. Fritting is a process that renders raw-glaze materials either nontoxic or nonsoluble. Lead or alkaline fluxes (borax or soda ash) are melted in a frit kiln with silica or with silica and a small amount of alumina. When the glaze becomes liquid, a plug is pulled in the bottom of the frit furnace, and the contents are discharged into a container filled with water. The fractured particles are then ground to the necessary fineness. Small amounts can be made in the studio using a crucible. One disadvantage of studio manufacture is the extremely long grinding time necessary to pulverize the frit to adequate fineness.

Many different types of frit glazes are commercially available. Frit composition is complicated, for nontoxic or nonsoluble elements must be completely absorbed within a satisfactory firing range and without creating later adjustment problems. A frit glaze is seldom a complete glaze for several reasons. Since it is usually colorless, opacifiers or colorants must be added. The frit has little ability to adhere, so a small amount of plastic clay or bentonite is usually necessary. Adjustments for the final firing ranges must also be made. Frits have extensive commercial use where large amounts of standard glaze are employed. For the studio potter, frits are of most value in eliminating the lumpy quality of borax needed in crystalline, copper reds, and similar glazes. Purchased in 100-pound lots, low-fire frits

364, 365. Dick Evans, U.S.A.
Details of Figure 363
showing the color and textural effects
obtained by the layers of lusters
and numerous firings.

366. Maija Grotell, U.S.A.
Large bowl. Wax-resist decoration
with mottled effects created
by an Albany slip under a Bristol glaze.

might well be used in schools to replace the small and expensive colored glaze packets often purchased. The addition of a few color oxides and kaolin would not raise the cost substantially.

Bristol Glazes Bristol glazes are very similar, in most respects, to the typical porcelain glaze, except that a relatively large amount of zinc oxide is added. In most cases, this tends to lower the melting point and to add a certain opacity to the glaze. Calcium and barium should be included in the fluxes. Most Bristols fall into the cones 5 to 9 range, although formulas have been successfully developed for cones 3 to 14. The most common use of the Bristol glaze is for architectural tile and bricks.

Since a large amount of clay is normally used, the ware is generally given a single firing, and there is no problem of shrinkage. However, by calcining part of the clay, the glaze can be fitted to double firings. The commercial single fire usually takes 50 to 60 hours, not only because of the thickness of the ware being fired but also because of the extremely viscous nature of the Bristol glaze. It is this quality of the glaze that makes it valuable to the studio potter. Interesting effects can be achieved by using a Bristol glaze over a more fluid glaze that breaks through in spots. The application of the glaze must be perfect, because its viscosity prevents any cracks that may occur from healing. Moreover, in firing, the edges of the cracks will pull farther apart and bead. In general, Bristol glazes are shiny, but they can be matted by increasing the amount of calcium while reducing the silica content.

Slip Glazes Slip glazes are made from raw natural clays that contain sufficient fluxes to function as glazes without further preparation beyond washing and sieving. In practice, additions are often made to enable the slip glaze to fit the body or to modify the maturing temperature, but these changes are minor.

Slip glazes were commonly used by early American stoneware potteries that produced such utilitarian objects as storage crocks, bowls, mugs, and pitchers. Albany slip clay is the only commercial variety that is used widely. It fires brown-black at cones 6 to 10. The addition of 2 percent cobalt to Albany slip will result in a beautiful semigloss jet black. Many slip clay deposits are not recognized as such. They are particularly common in the Great Lakes Region—Indiana, Michigan, Minnesota, Wisconsin—and, like those in New York, are probably of glacial origin.

Barnard slip clay is somewhat similar to Albany, but it is lower in alumina and silica and has a much higher iron content. Red Dalton is higher in alumina and silica, but lower in fluxes. All fire to a brownish black and can be used in a combination or, depending upon the firing temperature, with added fluxes. Because of the natural contraction of slip clay during drying, the ware is best glazed and decorated in the leather-hard stage.

367. Earl J. Hooks, U.S.A.
Encapsulated Man.
Wheel-thrown with coils
and modeling,
fired to cone 9
with Albany slip and oxides;
height 9″ (22.5 cm).

Frequently, earthenware clays can be used as slip clays when fired high enough and with the addition of small amounts of flux. Most slip clays fire from cone 4 to cone 12. Slip-clay fluxes are generally the alkaline earth compounds, plus iron oxide in varying amounts. A high iron content serves also to produce a color ranging from tan to dark brown.

The potter must be careful in using slip clays, for they are generally mined in small pits, and their composition will vary slightly. Each new shipment of material should be tested before being used in quantity. Some Albany slip is so lacking in the usual brown colorant that the resulting glaze is a pale, semitransparent tan. Studio potters should pay more attention to this group of glazes. Slip clays are easy to apply, adhere well, and fire with few, if any, defects. The composition, chemically, is most durable, and, since additions are few, much time can be saved in glaze preparation. Slip clays are particularly well suited for single-fire glazes.

Terra Sigillata Roman terra sigillata relief ware, black Etruscan pottery, and the so-called "black varnish" of the Greek red and black ware all have essentially the same semiglaze finish. These glazes are actually slips fired to low temperatures so that the surface is easily scratched and not completely waterproof. However, the unusual decorative qualities of the soft black and red colors have made terra sigillata ware popular with hand potters.

368. Rhyton (drinking cup). Greek, found in an Etruscan tomb. Late 5th century. Museo Municipale, Tarquinia, Italy.

left: 369. William C. Alexander, U.S.A.
Covered jar. Earthenware,
glazed and fired to cone 010
in terra sigillata technique;
height 6″ (15 cm).

below: 370. Julian and Maria Martinez, U.S.A.
Jar. c. 1925–50.
Burnished earthenware,
heavily reduced in dung firing;
height 7″ (17.5 cm).
Museum of the American Indian, New York.
This traditional Pueblo Indian ware
was made by two famous potters
from San Ildefonso, New Mexico.

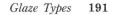

To prepare the slip, mix a low-firing, high-iron-content clay body in a dry state with a large quantity of water. To make a thinner slip, 3 or 4 percent soda ash will help to flocculate the clay. A large, plastic garbage can serve as a good container. Allow the slip to settle for a day or two, and then siphon off the clear water on the surface. Pour off the upper portion of slip and discard the coarser clay that has settled to the bottom. Adding more water to the slip and repeating the process will ensure that only the finest colloidal clay particles remain.

Like the higher-fire slip glazes described above, the terra sigillata should be applied when the body is leather hard. This reduces flaking that can result from the different shrinkage rates of the body and the glaze. For a smoother surface, burnish the glaze with a hardwood or bone tool. The glaze can be sprayed on to form an overall coating or brushed on to create a pattern.

The firing technique is an important factor in revealing the decoration. If the atmosphere is oxidizing, the color will be a soft, semigloss red; in a reducing fire, the color will be black. The covered jar in Figure 369 has been heavily reduced, causing the red iron oxide slip to become black. However, the reduction was followed by an oxidizing atmosphere, which changed the open and more porous body not covered with slip back to its original orange-tan color. The feather pattern vase in Figure 370 was fired in a smoky reduction atmosphere. The slip design was applied on top of an overall coating of slip that had been carefully burnished. Thus, the design is revealed by the difference in light refraction between the mat and burnished surfaces.

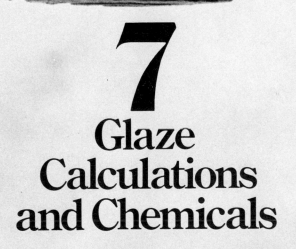

7
Glaze
Calculations
and Chemicals

In the previous chapter the characteristics of some common glazes were discussed and a trial-and-error method was suggested by which the novice potter might gain a rudimentary understanding of the properties of the common glaze materials. The development of the various types of ceramic glazes evolved over several thousand years through just such a trial-and-error method. Glaze formulas were passed on from generation to generation in the usual tradition of the crafts. This progression was not steady, because local economies were often interrupted by the migrations of people due to wars, famine, and pestilence. As a result, techniques would not only evolve and change but sometimes be lost and forgotten. Since the compounding of glazes was a more complicated and valuable task than the more ancient use of clay slips, glaze recipes came to be jealously guarded family secrets. Thus, while we find much in ancient literature about the beauty of the pottery, little is ever revealed about actual techniques. The scientific formulation of glazes is only about a century old. During this time respect for the ancient potter has increased, because attempts to duplicate Chinese glazes and Hispano-Moresque decorations are often unsuccessful.

In spite of all the research over the past hundred years, glaze making is still dependent upon experience. The following section on glaze calculations will be helpful in comparing one glaze to another and in finding solutions for glaze accidents. However, commercial glaze chemicals are not pure, as a refined drug might be, and they contain numerous impurities not listed in the molecular formulas. Compare, for example, the basic formula for feldspar with the possible variations (p. 311). Similar variations, with the presence of numerous impurities, exist in the other chemicals briefly described in this section, but because of the extreme complexity involved, only the major components are listed. Thus, in case mishaps occur, you should be aware of the variability of many of our common raw chemicals.

371. Hispano-Moresque dish,
from Manises, Spain. 15th century.
Earthenware, tin-enameled;
diameter 17⅝″ (44 cm).
Metropolitan Museum of Art,
New York (Cloisters Collection, 1956).

Calculations

All matter composing the earth is made up of approximately one hundred chemical elements in the form of atoms. These elements occur in nature not in a pure form but in compounds, which are groups of atoms held together by an electrical attraction or bond. The atom is much too small to be weighed, but it is possible to determine the relative weights of atoms to each other. Oxygen, symbolized by the letter O, has been given the atomic weight of 16, because it is sixteen times heavier than hydrogen, the lightest atom. Other atoms are assigned weights corresponding to their proportionate weights in relation to hydrogen.

Silica, mentioned frequently in the chapters on clay and glazes, is a major ceramic compound and is found in every clay and glaze. The *molecular formula* for silica (or, more precisely, silicon dioxide) is SiO_2. The atomic weight table in the Appendix (p. 308) lists the weight of silicon as 28. Since two oxygen atoms weigh 32, the total molecular weight of the compound silicon dioxide is 60.

Silica can be added to a clay body or glaze in the silicon dioxide form, but it is most commonly found as part of a more complex compound, such as kaolin ($Al_2O_3 \cdot 2SiO_2 \cdot 2H_2O$), or potash feldspar ($K_2O \cdot Al_2O_3 \cdot 6SiO_2$).

The RO, R₂O₃, RO₂ System

There are three principal components in a glaze. One of these is silica (SiO_2), which gives the glaze its glassy, transparent quality. The second is alumina (Al_2O_3), a refractory element, which contributes toughness and abrasion resistance to the glaze. Since neither of these oxides will melt at temperatures below 3100°F (1704°C), the potter must add a third ingredient, a flux, such as lead oxide or sodium, that will lower the melting point and combine with silica and alumina to form, after firing, a glassy coating on the body.

With rare exceptions, the glaze components commonly used are not single refined oxides but complex compounds that are available commercially at reasonable cost. In order to compare glazes or to understand the effects of these varied chemicals, it is necessary to separate the component oxides into the three major parts of the glaze formula. The symbol RO refers to the fluxing agents—chiefly metallic or alkaline elements that usually form

RO (Bases)	R₂O₃ (Neutrals)	RO₂ (Acids)
Fluxing agents	Refractory elements	Glass formers
Li_2O	(Amphoteric oxides)	SiO_2
Na_2O	Al_2O_3	TiO_2
K_2O	B_2O_3	ZrO_2
CaO	Fe_2O_3	
MgO	Sb_2O_3	
BaO	Cr_2O_3	
ZnO		
FeO		
MnO		
PbO		

their oxides by combining with one atom of oxygen, such as CaO or PbO. Most have one atom of the metallic or alkaline element, the exceptions being Li_2O, Na_2O, and K_2O. Similarly, alumina (Al_2O_3) can be symbolized by R_2O_3 and silica (SiO_2) by RO_2. The table on page 195 will better illustrate this division of the components of a glaze.

In the first column are the RO oxides that have the effect of fluxes in either a glaze or a body. They are also called the *base oxides*. Some of the *neutrals* or amphoteric oxides can function as either a base or an acid oxide. However, the major oxide in this group, alumina (Al_2O_3), always has a refractory effect in a glaze. On the other hand, red iron oxide (Fe_2O_3) is an active flux as well as a colorant. Boric oxide (B_2O_3) can react as either a base or an acid. Silica (SiO_2) is the major oxide in the *acid* column. The contribution of TiO_2 and ZrO_2 to a glaze is opacity, not their glass-forming effect. With minor exceptions, the RO, R_2O_3, and RO_2 method of categorizing the main components of a glaze works very well.

The Empirical Glaze Formula

In the interests of simplifying calculations, glaze batches are usually reduced to an *empirical formula*. This is a glaze formula in which the various active ingredients are expressed in molecular proportions. By contrast, the *batch recipe* is a proportion expressed in the actual weights of the raw chemical compounds making up the glaze. Since the materials used in the typical glaze batch are rather complex compounds, it is a distinct advantage to be able to define the glaze in terms of single oxides that bear the same proportional relationship to each other as when in their more complex form in the glaze batch. These oxides are grouped into RO, R_2O_3, and RO_2 units.

Before a batch recipe is converted into an empirical formula, it is first necessary to know the chemical formulas of the individual raw materials, as well as their equivalent weights. The molecular formulas and equivalent weights of the molecular compounds for all commonly used ceramic materials are listed in the Appendix (pp. 309–310). The commercial name of the raw material is in the first column, its molecular formula in the second. Many compounds are designated by more than one name, such as whiting or calcium carbonate.

The molecular weight of a compound is the sum of the atomic weights of its constituent elements. The equivalent weights of the RO, R_2O_3 and RO_2 units will often be the same as the molecular weight of the compound, but in many cases these equivalent weights vary. This is true of potash feldspar:

Raw material	Formula	Molecular weight	Equivalent weights		
			RO	R_2O_3	RO_2
feldspar (potash)	$K_2O \cdot Al_2O_3 \cdot 6SiO_2$	556	556	556	92

According to the given formula, when one molecular unit of potash feldspar is added, the glaze will have one unit of potassium oxide, one unit of alumina, and six units of silica. Since one unit each of potassium oxide and alumina form the compound, their individual equivalent weights are 556. And since six units of silica are necessary to form the compound, the equivalent weight of silica is 1/6 of the compound weight, or 92. The equivalent weights of the oxides in a compound are the same as its molecular weight if the oxide in question appears only once. However, if more than one unit of an oxide occurs, then its equivalent weight will be found by dividing the compound molecular weight by the number of times the oxide in question appears.

These definitions will become clearer in the actual procedure of converting the glaze batch recipe at right to an empirical formula. The recipe is for a lead glaze resistant to food acids, maturing at cone 06.

Before we can go into the actual calculations, we must first find the molecular formula of each of the compounds making up the glaze, plus the equivalent weights of the oxides contained in these compounds. It is convenient to put this information in table form, as illustrated below. By checking over the raw material formulas, we can determine which of the oxides should be indicated in the spaces to the right of the table.

Raw materials	Parts by weight
soda feldspar	18.95
gerstley borate	9.78
white lead	36.78
boric acid	4.90
kaolin	6.80
silica	21.70
zirconium oxide	.83
	99.74

Batch to Empirical Formula

Raw material and formula	Batch weights	Equivalent weights			PbO	CaO	Na_2O	B_2O_3	Al_2O_3	SiO_2	ZrO_2
white lead $[2PbCo_3 \cdot Pb(OH)_2]$	36.78 ÷	(RO)	258	=	.1425						
gerstley borate $(2CaO \cdot 3B_2O_3 \cdot 5H_2O)$	9.78 ÷	(RO) (R_2O_3)	206 137	= =		.0474		.0713			
boric acid $(B_2O_3 \cdot 3H_2O)$	4.90 ÷	(RO)	124	=				.0395			
soda feldspar $(Na_2O \cdot Al_2O_3 \cdot 6SiO_2)$	18.95 ÷	(RO) (R_2O_3) (RO_2)	524 524 87.3	= = =			.0361		.0361	.2165	
kaolin $(Al_2O_3 \cdot 2SiO_2 \cdot H_2O)$	6.80 ÷	(R_2O_3) (RO_2)	258 129	= =					.0263	.0527	
silica (flint) (SiO_2)	21.70 ÷	(RO_2)	60	=						.3616	
zirconium oxide (ZrO_2)	.83 ÷	(RO_2)	123	=							.0067
Totals	99.7				.1425	.0474	.0361	.1108	.0624	.6308	.0067

The batch weights of the raw materials are divided by the equivalent molecular weights of the particular oxides concerned, giving the molecular proportions in the form of single oxides. By arranging these oxides with the amounts calculated into their appropriate RO, R_2O_3, and RO_2 groups, we find that the glaze batch has the following empirical formula:

RO		R_2O_3		RO_2	
.1425	PbO	.1108	B_2O_3	.6308	SiO_2
.0474	CaO	.0624	Al_2O_3	.0067	ZrO_2
.0361	Na_2O				
.2260					

The total of the RO oxides comes to .2260 instead of the desired unit of one. By dividing each of the above figures by .2260 we will have the following empirical formula. The RO is now .9999.

RO		R$_2$O$_3$		RO$_2$	
.6305	PbO	.4905	B$_2$O$_3$	2.7914	SiO$_2$
.2097	CaO	.2770	Al$_2$O$_3$	.0296	ZrO$_2$
.1597	Na$_2$O				
.9999					

By rounding off the above figures to avoid unnecessary calculations we obtain the following empirical glaze formula.

RO		R$_2$O$_3$		RO$_2$	
.63	PbO	.49	B$_2$O$_3$	2.80	SiO$_2$
.21	CaO	.28	Al$_2$O$_3$	.03	ZrO$_2$
.16	Na$_2$O				

Considerable research has been done on the properties of ceramic materials, and some reasonable predictions can be made about the probable change that a particular chemical will cause in a known type of glaze. There are, however, many variables, such as the length of the glaze grinding time, the thickness of application, the reactions between glaze and body, the kiln atmosphere, and the rate of temperature rise and fall. Since each or all of these conditions can markedly affect a particular glaze, glaze experimentation is something less than a true science. Successful work depends largely upon the overall experience and care of the operator in controlling these factors as they interact with one another.

The Batch Recipe

To convert an empirical formula to a batch recipe, it is necessary to reverse the procedure explained in the previous section. As before, the easiest method is to draw up a chart on which to compile the information. This type of conversion will require slightly greater familiarity with raw chemical compounds, because we must select those compounds containing the proper oxides without adding any unwanted elements. The parts of compounds that pass off in the kiln as gases or water vapor are ignored. To make the process clearer, let us take our previous empirical glaze formula and convert it back into a batch recipe.

RO		R$_2$O$_3$		RO$_2$	
.63	PbO	.49	B$_2$O$_3$	2.80	SiO$_2$
.21	CaO	.28	Al$_2$O$_3$	.03	ZrO$_2$
.16	Na$_2$O				

The general procedure is as follows: First, if any alkaline (RO) fluxes are present (Na$_2$O or K$_2$O), it is best to include as much as possible in a soda or

372. Donald Frith, U.S.A.
Covered jar.
Porcelain with petal-like additions
and copper-red reduction glaze,
height 9″ (22.5 cm).

Formula to Batch Recipe

Raw material and formula	Oxides in formula: Equivalents needed:	Na₂O 0.16	CaO 0.21	PbO 0.63	B₂O₃ 0.49	Al₂O₃ 0.28	SiO₂ 2.80	ZrO₂ 0.03
soda feldspar ($Na_2O \cdot Al_2O_3 \cdot 6SiO_2$)								
0.16 equivalents		0.16				0.16	0.96	
remainder			0.21	0.63	0.49	0.12	1.84	0.03
gerstley borate ($2CaO \cdot 3B_2O_3 \cdot 5H_2O$)								
0.105 equivalents			0.21		0.315			
remainder				0.63	0.175	0.12	1.84	0.03
white lead [$2PbCO_3 \cdot Pb(OH)_2$]								
0.21 equivalents				0.63				
remainder					0.175	0.12	1.84	0.03
boric acid ($B_2O_3 \cdot 3H_2O$)								
0.175 equivalents					0.175			
remainder						0.12	1.84	0.03
kaolin ($Al_2O_3 \cdot 2SiO_2 \cdot 2H_2O$)								
0.12 equivalents						0.12	0.24	
remainder							1.60	0.03
silica (flint) (SiO_2)								
1.60 equivalents							1.60	
remainder								0.03
zirconium oxide (ZrO_2)								
0.03 equivalents								0.03

potash feldspar. This is a cheaper source of the flux, and, equally important, it is nonsoluble and not as likely to become lumpy in a glaze as borax. We then fill out the other single oxides, trying to save the alumina for next to last and taking out the silica at the end. Alumina and silica are often included in other compounds, and the balance can easily be taken care of last in the form of either kaolin or silica. Since silica is always present in larger amounts than alumina and is available in a cheap, pure form, it can safely be saved for the last.

Several of the calculations in the table on page 199 may seem incorrect at first, so perhaps we should point out a few of these seeming inconsistencies. In the first addition, when we take 0.16 equivalents of soda feldspar, we get six times as much SiO_2 as either Na_2O_3 or Al_2O_3, because the formula for soda feldspar is $Na_2O_3 \cdot Al_2O_3 \cdot 6SiO_2$. Similarly, gerstley borate has two units of CaO and three units of B_2O_3 for each equivalent of the compound.

Now that we have the needed molecular equivalents of the chemical compounds, we can find the gram (or pound) batch weights by multiplying each equivalent by the molecular weights of the chemical compound. Thus we have the following set of calculations:

Raw material	Equivalents		Molecular weights		Batch weights
soda feldspar	.16	×	524	=	83.84
gerstley borate	.105	×	412	=	43.26
white lead	.21	×	775	=	162.75
boric acid	.175	×	124	=	21.70
kaolin	.12	×	258	=	30.96
silica	1.60	×	60	=	96.00
zirconium oxide	.03	×	123	=	3.69
					442.20

By dividing the individual batch weights by 442.20, we arrive at a batch recipe expressed in percentages. This is our original glaze recipe (left).

Limit Formulas

In the glaze experiments described in Chapter 6 (pp. 166–169), no definite limits were mentioned regarding the ratio between the RO, R_2O_3, and RO_2 parts in a glaze. This is because the major purpose of these glaze tests was to gain familiarity with the qualities of the various glaze chemicals. The previous analyses have shown that there are general limits to the amounts of alumina and silica that can be used successfully in relation to a single unit of flux. The firing temperature and the type of flux are also important factors in establishing limits.

In the several limit formulas opposite, a number of possible fluxes are indicated; however, the total amount used must add up to a unit of one. In general, a higher proportion of alumina will result in a mat surface, provided the kiln is cooled slowly. Barium will also tend to create a mat surface. A study of these formulas indicates how the ratio of alumina and silica rises as the temperature increases. While not intended to take the place of glaze formulas, the listing should be a helpful guide to those seeking to change the temperature range of a favorite glaze. Some glaze chemicals are quite

Original Batch Recipe

Raw materials	Parts by weight
soda feldspar	18.95
gerstley borate	9.78
white lead	36.78
boric acid	4.90
kaolin	6.80
silica	21.70
zirconium oxide	.83
	99.74

complex, and under certain conditions an addition to a glaze will not have the desired effect. By converting the batch recipes to empirical formulas and comparing them with the suggested limits, one ought to be able to detect the direction of the error.

Limit Formulas

Cone 08-04   Lead glazes

PbO	0.2–0.60	Al_2O_3	0.15–0.20
KNaO	0.1–0.25	B_2O_3	0.15–0.60
ZnO	0.1–0.25		
CaO	0.3–0.60	SiO_2	1.5–2.50
BaO	0 –0.15		

Cone 08-04   Alkaline glazes

PbO	0 –0.5	Al_2O_3	0.05–0.25
KNaO	0.4–0.8		
CaO	0 –0.3	SiO_2	1.5–2.5
ZnO	0 –0.2		

Cone 2-5   Lead calcium glaze

PbO	0.4–0.60	Al_2O_3	0.2–0.28
CaO	0.1–0.40		
ZnO	0 –0.25	SiO_2	2.0–3.0
KNaO	0.1–0.25		

Cone 2-5   Lead-borax glaze

PbO	0.2 –0.3	Al_2O_3	0.25–0.35
KNaO	0.2 –0.3	B_2O_3	0.20–0.60
CaO	0.35–0.5		
ZnO	0 –0.1	SiO_2	2.5–3.5

Cone 2-5   Colemanite glaze

CaO	0.2–0.50	Al_2O_3	0.2–0.28
ZnO	0.1–0.25	B_2O_3	0.3–0.6
BaO	0.1–0.25		
KNaO	0.1–0.25	SiO_2	2.0–3.0

Cone 8-12   Stoneware glaze

KNaO	0.2–0.40	Al_2O_3	0.3–0.5
CaO	0.4–0.70	B_2O_3	0.1–0.3
MgO	0 –0.35		
ZnO	0 –0.30		
BaO	0 –0.30	SiO_2	3.0–5.0

Variables in Glaze Formulation

Potters are frequently disappointed when a glaze obtained from a friend or from a textbook produces quite unexpected results. Several factors may be involved in this problem. Ingredients that are more finely ground than usual will melt at a slightly lower temperature. In the same way, fritted glaze additions melt more quickly than do raw compounds of a similar composition. Occasionally the thickness of application or reaction with the clay body will produce slightly different results. More distressing and troublesome is the variable nature of such major glaze ingredients as Cornwall stone and the feldspars.

In attempting to alter a glaze that has proved unsatisfactory, the potter has several simple remedies. If the glaze is too runny, the addition of flint or kaolin usually will raise the melting point; if it is too dry, an increase of flux will develop a more fluid glaze. Sometimes, however, the effect is quite the opposite, and in such cases the student, quite justifiably, may feel that the instructor who suggested the change does not know a great deal about glaze chemistry.

The real culprit in many glaze failures is the chemical phenomenon known as a *eutectic*. A eutectic is the lowest point at which two or more chemicals will combine and melt. It is much lower than the melting point of

373. Hiroaki Morino, Japan. Bowl. Stoneware with barium blue glaze and trailed luster decoration, height 8″ (20 cm).

any of the individual chemicals. For example, lead oxide has a melting point of 1616°F (880°C), and silica melts at 3119°F (1715°C). One might expect that a half-and-half mixture of lead and silica would melt at the halfway point, 2364°F (1300°C), yet the actual melting point is much lower, about 1470°F (800°C). The lowest melting point of lead and silica (the eutectic point) occurs at about 945°F (510°C), with a mixture of approximately 90 percent lead oxide and 10 percent silica. The line diagram in Figure 374 illustrates the relatively simple reaction between lead oxide and silica and the eutectic point at E.

In an actual glaze—compounded of complex minerals and containing several fluxes, alumina, and even different types of silica—the firing reaction is much more complicated. It is quite possible for there to be two and even more eutectic points.

Figure 375 shows a hypothetical reaction, with two eutectic points, between several fluxes and silica. The vertical movement represents the changing temperature of fusion as a portion of flux is replaced with a like amount of silica. Glazes that fall in areas B and C are more troublesome to potters, since a slight change in composition or temperature is critical. These are generally high-gloss glazes. In area B a small increase in silica will increase the gloss and raise the melting temperature, but in area C an increase in silica will lower the melting temperature and create a very runny glaze. The points E1, H, and E2 are especially troublesome, for a very slight temperature rise will change the character of the glaze. The most satisfactory glazes fall in the lower ranges of A and D. Because of the flattened curve in these areas, a slight change in temperature or silica is not likely to cause a great variation in the fired glaze. The alumina, calcium, zinc, and dolomite mat glazes fall in the lower area of A. As the silica is decreased in area A, the glazes become more mat and finally become rough and incomplete with a very low proportion of silica. Transparent and majolica glazes fall in the lower area of D; these become less glossy as the ratio of silica and the temperature are raised. Although the area D glazes can be glossy like the unpredictable glazes in B and C, they are quite stable and little affected by slight changes in silica or temperature. Ash glazes fall in all areas; those in areas B and C are runny and unpredictable.

Figure 375 is a purely theoretical attempt to visualize the reactions between the fluxes and silica. It does not represent an actual glaze, since the function of alumina is ignored. The more usual method of diagramming a glaze is shown in Figure 376. Here we have the three major components of a glaze: fluxes, silica, and clay (alumina-silica). The small triangle at each apex contains 100 percent of the compound used. As we move along the base line of the silica-clay axis, the ratio becomes 90 percent silica to 10 percent clay (kaolin), then 80 percent silica to 20 percent clay, and so forth. Pro-

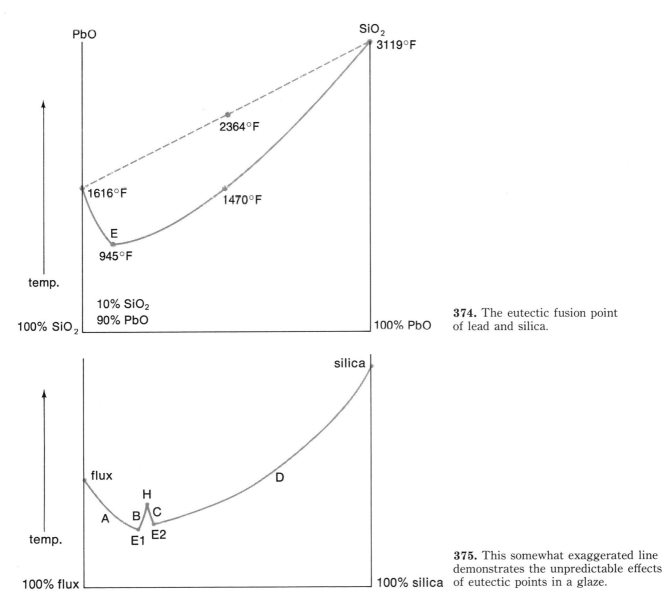

374. The eutectic fusion point of lead and silica.

375. This somewhat exaggerated line demonstrates the unpredictable effects of eutectic points in a glaze.

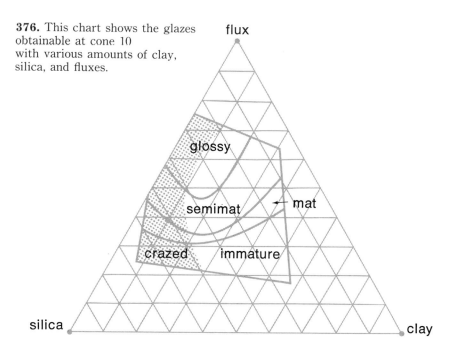

376. This chart shows the glazes obtainable at cone 10 with various amounts of clay, silica, and fluxes.

gressing vertically, the triangles contain an increasing amount of the third glaze component, the fluxes. The roughly square section in the center covers those glaze tests that at cone 10 (2426°F, 1330°C) fuse to form a glaze. As the gradient indicates, there is a change from mat to glossy as the fluxes are increased, and an area of crazed glazes where the alumina content is low. The clay content also has a decisive effect upon whether a glaze is to be glossy or mat. As indicated in both Figures 375 and 376, the mat and semimat glazes cover a much wider range of possible combinations at a given temperature. The sharp gradient of the glossy area in Figure 376 would suggest that the eutectic points for this particular glaze would fall in this range.

The use of a triaxial diagram for planning experiments has many applications in ceramics. It takes much time to complete the entire sequence, and considerable effort can be saved by concentrating on those areas in which meaningful results can be expected. This system is especially helpful in gaining knowledge about the relative fluxing power of various compounds, their effects on colorants, and blending of colorants and opacifiers.

Ceramic Chemicals

The chemicals used by the potter are generally not pure single oxides but more complex compounds that are available for industrial uses in a moderately refined form at low cost. Because of differences either in the original mineral or in refining methods, the ceramic chemicals available from different dealers can vary slightly. Even items from the same supplier can change minutely from year to year. Commercial potteries constantly check new shipments of chemicals, but this is seldom done in the small studio. If a favorite glaze reacts strangely, you should consider this factor, provided, of course, there was no deviation from the normal glazing and firing procedure. The feldspars, in particular, vary in their fluxing power. It is for this reason that we have not stressed the importance of a glaze formula but rather the experimental knowledge of the properties in glaze ingredients.

The batch glazes listed in the Appendix (pp. 316–319) are mainly for purposes of illustration, and they may have to be adjusted slightly to fit the materials available.

For the convenience of students converting an empirical glaze formula into a batch recipe, a listing follows that gives the major sources of the various oxides in the RO, R_2O_3, and RO_2 groups. A more complete chemical description will be found in the alphabetized list at the end of this chapter.

Sources of Base (RO) Oxides

Barium oxide (BaO) is a very active flux under some conditions. Its glass formation has a brilliancy second only to the lead silicates. Barium's effect on the thermal expansion of the glaze is less than that of the alkalies and calcia. Like lead, its fumes are toxic. It is one of the alkaline earth minerals, a category that also includes calcium, strontium, and radium. The best source for barium is:

 barium carbonate ($BaCO_3$)

Calcium oxide (CaO), in comparison with the other alkaline oxides, produces a glaze more resistant to abrasion, mild acids, and weathering. It also lowers the coefficient of thermal expansion, thereby increasing tensile strength. Although it is often used in small amounts with other fluxes in low-fire glazes, calcium should not be used as the sole flux at temperatures below cone 3. As with alumina, an excess of calcia tends to produce mat textures. Sources of calcium are:

 calcium carbonate ($CaCO_3$), also called whiting
 calcium borate ($2CaO \cdot 3B_2O_3 \cdot 5H_2O$), more commonly known as colemanite or gerstley borate
 dolomite [$CaMg(CO_3)_2$]
 calcium fluoride (CaF_2), better known as the mineral fluorspar
 bone ash, refined [$Ca_3(PO_4)_2$]
 wollastonite ($CaSiO_3$)

Lead oxide (PbO) has been mentioned frequently as one of the major low-fire fluxes. There are several reasons for its popularity. It combines readily with all other fluxes and has a lower coefficient of expansion than do the alkaline fluxes. Lead gives greater brilliancy to the glaze, although at times this can be a disadvantage. Lead glazes melt and flow well and thus tend to reduce pinholes and other defects of the more viscous type of glaze. The chief drawbacks are the poisonous nature of lead compounds (unless they are carefully compounded) and their susceptibility to attack by strong fruit acids. Lead tends to blacken or develop a film if slightly reduced. The surface of a lead glaze will scratch easily unless an alkaline flux is added. There are many forms of lead, such as:

 litharge (PbO), a lead oxide
 red lead (Pb_3O_4), a lead oxide
 white lead [$2PbCO_3 \cdot Pb(OH_2)$], also called lead carbonate
 lead monosilicate, the fritted lead silicate composed of approximately 16
   percent SiO_2 and 84 percent PbO
 lead bisilicate, another commercial lead silicate, with the approximate
   composition of 65 percent PbO, 33 percent SiO_2, and 2 percent Al_2O_3
 lead sulfide (PbS), also called galena

Lithium oxide (Li_2O) is more commonly used by glass manufacturers, but it has several important qualities that make its occasional use in glazes

377. Robert A. Sedestrom, U.S.A.
Double Barreled Teapot.
Slip-cast porcelain with
sprayed glossy and crystalline glazes
and copper, manganese, and nickel,
oxidation-fired to cone 9;
height 10¼″ (25.5 cm).

valuable. Lithium (the oxide or carbonate) is expensive, because it is present in very small quantities (3 to 8 percent) in the producing ores. It has a much lower atomic weight than does either sodium or potassium (ratio of 1:3 and 1:5); therefore, a smaller amount of material can be used without lessening the fluxing action. This has the effect of decreasing tensions caused by thermal expansions and contractions and thus promoting a more durable glaze. Lithium is one of the alkaline metals, a category that also includes sodium, potassium, rubidium, and cesium. Sources of lithium are:

lepidolite ($LiF \cdot KF \cdot Al_2O_3 \cdot 3SiO_2$)
spodumene ($Li_2O \cdot Al_2O_3 \cdot 4SiO_2$)
lithium carbonate (Li_2CO_3)
petalite ($Li_2O \cdot Al_2O_3 \cdot 8SiO_2$)
amblygonite ($2LiF \cdot Al_2O_3 \cdot P_2O_5$)

Magnesium oxide (MgO) is frequently found combined with the feldspars and limestones. It lowers the thermal expansion more than do other bases, and it is as satisfactory as the alkaline fluxes in developing a durable glaze. In some combinations it will produce a slight opacity. Used with low-fire glazes, magnesium has a refractory effect and lends opacity and a mat quality; it fluxes easily at higher temperatures and becomes quite fluid. Sources of magnesium are:

magnesium carbonate ($MgCO_3$)
dolomite [$CaMg(CO_3)_2$]
talc (varies from $3MgO \cdot 4SiO_2 \cdot H_2O$ to $4MgO \cdot 5SiO_2 \cdot H_2O$). In the solid and more impure form it is also known as steatite or soapstone.
diopside ($CaO \cdot MgO \cdot 2SiO_2$)

Potassium oxide (K_2O) is similar in fluxing action to sodium. It has a lower coefficient of thermal expansion, thus increasing the hardness and brilliance of a piece and lowering the fluidity of the glaze. Sources of potassium are:

potassium carbonate (K_2CO_3), more commonly known as pearl ash
potash feldspar ($K_2O \cdot Al_2O_3 \cdot 6SiO_2$)
Cornwall stone, a complex compund of variable composition, roughly similar to a feldspar and having fluxes of calcium, sodium, and potassium ($1RO \cdot 1.16Al_2O_3 \cdot 8.95SiO_2$)
Carolina stone, a domestic product similar to Cornwall stone
volcanic ash (see analysis in Appendix, p. 310)
plastic vitrox ($1RO \cdot 1.69Al_2O_3 \cdot 14.64SiO_2$)

Sodium oxide (Na_2O) is one of the more common low-fire fluxes. It has the highest coefficient of expansion of all the bases and generally gives a lower tensile strength and elasticity to the silicates formed than do most other fluxes. The usual ceramic sources of sodium are:

sodium chloride (NaCl)
sodium carbonate (Na_2CO_3), more frequently called soda ash
sodium bicarbonate ($NaHCO_3$)
borax ($Na_2O \cdot 2B_2O_3 \cdot 10H_2O$)
soda feldspar ($Na_2O \cdot Al_2O_3 \cdot 6SiO_2$)
cryolite (Na_3AlF_6)
nepheline syenite ($K_2O \cdot 3Na_2O \cdot 4Al_2O_3 \cdot 9SiO_2$)

378. Hiroaki Morino, Japan.
Cube with playing card design
Stoneware slab form
with modeled additions, iron stain,
and low-fire stencil decoration;
height 14″ (35 cm).

Zinc oxide (ZnO) can contribute several different qualities to a glaze. It can be used to replace some of the more soluble alkaline fluxes. Zinc is second only to magnesium in reducing thermal expansion and to calcium in increasing the strength and resistance of a glaze. It contributes some opacity to the glaze and is helpful in reducing crazing defects. The major zinc compound used in ceramics is:

   zinc oxide (ZnO)

Sources of Neutral (R_2O_3) Oxides

Unlike the RO group, which has numerous similar compounds, the R_2O_3 group is almost limited to alumina (Al_2O_3) and a few oxides that have the same oxygen ratio. The greatest difference between a glass and a glaze is the presence of alumina in the glaze. The alumina content is a most important factor in a successful glaze. It controls the fluidity of the melting glaze and enables it to withstand the temperatures needed to mature the body. Greater amounts of alumina increase the hardness of the glaze and its resistance to abrasions and acids. Crystalline glazes must necessarily be low in alumina, since alumina prevents the devitrification that accompanies the crystal formation.

Alumina (Al_2O_3) in a glaze can vary from 0.1 to 0.9 molecular equivalents, depending upon the firing temperatures. The equivalent ratios between the alumina and the silica groups can be from 1:4 to 1:20. For glossy glazes the ratio is about 1:10. As mentioned before, an increase of alumina will tend to produce mat textures. A glossy porcelain glaze firing from cones 10 to 12 will have an alumina-silica ratio of between 1:7 and 1:8, whereas the mats will be 1:3.2 to 1:3.8. Alumina also has an effect on the colors developed. The normal blue of cobalt oxide will become a rose pink in the absence of alumina. Chromium oxide, which usually gives various green tones, will tend to become reddish in the presence of excess alumina. Sources of alumina are:

   alumina hydrate [Al(OH)$_3$]
   feldspar and Cornwall stone, see sections under RO oxides
   kaolin or china clay ($Al_2O_3 \cdot 2SiO_2 \cdot 2H_2O$), see sections under clay
   nepheline syenite ($K_2O \cdot 3Na_2O \cdot 4Al_2O_3 \cdot 9SiO_2$)
   plastic vitrox (1RO $\cdot$ 1.69$Al_2O_3 \cdot$ 14.64SiO_2)
   pyrophyllite ($Al_2O_3 \cdot 4SiO_2 \cdot H_2O$)

Antimony oxide (Sb_2O_3) is primarily used as an opacifier and a coloring agent. It is found in:

   antimonious oxide (Sb_2O_3)
   basic antimonate of lead [Pb$_3$(SbO$_4$)$_2$], also known as Naples yellow

Boric oxide (B_2O_3) is one of the neutral oxides (R_2O_3), which, by our previous definition, can react either as bases or acids. The refractory properties of alumina are more like those of the acid silica than any of the bases. Boric oxide has a number of characteristics similar to alumina: the alumina of mat glazes can be satisfactorily replaced by boric oxide; color effects do not change by this substitution; both alumina and boric oxide harm underglaze red and green colors; and both can form mixed crystals. On the whole, however, boric oxide functions as a flux, since in comparison with silica it increases elasticity, lowers tensile strength, and, in limited quantities, lowers the thermal coefficient of expansion. Like lead, it increases the gloss and refractive index. Major compounds containing boron are:

boric acid ($B_2O_3 \cdot 2H_2O$)
borax ($Na_2O \cdot 2B_2O_3 \cdot 10H_2O$)
colemanite ($2CaO \cdot 3B_2O_3 \cdot 5H_2O$), also called calcium borate
gerstley borate ($2CaO \cdot 3B_2O_3 \cdot 5H_2O$)

Chromic oxide (Cr_2O_3) is derived from the mineral *chromite* ($FeCr_2O_4$). It is used as a colorant in glazes. The fact that the mineral form is a natural spinel would indicate its use as a stain.

Red or **ferric iron oxide** (Fe_2O_3) is commonly used as a coloring agent to form brownish-red hues and also to modify copper and cobalt. It would serve well as a flux except for its strong coloring action. Its presence in many compounds is regarded as an impurity, and considerable effort goes into removing iron flecks from white-ware bodies. Red iron oxide conforms to the R_2O_3 oxide ratio but has none of the refractory qualities that alumina has.

Sources of Acid (RO_2) Oxides

The important oxide in this group, silica, has a refractory effect on glaze, while the others function largely as opacifiers or coloring agents.

Silica (SiO_2), also called flint, combines readily with the bases to form glassy silicates. It is the most common element in glazes, comprising about 50 percent by weight. In a glaze it has the effect of raising the melting point, decreasing fluidity, increasing resistance of the glaze to water and chemicals, increasing hardness and tensile strength, and reducing the coefficients of thermal expansion. The amounts of silica used depend upon the flux and the maturing point of the glaze, but it is generally between 1 and 6 molecular equivalents.

Silica is commonly obtained from sandstone, quartz sands, or flint pebbles. Silica is found combined with many ceramic materials. Below are listed a few of the more frequently used silica compounds.
ball clay ($Al_2O_3 \cdot 2SiO_2 \cdot 2H_2O$)
kaolin ($Al_2O_3 \cdot 2SiO_2 \cdot 2H_2O$)
soda feldspar ($Na_2O \cdot Al_2O_3 \cdot 6SiO_2$)
potash feldspar ($K_2O \cdot Al_2O_3 \cdot 6SiO_2$)
Cornwall stone ($1RO \cdot 1.16Al_2O_3 \cdot 8.95SiO_2$)
wollastonite ($CaSiO_3$)
petalite ($Li_2O \cdot Al_2O_3 \cdot 8SiO_2$)

Tin oxide (SnO_2) is used primarily as an opacifier in glazes. Although rather expensive, it remains popular because it has greater covering power than any other opacifier. The chief form of tin is:
tin oxide (SnO_2), also called stannic oxide

Titanium oxide (TiO_2) is probably the only other oxide in the RO_2 group that has some of the refractory qualities of silica. Its use in glazes, however, is entirely for its effect upon other colors and its action as an opacifier.
titanium dioxide (TiO_2)
rutile (TiO_2), an impure form containing iron and vanadium oxides

Characteristics of Ceramic Chemicals

Albany slip is a slip clay, which is a natural clay containing silica, alumina, and fluxes in the correct proportions to function as a glaze. It is mined in the vicinity of Albany, New York. Since it occurs in small pits, its composition and color will vary. Usually, it fires to a glossy brown-black at temperatures between cones 4 and 12. Occasionally, it may fire to a pale, nearly transparent tan. Slip clays are very easy to apply and fire with few, if any, defects.

Alumina hydrate [$Al(OH)_3$] is preferred to the calcined form (Al_2O_3) for some uses, since it has better adhesive qualities and remains suspended in the glaze longer. Introduction of alumina for mat effects is considered to be more effective in the hydrate form than in such compounds as clay or feldspar.

Antimonate of lead [$Pb_3(SbO_4)_2$], also known as Naples yellow, is primarily used as a paint pigment. It is a source of low-fire yellows. The presence of lead in Naples yellow is an advantage, since antimony will not produce a yellow unless combined with lead or iron.

Antimonious oxide (Sb_2O_3) is poisonous and slightly soluble in water. For a satisfactory effect as an opacifier, it must be used in glazes fired below cone 1. Antimony will also produce yellow and orange colors for glazes. The most common mixture, known as *yellow base,* has the following composition:

red lead	15 parts
antimony oxide	10 parts
tin oxide	4 parts

The mixture is calcined to cone 09, then ground and washed.

Barium carbonate ($BaCO_3$) is usually used in combination with other fluxes, since at lower temperatures it combines very slowly and acts as a refractory element to form mat textures. At higher temperatures it reacts strongly as a flux.

Barium chromate ($BaCrO_4$) will produce colors in the pale yellow to light green range. It is generally used in overglaze decoration, since it is fugitive at temperatures above cone 04.

Bentonite ($Al_2O_3 \cdot 4SiO_2 \cdot 9H_2O$) is of volcanic origin. The formula is not quite correct, since bentonite contains other impurities (see the analysis of South Dakota bentonite in the Appendix, p. 310). Bentonite generally fires to a light cream color and fuses at about 2400°F (1300°C). Its chief value is as a plasticizer for short clays. As such it is about five times as effective as ball clay. Purified bentonite will also make a stronger glaze covering and will help prevent settling in the glaze. An addition of about 3 percent is sufficient.

Bicarbonate of soda (see sodium bicarbonate)

Bismuth subnitrate ($BiONO_2 \cdot H_2O$) generally contains impurities such as arsenic, lead, and silver carbonates. It melts at a low temperature and will produce pearly metallic lusters under reducing conditions.

Bone ash in the unrefined state has a formula of $4Ca_3(PO_4)_2 \cdot CaCO_3$ with a molecular weight of 1340. The material generally available today is the refined calcium phosphate $Ca_3(PO_4)_2$ with a molecular weight of 310. It sometimes serves as a glaze flux but more commonly as a body ingredient in bone china, chiefly in the kind produced in England. It lowers the firing temperatures required and increases translucency.

Borax ($Na_2O \cdot 2B_2O_3 \cdot 10H_2O$) is, next to lead, the major low-fire flux. It has a strong action on all ceramic compounds and may even be used in small amounts in the high-fire glazes that tend to be overly viscous in nature. Borax has an effect on coloring oxides different from that of lead; for this reason it is often combined with lead. Borax absorbs moisture and should therefore be kept dry, or weight calculations will be inaccurate. As mentioned earlier, borax is very soluble in water and should not be applied to raw ware.

Boric acid ($B_2O_3 \cdot 2H_2O$) is a flaky material soluble in water. It is available in a fairly pure state at low cost. Although boron is one of the neutral oxides (R_2O_3), it functions more as a flux, since it increases the gloss in glazes. Unlike silica, an acid, boron lowers the expansion coefficient and helps to increase elasticity.

Cadmium sulfide (CdS) is a low-fire yellow colorant. It is usually combined in a stain made of cadmium, selenium, and sulphur frits. Unfortunately, it is fugitive above cone 010 and can be used only for overglaze decorations.

Calcium borate (see colemanite and gerstley borate)

Calcium carbonate (see whiting)

Calcium fluoride (see fluorspar)

Calcium phosphate (see bone ash)

Calcium zirconium silicate is a commercially produced opacifier with the composition of ZrO_2, 41.12 percent; SiO_2, 25.41 percent; CaO, 22.23 percent. It does not have the strength of tin but is considerably cheaper. It will reduce slightly the maturing temperatures of the lower-fire glazes.

Carolina stone is similar in composition to Cornwall stone but is mined domestically. However, it is not commonly available.

China clay (see kaolin)

Chromic oxide (Cr_2O_3) and other chromium compounds are often used in glazes to produce green colors. Dichromates are preferred because of the greater amounts of chromium per weight. Care must be taken in the glaze composition, for, when chromic oxide is combined with tin, a pink color results. Zinc and chrome will form a brown, and high-lead glazes may develop a yellow-lead chromate. Reducing conditions in the kiln will blacken the color. In fact, even adjacent tin-glazed and chrome-glazed pieces may affect each other in the kiln. Bright, low-temperature reds (below cone 010) can be produced by chrome oxide in a high-lead and low-alumina glaze.

Clay is a decomposed feldspathic-type rock consisting chiefly of silicates of aluminum but often containing numerous other ingredients, such as quartz, micas, feldspars, iron oxides, carbonates of calcium and magnesium, and organic matter (see Chap. 1).

Cobalt carbonate ($CoCO_3$) is used to introduce a blue color in glazes. When combined with manganese, iron chromate, or ochre, it will produce colors ranging from gray to black.

Cobalt oxide (Co_2O_3) is the major blue colorant. It is extremely strong and therefore is often fritted with alumina and lime or with lead for lower-fire underglaze colors. The frit allows a lighter and more even color dispersion. Color stains made of cobalt, alumina, and zinc are uniform at all temperature ranges. Small amounts of cobalt in combination with magnesium carbonate, silica, and boric acid will produce a variety of hues in the pink and lavender range.

Cobalt sulfate ($CoSO_4 \cdot 7H_2O$), unlike the other cobalt compounds mentioned, is very soluble in water. It melts at a low temperature and is primarily used in decorative work or luster ware.

Colemanite ($2CaO \cdot 3B_2O_3 \cdot 5H_2O$) is a natural hydrated calcium borate, which has the advantage of being only slightly soluble in water. Therefore, it does not develop the granular lumps in the glaze so characteristic of borax. Colemanite serves as a low-fire flux, since the boron present melts at a fairly low temperature. It tends to prevent crazing and also functions partially as an opacifier. Colemanite can be substituted for calcium in some glazes where calcium would harm the pink or red colors desired. In both high- and low-fire glazes, colemanite tends to develop a milky-blue opalescent color. Gerstley borate, a type of colemanite, is preferred by many potters because it has less tendency to settle in the glaze and is less variable in quality.

Copper carbonate ($CuCO_3$) is a major green colorant in glazes. The carbonate form is preferred to the oxide form in the production of blue-greens or copper reds under reducing conditions.

Copper oxide is available in two forms: *cupric* or black copper oxide (CuO), or *cuprous* or red copper oxide (Cu_2O). Copper is one of the few colorants that does not change greatly under normal oxidizing conditions. Additions of 2 percent or more of copper will decrease markedly the acid resistance of lead glazes. Lead fluxes tend to produce a blackish green. When copper and tin are combined with an alkaline flux, a turquoise will result. Potash will induce a yellowish green, while zinc and copper with fluxes of sodium, potassium, and barium will develop a blue tinge.

Cornwall stone is a complex mixture derived from an English deposit of partially decomposed granite rock. It is composed of quartz (flint), feldspar, lepidolite, tourmaline, fluorspar, and small quantities of other minerals. Cornwall stone has characteristics that lie between those of kaolin and feldspar. It is a major ingredient of many English glazes and bodies and is subject to less firing strains than kaolin and feldspar. Because of the more intimate mixture of naturally occuring minerals, a smaller amount of alkali flux is necessary than would otherwise be needed. Since less bulk is required, there is less shrinkage of both the unfired and the fired glaze, thus minimizing glaze defects. Cornwall stone is roughly similar to *petuntze,* the feldspathic rock used for centuries by the Chinese as a major ingredient in their porcelain bodies and glazes. Like feldspars, Cornwall stone has variable composition; samples differ in the percentages of silica, potassium, sodium, and so on. If Cornwall stone is not available, a substitution of 67 parts feldspar, 22 parts flint, and 11 parts kaolin can be made for 100 units of Cornwall stone. However, as previously noted, the new glaze will not have identical characteristics. The analysis of Cornwall stone is found in the Appendix, p. 310.

Cryolite (Na_3AlF_6) is used primarily as a flux and an opacifier for enamels and glasses. It has a limited application in glazes and bodies as a source of fluxes and alumina. In some glazes, an addition of cryolite will promote crazing.

Dolomite [$CaMg(CO_3)_2$] is a double carbonate of calcia and magnesia. Its inclusion in a glaze is a good method of introducing both calcia and magnesia, since glazes with magnesia usually have a large proportion of calcium. Dolomite contains the equivalent of 44 percent magnesium carbonate and 56 percent calcium carbonate. Dolomite will also promote a longer and lower-firing range in clay bodies. Below cone 4, the addition of a small amount of a lower-firing alkaline flux to the dolomite will greatly increase this effect.

Epsom salts (see magnesium sulfate)

Feldspar is a crystalline rock composed of the aluminum silicates of potassium, sodium, and calcium. These silicates are never found in a pure state but in a mixture with one or the other predominating. For convenience in ceramic calculations, their formulas are usually given as follows:
potash feldspar (microcline) $K_2O \cdot Al_2O_3 \cdot 6SiO_2$
soda feldspar (albite) $Na_2O \cdot Al_2O_3 \cdot 6SiO_2$
lime feldspar (anorthite) $CaO \cdot Al_2O_3 \cdot 6SiO_2$

The feldspars are a major component of porcelain and white-ware bodies and are often the only source of body flux. If the feldspar content of the body is high, the substitution of soda spar for potash feldspar will reduce the vitrification point by as much as 100°F (38°C). Feldspars are a cheap source of glaze flux and have the additional advantage of being nonsoluble. Because of the presence of Al_2O_3 and SiO_2, the feldspar cannot be considered a flux at low temperature ranges, even though some flux is contributed to the glaze. The fluxing action is increased by the fineness of the particle size. Potash forms a harder glaze than does soda and decreases the thermal expansion. Thus, unless soda is desired for color purposes, potash feldspar should be preferred in the glaze composition. (See Appendix, p. 311, for a comparative analysis of feldspars.)

Ferric chloride ($FeCl_3 \cdot 6H_2O$) is more commonly called *chloride of iron.* It is very soluble in water and must be stored in airtight containers. Ferric chloride serves as a luster decoration on glass or glazes and produces an iridescent gold-colored film under proper conditions.

Ferric oxide (see iron oxide)

Ferrous oxide (see iron oxide)

Flint (see silica)

Fluorspar (CaF_2), also called *calcium fluoride,* may serve as a source of flux in glaze and body compositions. The particle size must be less than 100 mesh when used in the body, or pinholes are likely to form in the glaze. Fluorspar fluxes at a lower temperature than do other calcia compounds. When it is combined in a glaze with copper oxides, some unusual blue-green hues can be developed.

Galena (see lead sulfide)

Gerstley borate ($2CaO \cdot 3B_2O_3 \cdot 5H_2O$) is given the same formula as colemanite, but it usually also contains a small amount of sodium. Most dealers now supply gerstley borate when colemanite is ordered, since the latter is quite variable in quality. It is an excellent source of calcium and boron and gives a slight opalescent color to the glaze.

Ilmenite ($TiO_2 \cdot FeO$) is the mineral source of titanium and its compounds. When coarsely ground into a powderlike sand, it produces dark specks in the glaze.

Iron chromate ($FeCrO_4$) combined with manganese and zinc oxide will produce underglaze brown colors; combined with cobalt it will form a black stain. Used alone, it is fugitive above cone 04.

Iron oxides have three forms: *ferrous oxide* (FeO), *ferric oxide* or hematite (Fe_2O_3), and *ferrous-ferric oxide* or magnetite (Fe_3O_4). Iron is the oxide most frequently used to produce tan or brown bodies and glazes. Were it not for its pronounced color, it could serve as a flux. It is responsible for most of the low-firing characteristics and the red color of many earthenware clays. A pink stain can be made with a smaller amount of iron, plus alumina, calcium, and flint. When reduced in a suitable glaze, iron will form gray-greens characteristic of the Chinese celadons.

379. Alan Peascod, Australia. Jar. Stoneware with incised decoration and mat iron glaze, height $33\frac{3}{4}''$ (53 cm).

Kaolin ($Al_2O_3 \cdot 2SiO_2 \cdot 2H_2O$) is also called *china clay* or *pure clay*. Because of its composition and relative purity, kaolin is the highest-firing clay. It is an important ingredient of all white-ware and china bodies, since it fires to pure white. For glazes, kaolin constitutes a major source of Al_2O_3 and SiO_2. The chief residual deposits in the United States are in North Carolina, and sedimentary deposits are found in South Carolina and Georgia. For bodies, the more plastic sedimentary types are preferred. The sedimentary kaolin deposits of Florida are even more plastic and are often termed ball kaolin or EPK (see Chap. 1, p. 3).

Lead antimonate (see antimonate of lead)

Lead bisilicate (see lead silicate)

Lead carbonate [$2PbCO_3 \cdot Pb(OH)_2$], more commonly called *white lead,* is a major low-fire flux that imparts a lower surface tension and viscosity over a wide temperature range. This results in a smooth, brilliant glaze with few surface defects. Lead may comprise all the flux in the low-temperature range, or a lesser amount at cone 4. (See glaze recipes in Appendix, p. 316.) Unless properly compounded, lead glazes can be poisonous, because the harmful lead may be released when in contact with tea, citric-acid fruit juices, salad dressings containing vinegar, or other acids. Lead should be handled only when it is fritted. Otherwise, it may be absorbed into the body by inhaling the lead powder or through a cut in the skin. Copper oxide in amounts greater than 2 percent and combinations of iron oxide and manganese dioxide greater than 5 percent increase the toxic lead release. Larger amounts of alumina, silica, calcium, and zirconium increase the acid resistance of lead glazes. Additions of sodium, potassium, and barium all decrease acid resistance (see pp. 171, 172, 242).

Lead oxide occurs in two types: *litharge* or lead monoxide (PbO), and *red lead* or minium (Pb_3O_4). Litharge is a yellow powder that has greater use in Europe than in the United States. Since litharge occasionally contains impurities and has larger particles than does the carbonate form, the latter is the preferred lead compound. Because of the greater amount of oxygen, red lead often replaces litharge. Ceramic grades of red lead are seldom pure but usually contain 75 percent red lead and about 25 percent litharge. Red lead contains more PbO by weight than does the carbonate form.

Lead silicate is a frit made of lead and silica to eliminate the toxic effects of the lead compounds. The two most common types are: *lead monosilicate,* with a composition of 15 percent SiO_2 and 85 percent PbO; and *lead bisilicate,* which has a formula of 65 percent PbO, 34 percent SiO_2, and 1 percent Al_2O_3.

Lead silicate, hydrous [$2PbSiO_2 \cdot Pb(OH)_2$] has a molecular weight of 807. This material is the basic silicate of white lead. It is used as a substitute for lead carbonate when the CO_2 released by the carbonate forms pinholes or is otherwise objectionable in the glaze.

Lead sulfide (PbS), also called *galena,* is the black powder that is the raw source of all lead compounds. It has a very limited use in glazes.

Lepidolite ($LiF \cdot KF \cdot Al_2O_3 \cdot 3SiO_2$), also called *lithium mica,* contains from 3 to 6 percent lithia. It has some use as a body ingredient in chinaware and is a source of flux, Al_2O_3, and SiO_2 in higher-temperature glazes. It will tend to brighten most glazes, lower thermal expansions, and reduce brittleness (see lithium carbonate).

Lime (CaO), calcium oxide (see whiting)

Litharge (PbO) (see lead oxide)

Lithium carbonate (Li_2CO_3) is a common source of *lithia,* which is a strong flux in the higher temperature ranges. With lithia, greater amounts of Al_2O_3, SiO_2, and CaO can be used in alkaline glazes, thus producing a more durable glaze while retaining the unusual copper blues characteristic of the alkaline glazes. It can be used in place of lead in the medium temperature ranges when volatilization is a problem. When substituted for sodium or potassium, it reduces glaze expansion and promotes crystallization. Other sources of lithia are *lepidolite* and *spodumene.*

Magnesium carbonate ($MgCO_3$), also called *magnesite,* acts as a refractory element at lower temperatures, changing to a flux at higher temperatures. It is valuable for slowing down the fluid qualities of crystalline and other runny glazes. It also improves glaze adhesion. Because magnesium carbonate has some solubility in water that causes drying and firing shrinkages, it is best added to glazes in the form of dolomite [$CaMg(CO_3)_2$]. It has a slight tendency to promote opacity in glazes.

Magnesium sulfate ($MgSO_4 \cdot 7H_2O$) is better known as *epsom salts.* It serves to thicken glazes applied to nonporous bodies. Usually 1 percent, dissolved in hot water, will be sufficient and will have no apparent effect on the glaze.

Magnetite (see iron oxides)

Manganese dioxide (see manganese oxide)

Manganese oxide (MnO_2) is primarily a colorant. It should not be used in concentrations greater than 5 percent in either body or glaze, because blisters may develop. The usual colors produced are in the brown range. With cobalt, a black results; with the proper alkaline fluxes, purple and dark reddish hues can be produced. When it is fritted with alumina, a pink colorant will be formed.

Naples yellow (see antimonate of lead)

Nepheline syenite ($K_2O \cdot 3Na_2O \cdot 4Al_2O_3 \cdot 9SiO_2$) is a material roughly similar to feldspar (see Appendix, p. 310, for composition). In glazes, nepheline syenite can substitute for potash feldspar but will lower the maturing point. It also produces a greater firing range and increased thermal expansion, which in turn will reduce crazing tendencies in the glaze.

Nickel oxide is used in two forms, *green nickel oxide* or nickelous (NiO), and *black nickel oxide* or nickelic (Ni_2O_3). The function of nickel in a glaze is almost solely as a colorant. Depending upon the flux used and the ratio of alumina, a variety of colors can be produced: with zinc, a blue; with lime, a tan; with barium, a brown; and with magnesia, a green. None of these hues are particularly brilliant. In general, nickel will soften and alter other coloring oxides. In addition, 5 to 10 percent nickel in a suitable glaze promotes the formation of a crystalline structure.

Ochre is a term given to clays containing varying amounts of red iron or manganese oxides. Their primary function is in paint manufacturing. However, they can be used as glaze or slip colorants to impart tan, brown, or brick-red hues.

Opax is a standard commercially produced opacifier with the composition listed in the table at right.
Opax does not have the power of tin oxide, but it is considerably cheaper, and for this reason it often replaces part of the tin oxide in glaze recipes.

Pearl ash (see potassium carbonate)

Petalite ($Li_2O \cdot Al_2O_3 \cdot 8SiO_2$), lithium-aluminum silicate, is chiefly used as an auxiliary body flux to reduce thermal expansions and increase shock resistance in ovenware bodies. At about cone 06 it converts into beta spodumene, which has almost no volume change when heated or cooled. It serves as a source of lithia and silica primarily for medium- and high-temperature glazes.

Plastic vitrox ($1RO \cdot 1.69Al_2O_3 \cdot 14.64SiO_2$) is a complex mineral mined in California that is a source of silica, alumina, and potash in both glaze and body formulas. It resembles potash feldspar and Cornwall stone in composition. (See Appendix, p. 310 for comparative analysis.)

Potash feldspar (see feldspar)

Potassium carbonate (K_2CO_3) is more commonly called *pearl ash*. It is used primarily to modify color effects. When pearl ash is substituted for the lead, sodium, or calcium content in a glaze, the colors resulting from copper oxide can be changed from the usual green to either a yellow-green or a bright blue.

Potassium dichromate ($K_2Cr_2O_7$) is used in glazes as a green colorant. When it is calcined with tin, low-fire stains developing pink and red hues are formed (see chromic oxide). Because potassium chromate is very poisonous, it should be handled with caution.

Praseodymium oxide (Pr_6O_{11}), a black oxide, is a rare earth compound used in ceramics as a yellow colorant. It is commonly combined with zirconium oxide and silica to form a glaze stain that is stable at all normal firing temperatures.

Pyrophyllite ($Al_2O_3 \cdot 4SiO_2 \cdot H_2O$) is used primarily in wall-tile bodies, where it decreases thermal expansions, crazing, and moisture expansions to which tile is subjected. Since it is nonplastic, it has limited use in throwing or handbuilding bodies.

Red lead (see lead oxide)

Rutile (TiO_2) is an impure oxide of titanium containing small amounts of iron and vanadium. It serves as a tan colorant in glazes and imparts a mottled or streaky effect.

Opax

Oxide	Percent
ZrO_2	90.84
SiO_2	6.48
Na_2O	1.11
Al_2O_3	0.91

Selenium (Se) is a glass colorant. It has a limited application in ceramic glazes and overglaze colors, primarily as cadmium-selenium red frits. These frits, unfortunately, are fugitive at higher temperatures.

Silica (SiO_2) is also called flint or, in foreign publications, quartz. It is commonly obtained from sandstone, quartz sands, or flint pebbles. True flint is obtained from England, France, and Denmark. This cryptocrystalline flint has a different specific gravity (2.33) from that prepared from quartz sand or sandstone (2.65). For glaze purposes, we are interested in the silica (silicon dioxide) derived from flint.

When used alone, silica melts at the extremely high temperature of 3119°F (1700°C) and forms an unusually hard and stable crystal. It combines under heat, however, with a variety of fluxes at much lower temperatures to form a glass, and with the alumina compounds to form the more refractory body structure. An increase in the silica content of a glaze has the effect of raising the maturing temperature as well as increasing hardness and resistance to wear. In a glaze, the addition of silica decreases its thermal expansions; in a body it increases them.

Silicon carbide (SiC) has many industrial uses. Its value in ceramics is as the sole or major ingredient in high-temperature kiln furniture and muffles. When added to an alkaline glaze in small amounts (0.5 percent), the carbon will reduce the copper oxides to form localized copper reds.

Silver chloride (AgCl) is the major silver compound used in luster overglaze preparations (see lusters, p. 225). When silver chloride is combined with bismuth and with a resin or fat oil as a binder, an overglaze metallic luster with greenish or yellow tints will form.

Soda ash (see sodium carbonate)

Sodium aluminate ($Na_2O \cdot Al_2O_3$) is used to prevent casting slips from settling and to increase the strength of dry ware.

Sodium bicarbonate ($NaHCO_3$), also called bicarbonate of soda, has some use in casting slips and in forming stains with cobalt sulfate. Sodium carbonate (Na_2CO_3) is the sodium form more commonly used as a flux. Many potters are experimenting with sodium bicarbonate for salt glazing, as a less toxic alternative to sodium chloride (common salt).

Sodium carbonate (Na_2CO_3) is commonly called *soda ash*. It is a very active flux, but because of its solubility it is more often used in glazes as a frit ingredient. Small quantities of soda ash, functioning as a deflocculant, will reduce the water of plasticity required in a clay body. This increases workability and strength of the plastic body and reduces shrinkage from the wet to the dry state.

Sodium silicate is a compound that can vary from $1Na_2O \cdot 1.6SiO_2$ to $1Na_2O \cdot 3.75SiO_2$. It usually comes in liquid form and is the major deflocculant for casting slips. Like soda ash, it greatly reduces the water required to make the clay into a slip form. In doing so, it lessens the rate of shrinkage, the strains of drying, and breakage in the green and dry states.

Sodium uranate ($Na_2O \cdot UO_3$), more commonly called *uranium yellow,* has unfortunately not been available in the United States since World War II

380. Janet Mansfield, Australia. Jug. Stoneware with pebbled surface characteristic of salt glazes, height 16¾″ (42 cm).

because of restrictions placed on uranium by the Atomic Energy Commission. Uranium yellows are still available, however, in Europe. Uranium compounds formerly were the best source of yellow colorants. When uranium compounds are combined with various fluxes or with tin and zirconium oxide, a variety of hues from bright yellow through orange to vermilion red can be developed (see also uranium oxide).

Spodumene ($Li_2O \cdot Al_2O_3 \cdot 4SiO_2$) is an important source of lithia. The use of lithia, which is an active flux, helps to develop unusual copper-blue hues. Spodumene is also added to white ware and porcelain bodies. As a replacement for feldspar, it will reduce the vitrification temperature as well as the shrinkage rate. Strange as it may seem, the crystalline form of spodumene expands, instead of shrinking, at about 1700°F (927°C). When a mixture of 60 percent spodumene and 40 percent lead bisilicate is used, a nonplastic, press-formed body can be made that will have zero absorption and zero shrinkage at 1970°F (1077°C).

Stannic oxide (see tin oxide)

Steatite, a hydrous magnesium silicate, is a massive variety of talc. Most steatite is used in powdered form for electrical insulators. It has very little shrinkage, and occasionally the rocklike nuggets are turned down on a lathe for special projects. Steatite was used by the Egyptians almost 5000 years ago for the creation of beads and small figurines. These were generally covered with a turquoise alkaline copper glaze (see talc).

Talc varies from $3MgO \cdot 4SiO_2 \cdot H_2O$ to $4MgO \cdot 5SiO_2 \cdot H_2O$. In the solid and more impure form, it is also known as steatite or soapstone. Talc is occasionally used in glazes, but it is more frequently employed as a major ingredient in white-ware bodies firing at moderate temperatures (cones 04 to 6). Like dolomite, it will lower the firing temperatures of the other body ingredients, usually kaolin, ball clays, and feldspars. Talc will promote a slight opacity in glazes.

Tin oxide (SnO_2), also called *stannic oxide,* is the most effective of all opacifiers. From 5 to 7 percent will produce a completely opaque white glaze. An excess will create a dull surface. Tin also has wide use in stains, since it has considerable effect on the color qualities of most color-forming oxides. Because of its relatively high price, tin substitutes are frequently used.

Titanium oxide (TiO_2), or more correctly titanium dioxide, is a major opacifier when used either alone or in a frit. Like rutile, which is an impure form containing iron, titanium will encourage a semimat surface texture.

Uranium oxide, [U_3O_8(black)], is a depleted nuclear fuel that was used formerly as a yellow colorant in low-fire lead glazes. The tin-vanadium, zirconium-vanadium, and praseodymium yellow stains have greater flexibility and no radiation hazard. They are more readily available and are preferred by most potters.

Vanadium pentoxide (V_2O_5) is a rather weak yellow colorant when used alone. When fritted in the proper composition with tin, it produces a strong yellow color. This stain, known commercially as tin-vanadium stain, has largely replaced the uranium yellows, which are no longer available. It has a wide firing range (cones 06 to 14), is transparent, and is not affected by a reduction firing.

Volcanic ash occurs in many regions of the western United States. It was formed from the dust of volcanic glass erupted in prehistoric times. Since the material often floated through the air many miles before being deposited, it is extremely fine and can be used with little preparation. Its composition is roughly similar to that of a granite-type rock (see the formula in the Appendix, p. 310). In most glazes volcanic ash can be substituted for roughly 70 parts of feldspar and 30 parts of flint. A low-fire cone 04 glaze can be compounded of 60 percent ash and 40 percent borax and lead or just lead.

White lead (see lead carbonate)

Whiting ($CaCO_3$) is a calcium carbonate produced domestically by processing marble or limestone. European whiting is generally obtained from chalk deposits, such as those at the famous cliffs of Dover. Whiting is the major high-fire flux, although it has a limited use in bodies where a small amount will lower vitrification temperatures and reduce porosity. As a flux, it produces much harder and tougher silicates than will either the lead or alkaline compounds. For this reason, small amounts of whiting are often added to the lower-fire glazes, although it is most effective at cone 4 and above. As with other fluxes, calcium has an effect upon the coloring oxides, particularly chrome greens.

Wollastonite ($CaSiO_3$) is a natural calcium silicate. As a replacement for flint and whiting, it reduces firing shrinkage and improves heat shock. It is used in both bodies and glazes.

Zinc oxide (ZnO) is a difficult compound to classify. At high temperatures it is an active flux. When used to excess in a glaze low in alumina and cooled slowly, zinc will produce crystalline structures. Opacity will develop if zinc is used in a high-alumina, low-calcium glaze, with no borosilicate fluxes, at cone 1 or higher. In general, zinc increases the maturing range of a glaze and promotes a higher gloss, brighter colors, reduced expansions, and, under some conditions, an opacity.

Zirconium oxide (ZrO_2) is seldom used alone as an opacifier in ceramics but is generally combined with other oxides and fritted into a more stable silicate form. Below are listed a few commercial zirconium silicates. None have the strength of tin oxide, but they are considerably cheaper.
> *calcium zirconium silicate:* 51.12 percent ZrO_2, 25.41 percent SiO_2, and 22.23 percent CaO
> *magnesium zirconium silicate:* 53.75 percent ZrO_2, 29.92 percent SiO_2, and 18.54 percent MgO
> *zinc zirconium silicate:* 45.78 percent ZrO_2, 23.08 percent SiO_2, and 30.52 percent ZnO
> *zirconium spinel:* 39.94 percent ZrO_2, 25.25 percent SiO_2, 19.47 percent ZnO, and 19.41 percent Al_2O_3

Most of the above compounds are used in combination with other opacifiers, such as tin or titanium compounds (see also opax and zircopax).

Zircopax is a standard commercially produced opacifier with the composition of 64.88 percent ZrO_2, 0.22 percent TiO_2, 34.28 percent SiO_2.

Guide to Use of Colorants

Color	Oxide	Percentage	Temperature	Atmosphere
black	cobalt	1–2	any	either
	manganese	2–4		
	cobalt	1		
	iron	8	any	either
	manganese	3		
blue	cobalt	½–1	any	either
turquoise	copper (alkaline flux)	3–5	low	oxidizing
slate blue	nickel (with zinc)	1–3	low	oxidizing
brown	rutile	5	any	reducing
	chromium (with MgO, ZnO)	2–5	low	either
	iron	3–7	any	oxidizing
	manganese	5	any	either
	nickel (with ZnO)	2–4	any	either
green	copper oxide	1–5	any	oxidizing
gray-green	iron	1–4	any	reducing
	nickel-magnesia	3–5	low	oxidizing
red	copper	1	any	reducing
	iron (high SiO_2, KNaO), CaO	2–5	low	oxidizing
pink	chrome and tin (1 to 18)	5	any	oxidizing
coral	chromium (with high PbO)	5	low	oxidizing
purple	manganese (with KNaO)	4–6	any	oxidizing
tan	iron	2	any	either
	manganese	2	any	either
	rutile	2	any	either
yellow	antimony yellow stain (with high PbO)	3–5	low	either
	praseodymium yellow stain	4–6	any	either
	uranium yellow and orange (with high PbO)	5–8	low	oxidizing
	zirconium-vanadium stain	5–10	any	either
	tin-vanadium stain	4–6	any	either

Colorants for Glazes and Decoration

Coloring Oxides Most studio potters obtain their glaze colors from the oxides or carbonates of the more common metals, such as iron, copper, nickel, tin, zinc, and manganese. Other oxides, such as vanadium and cobalt, although rarer and more expensive, are extensively used because of a lack of cheaper substitutes. The list of major colorants (above) indicates the oxide necessary and the amount generally used to produce a particular color.

381. Janet De Boos, Australia. Tea bowl. Freely thrown stoneware with opaque "shino"-type glaze, wood-fired to cone 10.

However, just because an oxide is listed as producing a green does not mean that it will produce a green in every case. A study of the previous section on ceramic materials will reveal that generally the particular color that develops from an oxide depends upon the type of flux used, the proportions of alumina or silica, and the firing temperature. In some cases, even the rate of cooling will have an effect upon the glaze. Therefore, the list of oxides and colors is merely for convenience in determining color possibilities. Before using the oxide, you should be aware of its characteristics and the characteristics of the glaze to which it is added.

It is common practice to use two or more colorants in order to modify harsh colors and to obtain subtle variations or mottled color effects. Copper and nickel are often added to soften powerful cobalt hues. Opacifiers will brighten colors. Rutile is a frequent addition, since it contributes a runny and speckled quality as well as slightly matting a glaze.

Opacifiers Opacifiers are, for the most part, relatively insoluble in the glaze melt. Tin oxide and zirconium oxide are the chief examples of this type. As such, they remain suspended in the glaze and, if dense enough,

Opacifiers

Color	Oxide	Percentage	Temperature	Atmosphere
pure white	tin	5	any	either
weak blue white*	titanium	8–12	any	either
white	zirconium	8–12	any	either
weak yellow white	antimony	10–12	low	oxidizing
white	opax (a frit)	10	any	either
white	zircopax (a frit)	10	any	either
*a yellowish coloration with lead flux				

prevent light from penetrating through to the body. Most opacifiers, and of course those of the greatest value, are white. However, some give a slight yellow, pink, or bluish cast to the glaze.

Another type of opacifier is titanium (or zinc under some conditions), which tends to form minute crystalline structures within the glaze. Having a different index of refraction from the major portion of the glaze, it thus breaks up and prevents much light penetration. This is the type of crystal formation associated with mat glazes. It is the reason why all mats must be, necessarily, either wholly or partially opaque.

Spinel Stains   Under certain circumstances, the use of a raw coloring oxide may be objectionable. For example, most metallic oxides are quite soluble in the melting glaze. In the previous section, we noted that the fluxes and other elements of the glaze had considerable effect upon color quality. Overglaze and underglaze decoration with any degree of precision or control is impossible with colorants that diffuse into, or flow with, the glaze. In these cases, a special type of colorant known as a spinel is used.

A spinel stain is a colored crystal that is highly resistant to attack by fluxes in the glaze and to the effects of high temperatures. In strict chemical terms, *spinel* refers to the mineral magnesium aluminate ($MgOAl_2O_3$). However, manganese, iron, and chromium may be present by replacement. The crystal is an octahedron variety of extreme hardness. The ruby gem is a red spinel. By calcining certain oxides together, some very stable colored spinels can be formed. In general, these follow the formula $RO \cdot R_2O_3$. The RO member can be MgO, ZnO, NiO, CaO, MnO, or FeO, and the R_2O_3 can be Cr_2O_3, Al_2O_3, or Fe_2O_3.

Preparation of a spinel stain is a long procedure, and it is not recommended unless it is necessary for advanced experimental work. A wide range of commercial stains, expertly prepared, are available at reasonable cost. However, the general idea of the preparation should be understood. Detailed information can be found in the reference texts listed in the Bibliography.

It is extremely necessary that the chemicals involved be mixed completely and intimately. To this end the raw chemicals should first be passed through an 80-mesh sieve. It is preferable that they be in the form of soluble salts, that is, the nitrates or sulfates of the oxides listed above. These are thoroughly mixed in a liquid solution. After the water has been evaporated, the dry mixture is placed in a crucible or a kiln and calcined. The temperature will vary with the mixture. If the mixture melts into a solid mass, it should be calcined in a pot furnace so that the crucible can be removed with tongs and the contents poured into water, thus preventing the spinel from hardening into a solid crystalline block. Afterwards, the material is broken up with an iron mortar and pestle into a coarse powder, which is then ball milled. For a uniform color without specks, the particle size of the spinel must be extremely small. This may necessitate grinding in the ball mill for well over a hundred hours. When it is sufficiently fine, the stain should be washed several times with hot water to remove any remaining soluble salts. Filters may be necessary at this point in the process to prevent the loss of fine particles.

Other Colored Stains   Besides the spinels, a number of other chemical compounds are calcined to produce stable colorants at certain temperatures. A discussion of a few of the better-known examples will serve to illustrate some of the numerous possibilities in the preparation of colorants.

An ultramarine blue can be formed by a silicate of cobalt. It is made by calcining cobalt oxide and flint, plus a flux such as feldspar.

Green stains can be developed by calcining fluorspar and chromium oxide.

Yellow stains, such as Naples yellow and yellow base, are made from antimony, lead, and tin. Calcium and sodium uranate can also be used, when available, to form various yellow and orange colorants.

Pink and red stains are made by a number of methods. One of the most unusual is the precipitation of colloidal gold upon kaolin, which is then calcined and ground to form the stain. Other red stains are formed from a mixture of tin, calcium, flint, and chromium. (For further information and specific details, consult the reference texts by Parmelee, Norton, and Koenig and Earhart listed in the Bibliography.)

Underglaze Colors   Underglaze colors were mentioned before briefly in the section on decoration (p. 122). As the term indicates, they are colors used under the glaze. Since they will eventually be fired at the same temperature as the glaze, the variety of colors available is less than for overglaze colors. For example, at the hard porcelain range of cone 14 (2548°F, 1398°C), most, if not all, of the delicate hues available in overglaze colors will burn out completely. This leaves only the blues, browns, grays, gold-pinks, reduction reds, and celadon hues available for use at these higher temperatures. It is advisable to run a series of firing tests before attempting any amount of decorative work at such temperatures. The basic reason for employing underglaze rather than overglaze colors is durability.

Underglaze colors are made up of a colorant, either a raw oxide or a spinel, a flux such as feldspar to allow the color to adhere to the body, and a diluent like silica, calcined kaolin, or ground bisque ware. The purpose of these last materials is either to lighten the color or to equalize shrinkage. It is rather important that the mixture be adjusted properly to the bisque ware and the final glaze. The glazed surface should show no change in gloss over the decoration.

Overglaze Colors   The major differences between overglaze colors and underglaze colors are the use of a lower melting flux and a wider range of colors. Since the overglaze decoration is to be applied to a previously fired glaze, the final firing need be only high enough to allow the flux to melt into the glaze and seal the color. This is usually about cone 020 to cone 015, approximately 1231° to 1549°F (666°–843°C). The flux is made of varying proportions of lead, borax, and flint, depending upon the color to be used with it. The mixture is calcined lightly, ground, and washed. The colorant, and if necessary, an opacifier, is then added, and the whole mixture is ball milled to an adequate fineness. A vehicle such as gum or oil is used to help the mixture adhere to the glazed surface. In commercial production, where decoration is standardized, printing methods are used. The colors of both types of decoration are applied by decals or silk screen. (See Chap. 4, p. 135 for application methods.)

Lusters   Since lusters are employed more as decoration than as a glaze, they are included in this section on decorative coloring materials. As was noted earlier in the discussion of glaze types (Chap. 6, p. 184), a luster is nothing more than a thin layer of metal that is deposited and fused upon the surface of the glaze. There are various methods by which this can be

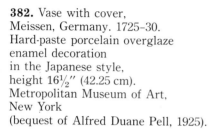

382. Vase with cover, Meissen, Germany. 1725–30. Hard-paste porcelain overglaze enamel decoration in the Japanese style, height 16½″ (42.25 cm). Metropolitan Museum of Art, New York (bequest of Alfred Duane Pell, 1925).

accomplished, some of them outlined below. Luster can give a variety of effects, depending upon the transparency or color of the composition and the type of glaze upon which it is applied. In Persian and Hispano-Moresque pieces it is very effectively combined with underglaze decoration. In fact, luster really comes into its own when it is used to enrich other types of decoration. The colors available in lusters are a transparent iridescent, a nacreous silver white, and metallic hues in a variety of yellows, greens, browns, and reds. (See Chap. 4, p. 138 for methods of application.)

Preparation of lusters will vary according to the specific method of firing to be employed. There are three types of preparation, the first being the most common.

1. A mixture composed of a resin, oil of lavender, and a metallic salt is brushed on the glazed ware. The ware is then fired in an oxidizing kiln to a low temperature of between 1100° and 1300°F (593°–704°C), at which point the carbon in the resin reduces the metallic salt to its metal form. Most lusters contain bismuth nitrate, an active flux, as well as the other metal salts. This is used in combination with zinc acetate, lead acetate, and alumina to produce a clear, iridescent luster. The various metal colorants are always used in the form of a salt that decomposes at the lower temperatures needed to form the luster coating. Yellows can be made with chrome alum and bismuth nitrate. Nickel nitrate, cobalt sulfate, manganese sulfate, and iron chloride will produce a variety of browns, shading from yellowish to reddish hues. Uranium nitrate, where available, develops a greenish yellow. Gold is commonly used to produce red hues and platinum to create silvery lusters. Many combinations of these colorants are used and results will be varied, depending in part upon the basic glaze and the firing schedule. In general, the luster mixture will consist of 1 part metallic salt, 3 to 5 parts resin, and 7 to 10 parts oil of lavender. The resin, usually gum dammar, is heated; when it becomes liquid, the nitrate or chloride is added. When the nitrate dissolves, the oil is slowly poured in. The solution is then filtered or cooled and decanted. The experiments in *Literature Abstracts of Ceramics Glazes,* by J. H. Koenig and W. H. Earhart, (see Bibliography) will help in creating formulas.

2. Another type of preparation is similar to that employed many centuries ago by Egyptian and Islamic potters, although it is seldom used today. The ancients developed luster and carried this decorative glaze to its highest level of artistic merit. The chief difference between their method and that described above is the use of a reduction fire to reduce the metal rather than having a reducing agent contained in the resin. The mixture, which is brushed on the glazed ware, consists of 3 parts metal, usually in a carbonate form, 7 parts red ochre, and an adhesive, such as gum tragacanth. Old recipes call for vinegar or wine, but gum is doubtless more efficient. In the firing cycle, the atmosphere is oxidizing until a low red heat is reached, whereupon reduction is started and continued to the temperature necessary to reduce the metal, usually from 1200° to 1300°F (649°–704°C).

3. The third method of developing a luster is also seldom used, but in rare cases it occurs by accident. The color is incorporated into the glaze, preferably in the form of a metallic salt. Various combinations can be used in proportions ranging from 0.5 to 8 percent of the total glaze. As in the resinate type of luster glaze, the use of bismuth, in addition to the other metallic salts, will aid luster development. The kiln is fired oxidizing to the

maturity point of the glaze, then cooled to between 1200° and 1300°F (649°–704°C). At this point the kiln is relit and fired for about 15 minutes with a reducing atmosphere. Accurate records should be kept on reduction firings, since variations of temperature and reduction periods will produce quite different results.

Binders

Various materials can be added to either a clay body or a glaze to increase the green or dry strength of the ceramic form, to aid glaze adhesion, and to lessen injury to the fragile glaze coating during the kiln loading. The several binders and waxes used in industrial production to increase the body strength are not really needed by the studio potter, since a plastic clay body is usually adequate in this regard.

Clay If the glaze contains an excess of 10 percent kaolin, additional binders may not be needed. However, if the clay content is low, the inclusion of about 3 percent bentonite will increase adhesion. It should be mixed with the dry ingredients. Macaloid and Veegum T are both refined colloidal magnesium aluminum silicate clays. *Macaloid* is similar to bentonite as a plasticizer in both clay bodies and glazes. *Veegum T* is useful both as a plasticizer and as an aid in suspending chemicals that tend to settle in the glaze. The addition of 2 or 3 percent to the glaze will prove helpful. Veegum T should be soaked in hot water.

Gums Traditionally, gum arabic or gum tragacanth has been used as a glaze binder. The granular gum crystals are soaked overnight in water and stirred vigorously the following day. Heating in a double boiler will speed up the process. Straining may be necessary. About one-quarter ounce will make a quart of creamlike mucilage binder. A couple of drops of carbolic acid are needed to prevent decomposition. One or two teaspoons of this solution per quart of glaze is usually adequate.

Gelatin Gelatin, another glaze binder, is an animal glue dissolved in 4 parts water and added to the glaze in a proportion of 1 to 6. The gelatin solution may also be brushed onto either a vitreous or a very porous bisqued surface for better adhesion of the glaze.

Methocel Methocel is a synthetic methylcellulose compound that will not deteriorate as the gums will and that also serves as an agent to prevent settling. The latter is a problem to which colemanite, in particular, is susceptible. Normally 1 to 2 percent methocel by dry weight is sufficient. However, do not attempt to add the dry powder to a liquid glaze. Instead, sift the powder into hot water in a double boiler, soak the mixture overnight, and then pour the resultant jellylike mass into a larger container of hot water. When all the methocel is dissolved, it can be added to the glaze ingredients. An electric mixer is useful for this step, since it greatly speeds up the combining of ingredients.

Temporary Binders In an emergency, sugar, syrup, or wheat flour can be used as a binder. Of course, all of these will ferment and therefore must not be stored without adding a few drops of formaldehyde to the glaze. The medium used in painting to produce acrylic pigments can also be used as a binder. Because it is a plastic, it does not decompose, although it may cause the glaze to settle.

8
Kilns and Firing

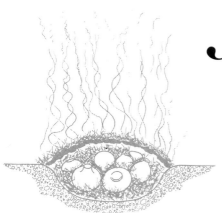

383. A primitive bonfire firing in a shallow pit.

A discovery was made in the far distant past that figurines or pots formed from plastic clay would become hard and durable when heated to a fairly high temperature. Primitive artisans seem to have had this knowledge by about 8000 B.C. Early potters fired their wares in what was little more than a bonfire. For many thousands of years pottery was fired in a shallow pit using twigs or even dry grass as a fuel. Continual additions of fuel made a glowing bed of coals that, within a couple of hours, raised the ware to a red heat. Since the ware consisted mainly of low-firing clays, containing a large percentage of iron, it could be brought to a moderate hardness at about 1500°F (800°C). The ware was then covered with ashes, broken pottery shards, and earth to contain the heat and allow slow cooling.

When pottery is smothered by ashes, the normal red iron (Fe_2O_3) in the clay body is converted by the lack of oxygen into the black oxide (FeO) form. Carbon impregnated in the surface of the ware also contributes to the dark color of most pit-fired pottery. The ware was still porous and, by modern standards, underfired, so it was often removed from the pit while still quite hot and rubbed with certain kinds of leaves whose gummy sap would provide a partially waterproof coating. Long after primitive kilns were developed, many cultures continued to make black ware fired in pits. The pots were often coated with a refined iron clay slip and burnished to obtain a smooth and almost glossy surface, such as is found in the Etruscan ware of the 6th century B.C. The technique is still followed today by many cultures, including the Southwest Indians.

The most recent firing techniques used in the Southwest are a considerable improvement over traditional pit firing, and they make a good introduction to firing methods for a beginning ceramics class. A heavy iron grating is placed on rocks 4 or 5 inches off the ground, forming a natural firebox. Sun-dried pots are inverted on the grating, and the firebox and spaces between the stacked pots are filled with small dry twigs. Then, thin metal sheets are placed over the pots to contain the heat. Gaps between the sheets serve as both stoking holes and exhaust vents. In the Southwest dry sheep dung is used as fuel, but sawdust or wood chips also work well. A red heat is reached in about 2 hours. When the firing has been completed, the next step is to add more fuel and then cover the "kiln" with earth. All vents must be blocked so that the smoldering fuel can completely reduce the iron in the clay body and turn it into a lustrous black.

A more unusual firing method to produce black ware employs an old 55-gallon oil drum in place of a pit. A series of 1-inch holes are punched out around the base of the drum. The drum is then filled with coarse sawdust and randomly spaced earthenware pots. It is essential that the fuel be perfectly dry. The addition of a small amount of fuel oil may be needed to start the coarse sawdust burning at the top. Once the fire is started, a loose sheet of tin with a few punched holes placed over the top will prevent the fire from burning too rapidly. The firing will be most successful on a warm, clear day in a sheltered outdoor location. This method requires patience, for the fire may smolder all night before finally burning itself out.

Early Kilns

By the 5th millennium B.C. slip-decorated ware had become quite common in Anatolia (modern Turkey)—indicating the use of some type of kiln that would allow for a controlled oxidizing fire. At first this kiln consisted of little more than a firebox and a connecting chamber with a vertical chimney vent dug into the side of a clay bank, hence the name *bank kiln*. Preliminary firings hardened the clay and dried out the kiln area. After successive firings the clay walls resembled a brick-lined chamber. It is possible that in such red-clay bank kilns the wood fires created enough heat to cause the clay ceiling to actually melt and drip on the pots below.

Eventually, clay bricks were made, and these permitted reinforcement of a firebox area and construction of a slotted kiln floor. Because loading through the narrow firebox area was laborious, the chimney was enlarged to become a firing chamber. The pottery was loaded from the top. Broken shards mixed with clay and straw and placed over the stacked pots contained the heat; a few openings were left to provide a draft. This design eventually developed into a beehive-shape kiln with a small side door to make the loading process easier.

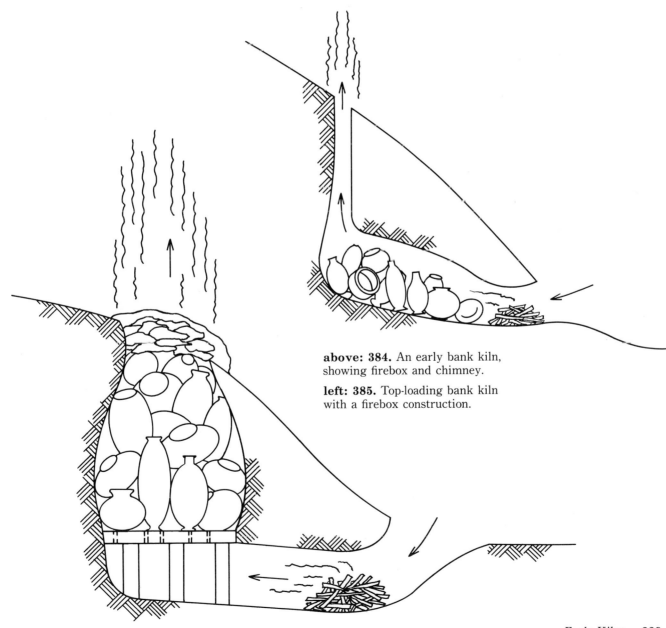

above: 384. An early bank kiln, showing firebox and chimney.

left: 385. Top-loading bank kiln with a firebox construction.

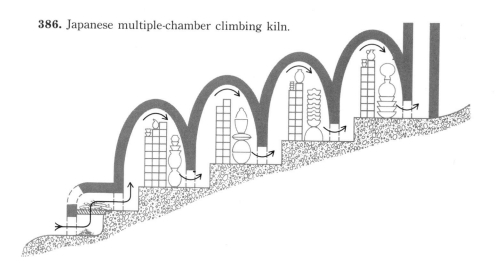

386. Japanese multiple-chamber climbing kiln.

During the Greek and Roman eras the typical kiln continued to be a round, dome-shape design of a moderate size, seldom more than 5 or 6 feet in diameter. Because the heat traveled directly upward from the firebox—through the ware and finally out the chimney vent above—the plan is termed an *updraft* design. Unfortunately, the pottery closest to the firebox usually became hotter than the ware placed above, so that firings tended to be unpredictable.

By the Renaissance a somewhat larger kiln had appeared in Italy, rectangular in design, with an arched firebox and chamber. It was updraft in design and probably also fired unevenly. Except for the long arched kiln used for salt glazing in the German region, most European kilns continued to be developments on the Greek domed kiln. As they grew larger, multiple firing ports were introduced, and coal eventually replaced wood as a fuel. The larger kilns required taller chimneys. This design evolved into the *bottle kiln,* with the glaze chamber below and the tall upper chamber used for a bisque fire. The glazed ware usually required *saggers*—clay boxes in which the ware was placed to protect the surface from ash and cinder particles drawn through the kiln during firing. It was not until after 1710 that the first porcelain was produced in Europe and only during the Industrial Revolution that large high-firing kilns were perfected.

Bank kilns evolved at an early age in the Orient. However, unlike the Middle East, China had numerous deposits of high-firing clays—both stoneware and fireclay, as well as kaolin—and by the Han Dynasty (206 B.C.–A.D. 220) a true high-fire stoneware was produced. Thus, Oriental kilns had to reach much higher temperatures than the bank kilns were capable of. The Chinese developed a high-fire kiln, usually quite long, built on a slope to create a natural draft. The arched chamber, domed in the lower firebox end, tapered as it ran up the slope, thus increasing the draft and equalizing the temperature. This chamber was large, often 15 feet high. To ensure even temperatures the kiln was divided into separate chambers, with the major firebox at the base but with individual fireboxes for each chamber.

The Koreans, by contrast, used a long, tubelike kiln, half buried in a sloping hillside. Since the kiln might be 150 feet long, the main firebox was supplemented by numerous stoke holes along its entire length. Great skill was needed to maintain an even firing over a period of three days. These kilns were adapted by the Japanese in the 16th century to create a series of chambers. Although the Japanese kilns had chambers smaller than those in

387. Detail of a climbing kiln, showing the chamber doorways and saggers.

the Chinese version, there might be as many as twenty. Usually, each chamber was about 8 feet wide and 5½ feet high.

These kilns are *downdraft* designs, since the flame and heat are deflected by the wall of saggers up and downward through the stacked ware to the floor openings and into the next chamber. Stoke holes are needed in each chamber. Because the heat rises through the kiln, less time is needed to fire the successive chambers. Figure 387 shows a typical Japanese climbing kiln with the square fireclay saggers outside each chamber. The kiln is built of large fireclay bricks and a thick mortar; the chamber doors must be bricked up and mortared for each firing. In Japan, wood kilns are common now only in the smaller rural pottery towns, such as Mashiko and Shigaraki. The scarcity and expense of wood, as well as the polluting smoke produced during firing, have contributed to their decline. Even in Kyoto, long famous for its potters, most small potteries are using the more expensive but cleaner gas and electric kilns.

Modern Kilns

The kiln types employed by the ancients are still in use today, but they have been modified to accommodate new fuels, new materials, and, in the case of industry, the need for expanded and efficient large-scale production. Perhaps the most drastic change in kiln design in recent times was caused by the development of a new source of power—electricity. Since the electric kiln needs no chimney or fuel lines and is comparatively portable, simple, and safe to operate, it has played a large part in the current popularity of ceramics. It is especially convenient for the potter whose studio might be relatively temporary or for the school in which the original design provided for neither a chimney nor a source of fuel.

The fairly recent increase in the prices of all fuels—oil, gas, and electricity—presents a real challenge to the potter. Kilns must be designed to operate as efficiently as possible. When fuel was relatively cheap, the potter building a new kiln often scrimped on materials, using inexpensive but not the most effective ones. New products now on the market are both light and convenient, as well as efficient in firing. Combined with traditional materials they promise a fuel saving. Although the price of refractory and insulating materials has risen, the most efficient materials will doubtless pay for their cost over the long run.

Fuel Kilns

Whether wood, coal, oil, or gas is used as a fuel, the basic kiln design is much the same. A combustion area is needed either below or to one side of the kiln chamber. Wood or coal requires a larger firebox area equipped with a grate and an ash pit. Saggers, which protect the glazed ware from flying ash, take up much space; they can be replaced with an inner muffle chamber that serves the same purpose. Both fuel oil and manufactured gas contain sulphur, and this often causes dullness and blistering on the glaze surface. The updraft muffle kiln shown in Figure 388 was designed to eliminate this problem. The design, however, creates extra heat in the floor area, making an even firing difficult. Placing burners closer to the side wall will alleviate the problem to some extent. Most portable gas kilns are of the updraft type. They usually lack muffles and have small vertical burners spaced across the floor area.

The downdraft kiln illustrated in Figure 389 provides a more even heat distribution and has come to be the standard design preferred by most potters. This is especially true since the advent of cleaner natural gas, which has eliminated the need for a muffle. In this downdraft kiln the heat enters from multiple burners on each side, is deflected upward by the bag wall, and then is drawn down through the ware to a channel under the floor by the suction of the chimney. If the fuel supply and draft are adequate, it will ensure a heat deviation of no more than one cone from top to bottom.

For a smaller-size kiln, a layout such as that illustrated in Figure 390, with the burners placed to one side, may prove equally satisfactory. Numerous other burner arrangements have been tried, despite the fact that the design sketched in Figure 389 is most efficient. Some of these alternate plans are shown in Figures 391 to 393. A burner or a fan at the base of the stack will induce a draft early in the firing and may be needed for a tall chimney.

The kiln illustrated in Figure 394 is essentially the same as the one in Figure 389, except that the chimney area is enlarged to provide a separate bisque chamber. Unless the glaze temperature in the main area is unusually high, this chimney chamber will bisque at between cone 010 and cone 06. While most pottery classes have an ample supply of both pots and kilns to ensure a full load for each firing, the individual potter may experience firing delays. The double chamber permits a more even flow of work and simultaneous bisque and glaze firings at no extra cost.

388. Gas-fired updraft muffle kiln.

389. Standard design for a gas-fired downdraft kiln.

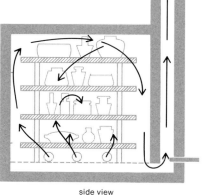

390. Downdraft gas kiln with burners on one side.

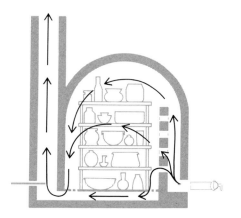

front view   side view

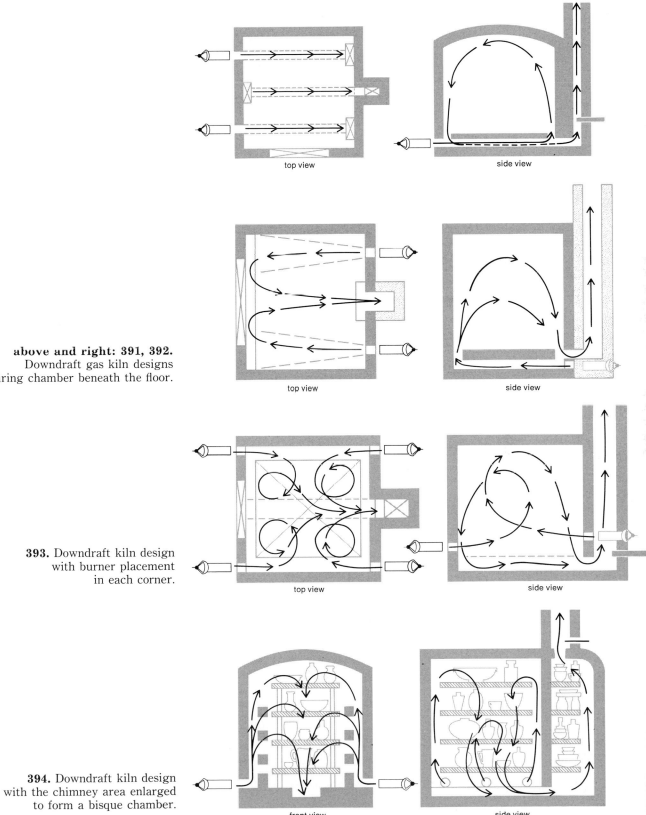

top view   side view

above and right: 391, 392.
Downdraft gas kiln designs
with the firing chamber beneath the floor.

top view   side view

393. Downdraft kiln design
with burner placement
in each corner.

top view   side view

394. Downdraft kiln design
with the chimney area enlarged
to form a bisque chamber.

front view   side view

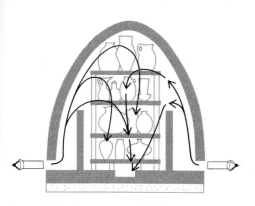

395. Catenary-arch kiln.

A kiln fired with fuel oil requires a slightly larger combustion area than one fired with natural gas. The catenary-arch kiln shown in Figure 395 is ideal for fuel oil, since the flare at the bottom provides the extra combustion area needed. Except for the arch construction, the design is similar to that of a gas kiln. The curve is established by suspending a chain from two points, thus forming a natural self-supporting arch. A proportion in which the base equals the height is the most stable and provides excellent heat distribution. Although the arch is self-supporting, tie rods are desirable from front to back, since some movement occurs during firing. Oil is a satisfactory fuel, cheaper than gas, but it has some drawbacks. A separate shedlike installation is desirable, since the fumes that are given off, together with the noisy blowers, make an oil-burning kiln impractical for use inside the potter's studio or the classroom.

Square kilns are more likely to fire evenly, and are easier to load, if the door width is larger than the depth of the chamber. It is assumed that the chambers of the kilns discussed have a loading area of about 10 to 20 cubic feet. However, many schools need a larger capacity. The physical strain incurred in stretching to load the heavy shelves and ware at the far end of a 30-cubic-foot chamber is too much for many people. In such cases a car kiln may be a good solution. This, again, is essentially the Figure 389 design,

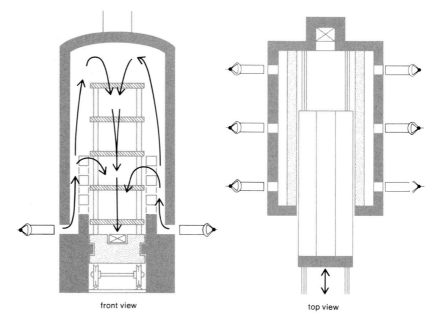

front view   top view

396. Downdraft car kiln design.

but the floor section is built on a steel frame and wheels, so that it can be rolled in and out of the kiln on a track. The door becomes an integral part of the car, instead of being bricked up in the usual fashion. There must be a close fit between the floor and the side walls, with a channel iron in the floor extending into a sand trough in the side wall to form a heat seal. In the car kiln the ware can be loaded from either side without undue strain.

In the case of a large kiln, more burners may be needed than the illustrations show. As a rule, a more even firing results from several smaller burners rather than two or more extremely large units. In the case of a long kiln, openings in the bag wall will need to be varied from front to back, because the draft, and the heat, may be greater at the rear, near the chimney.

Electric Kilns

The gas kiln, because of its cheaper operation, greater size, and ability to reduce, is preferred by most studio potters and university ceramics departments in the United States. In the Scandinavian countries, however, where electricity is relatively cheap and gas is not common, the electric kiln is almost universally used by the studio potter. The electric kiln has many advantages for the public school. It is almost as simple to operate as turning on a light switch, and there are no problems of burner adjustment or draft control. The small kiln, normally weighing about 300 pounds, can be wheeled anywhere. It requires only a 220-volt electrical outlet—a minor consideration compared to the gas kiln's demand of a high-temperature chimney and large-size gas lines. Room ventilation is not a problem, provided the clay body contains no sulphur or unusual impurities and that lead glazes are not used.

The electric kiln comes in two basic styles—the top loader and the front loader. In either type, a kiln with less than 18-by-18-inch interior should not be considered, for it is too small to fire most pieces. The heat comes from radiation produced by coiled elements recessed in the side walls; therefore, a kiln chamber bigger than 24 by 24 inches requires a large coil or strip element, which greatly increases the cost of the kiln. Because they must have a stand and a heavy frame to carry the door, plus flexible connections to the door elements, front-loading kilns are much more expensive. The top loader is cheaper and easier to load, so it is a more logical purchase.

There are three types of electric heating elements. Suitable for a low fire (up to 2000°F or 1098°C) are those made of coiled nickel-nichrome wire. The kanthol type is constructed of a different alloy and will produce temperatures up to cone 8 (2305°F or 1263°C) although some types will go higher. Larger and higher-firing industrial kilns use carbon compounds in the form of a rod from $\frac{1}{4}$ inch to 2 inches in diameter. Unfortunately, the special transformers needed are more expensive than the kiln itself, which makes this kiln more costly than gas or oil kilns.

Kiln Loading and Firing

The final step in the potter's art—the loading and firing of the kiln—is most important, for carelessness can easily ruin your previous efforts. It can also do permanent damage to the kiln. With the exception of some salt-glaze ware and commercial high-fire porcelain, most pottery is fired first at a low bisque temperature. Some clay bodies can be glazed successfully in the raw state, but the fragility of unfired clay and the difficulty of glazing some shapes make a double firing desirable, especially in schools, where techniques of glazing and loading are being taught.

Pyrometric Cones and Other Temperature Gauges

Pyrometric cones provide the most accurate method of measuring the *work heat* in the kiln. The name is inaccurate, for the pyrometric "cone" is actually a tetrahedron or pyramid shape. Large cones are $1\frac{3}{4}$ inches high, with a base $\frac{1}{2}$ inch across; small cones are $1\frac{1}{8}$ inches high and $\frac{1}{4}$ inch wide at the base.

Cones are compounded of a material similar to a glaze. When softened by heat, they bend; when the cone forms a half circle, the temperature in the kiln is that of the cone number (see Appendix, p. 314). The cone base is beveled to indicate the proper angle at which to press it into a pad of clay. A common practice is to use three cones—for example, 6, 8, and 9 if the firing is to reach cone 8. The bending of cone 6 warns that the kiln is approaching the proper temperature, and you should make burner or damper adjustments to stabilize the heat at this point. In a large kiln the cones are placed near both top and bottom, not too close to the door. As cone 8 bends, the burners can be cut back for a *soaking* period (holding the kiln at the same temperature). A softening of cone 9 indicates an overfiring. Kilns usually fire slightly hotter at the bottom, so a dryer glaze can be used there. If the cones are difficult to see, blowing into the peephole through a tube or inserting a metal rod near the cones will reveal them more clearly.

A slower rise in temperature, and the resulting longer period of chemical reaction, will permit a glaze to mature at a lower temperature than if the heat rise is rapid. This relationship between time and temperature is called the *work heat ratio,* and it is recorded by the pyrometric cone but not by the *pyrometer.* The pyrometer consists of a pair of welded wires of dissimilar metals, called a *thermocouple,* which is inserted into the kiln. When the kiln is heated, a minute electrical current indicates temperature change on a millivolt meter calibrated in degrees Fahrenheit (F) or centigrade (C). A pyrometer is convenient for making adjustments to produce the most efficient heat rise or to determine the proper time to begin a reduction. However, unless you have an exact and unvarying firing schedule, it is not completely dependable. In time, corrosion of the thermocouple tips affects the accuracy of the reading, but this can be adjusted to the proper cone by moving a tiny screw on the meter face.

Pyrometers are available in both low- and high-fire models. The rather inexpensive ones used by potters are seldom reliable over a wide range of temperatures; that is, if the cone 8 reading is correct, the cone 04 may be inaccurate. A slightly more expensive pyrometer has a thermocouple with wire tips completely enclosed in a porcelain jacket. This instrument is recommended for larger kilns in frequent use, for it is less apt to be damaged in kiln loading or by slight chemical reactions during firing. Optical pyrometers are also available; these are quite accurate but rather expensive. Glazed draw rings, which were common before the introduction of cones, can also be used to measure kiln temperature. Such clay rings are the only method of determining glaze buildup in a salt kiln.

The Bisque Fire

The bisque temperature is generally between cone 010 and cone 06, depending upon the clay body used. Fired bisque ware must be hard enough to endure normal handling in the glazing operation, yet sufficiently absorbent to permit glaze adhesion. Ware bisqued below cone 012 may crack during the glaze fire if too much flux is absorbed into the porous clay body. The stacking of a bisque kiln is quite different from that required for a glaze fire. In each case, however, at least 1 inch of free space must be left between the electrical elements and the ware. In a gas kiln 3 inches between the kiln wall and the ware is a desirable margin to allow free passage of heat and to avoid hot spots.

Raw ware must be completely dry before it is loaded in the bisque kiln. The accepted test for dryness is to hold the piece against your cheek. If it feels cold, there is still moisture in the clay.

Since there is no problem of glaze sticking, kiln wash is not needed, and pieces may touch each other. It is possible to stack one piece inside or on top of another, building to a considerable height. You must take care to make

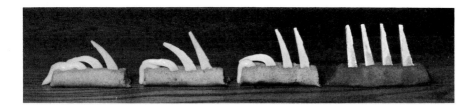

397. Pyrometric cones
pressed into pads of clay:
those at right have not been fired,
the three at the left indicate
different temperatures
reached in the kiln.

foot rims coincide for support and to avoid placing heavy pieces on more
fragile ones. Large, shallow bowls, which might warp, can be fired upside
down on their rims if the kiln shelf is even. Several smaller sizes can be
placed underneath. Covers should be fired in place to prevent warping, and
tall knobbed covers can often be reversed to save space.

Even though apparently dry, raw clay contains much moisture, and
firing should proceed at a low heat for several hours. Kiln doors should be
left ajar or peepholes left open for an hour or so to allow this moisture to
escape. Large, heavy pots or sculptural pieces must be fired slowly to
prevent the moisture contained in hidden air pockets from being converted
into steam, which would cause the piece to explode. Figure 398 shows a pot,
containing excess organic matter, that bloated in a too-rapid bisque fire.

398. Pottery shard
with a bloated base
from a too-rapid firing cycle.

Chemical Changes

Chemical changes in the body during firing are slight at first (Fig. 399).
When the temperature reaches 350° to 400°F (178°–204°C), all atmospheric
moisture should have left the ware, causing little or no shrinkage. Most of
the chemically combined water will leave the ware at temperatures between
950° and 1300°F (510°–705°C). During this "water smoking" period considerable shrinkage occurs as both the chemically combined water and gases
from organic material leave the body. The firing should not be too rapid, for
the body is very weak. As the temperature approaches 1750°F (955°C) and
continues to 1850°F (1010°C) tough needlelike crystals of alumina-silica
($3Al_2O_3 \cdot SiO_2$), called *mullite*, begin to form, but they are not fully developed until stoneware temperatures are reached. These crystals give toughness to the body, and as the temperature increases, additional free silica
forms a glass around them. Because of impurities and varying composition,
clay bodies achieve maximum hardness at different temperatures. Earthenware clay matures at about 2000°F (1090°C), stoneware at about 2350°F

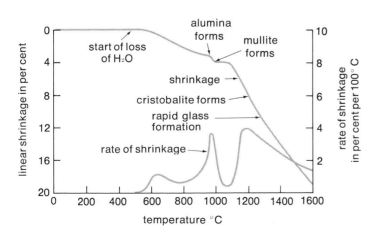

399. Linear shrinkage
and rate of shrinkage for kaolin
(F. H. Norton, *Elements of Ceramics,*
Addison-Wesley, 1952).

(1290°C), and pure clay (kaolin) at about 3000°F (1650°C). Porcelain fires in the same range as stoneware, normally between cones 8 and 10, although higher temperatures are possible.

Cooling Procedures

Cooling procedures are important to the maintenance of kilns. When the correct temperature has been reached, the electric kiln can simply be turned off and allowed to cool. In the fuel-burning kiln, the chimney damper must be closed immediately to prevent a cold draft of air from being sucked into the burner ports, which might crack both the ware and the shelves. Just as the kiln must be fired slowly, so must it be allowed to cool naturally. The damper can be opened after cooling overnight, and the peephole plugs can be removed, but the door must not be opened more than a crack until the temperature has dropped to 400°F (204°C). Even slower cooling may be desirable for extremely large or heavy pieces. An expensive kiln, which should give at least ten years' service before repairs are needed, may be ruined after a short time by careless firing and cooling.

The Glaze Fire

The glaze fire differs in several respects from the bisque fire: the loading is different, the kiln atmosphere may be varied, and the final temperature must be controlled carefully. Since mishaps may occur from runny glazes, all kiln shelves must be scraped and coated with a *kiln wash*. Kiln wash consists of equal parts of silica (flint) and kaolin in a creamy mixture. Several coats may be needed, each coat applied before the last is completely dry. A new shelf can be sprayed or brushed with aluminum paint before the kiln wash is applied. Dusting on a thin layer of coarse silica sand gives additional protection. The shelf edges must be cleaned to prevent this sand from sifting down on the ware below. All glazed ware should be "dry footed"—that is, all glaze cleaned off the base and about $\frac{1}{4}$ inch up the foot rim. Glazes that are runny, such as crystalline and copper-reds, can be placed on a pedestal made from high-firing insulating brick coated with kiln wash. This will facilitate any later grinding of the excess glaze.

A uniform load without tight spots will produce an even firing. Never try to fire a half load, since uneven temperatures are almost certain to occur. Staggering the shelves in a large kiln will create a more even heat flow. In the typical electric kiln, shelves should not be placed close to the bottom or the top, for a cold spot will develop in the center area. Test tiles must always be stacked near the middle, since there is usually some temperature variation from top to bottom. A center support is desirable for larger shelves. Damp clay pads used to level uneven posts should be dusted first with dry flint to avoid sticking. If the shelves are of moderate size, three posts will eliminate leveling problems. As in the bisque fire, covers are best fired in place, but you must make certain that the contact areas are clear of glaze. Placing glazed ware too close to the upper bag wall often results in shiny spots, although gaps in the bricks may even out the heat in this area. Glazed pieces should be at least $\frac{1}{4}$ inch apart, because heat radiation can also cause shininess. This may not be necessary with high-shrinkage bodies.

Reduction Firing

Reduction firing means that part of the firing cycle is conducted with an inadequate amount of oxygen to burn up all the fuel. As a result, the free carbon in the kiln atmosphere unites with, and thus reduces, the oxygen content of the metallic oxides in both the body and the glaze, thereby altering their color. In a forced-draft burner this is accomplished by cutting down on the air supply, while in a natural-draft burner the flue damper is cut back slightly, so that less air will be sucked into the kiln.

Excessive reduction is undesirable. Not only does the temperature drop rapidly, but the body may erupt with blisters or even crack, and the glaze becomes a dirty gray. In a natural-draft kiln a slight backing up of the flame at the burner ports will occur. This is all that is necessary for a reduction, not the belching of flame and smoke that some people seem to enjoy—until the blistered pots are unloaded. Because of atmospheric pressure built up during reduction, pull out the peep plugs cautiously, with your face turned away, for the flame will shoot out at least a foot. In a tall bricked-up door, inserting a section of curved sheet metal under the tie rod and pressing against the top bricks is helpful, since the door bricks may lean outward due to the pressure of the expanding gases in the kiln.

The atmosphere should be an oxidizing one during the first part of the firing cycle, in order to ensure the most efficient heat rise. The reduction needed to produce a rich body color is effective only at the temperatures below which the glaze begins to melt. When the maximum temperature has been reached, the damper can be adjusted to provide a neutral or slightly reducing fire. The usual practice is to cut back the burners slightly after the cones begin to bend to allow a half hour or so of an oxidizing *soaking heat* during which temperatures can stabilize and glazes become smoother.

The term *reduction fire* must not be confused with *reduction glazes*. The latter are glazes especially compounded to produce copper-red and celadon colors (see p. 178). In the firing of these glazes there may be little change in body color but rather a reduction of the coloring oxides in the glaze from an oxidic to a metallic form. Thus, copper-green becomes a rich red, and the iron brown-red is transformed into a gray-green or even a pale shade of blue. In a reduction glaze fire the reduction begins later than for a body reduction, but it must occur before the glaze begins to melt. Since the reduction causes the heat rise to diminish, there is usually an alternation of reduction and oxidation. Too much oxidation will bleach out the color. Copper-red color variations range from a mottled blue, green, and red to a deep purple-red or a pale pink, depending upon the reduction sequence, the glaze thickness, and the body color. In the case of both copper-red and celadon glazes the body should be porcelain. However, the celadon body may have 1 or 2 percent iron. This slightly gray body usually improves the celadon color.

A *localized reduction* can be obtained by adding 0.5 percent of silicon carbide (carborundum, 40-mesh or finer) to a suitable copper-alkaline glaze. The result is usually a speckled red-and-purple color. Its only real advantage is its adaptability to the electric kiln. An electric kiln can be reduced by popping a few moth balls through the peephole. The kiln should have heavy elements, which have a good oxidized coating from many previous firings. Continuous reductions will eat away the elements and corrode and eventually destroy the electrical connections, but an occasional one will do little harm to the kiln.

Raku Firing

Raku has become very popular in recent years for several reasons. Because of the rapidity of the firing procedure (usually less than 30 minutes) you can immediately see the result of the glaze and decoration. As a demonstration technique it is therefore a valuable teaching aid to show the otherwise long process of glazing, decorating, and firing a ceramic piece. In contrast to the traditional Japanese method, most contemporary potters end the raku firing with a heavy reduction to create unusual luster colors and smoked areas. Experts in raku firing gain control and have a good idea of what to expect, but perhaps the major interest for the novice is the unpredictable quality of the firing, when random brushed decorations develop striking contrasts, with copper-reds and lustered surfaces.

The raku body is made of a stoneware clay usually containing as much as 30 percent grog. Since neither the bisque nor the final glaze temperature is more than cone 04 (1940°F or 1060°C), the resulting body is always porous and rather fragile. A temporary brick kiln made from two layers of #20 insulating bricks and fired by two gas burners works well. A corbeled roof arch is formed by overlapping soft bricks held in place by several courses of heavy hard firebricks on the upper side walls. The removable kiln door is simply a stack of bricks held together by angle irons and bolts.

Raku pots should be preheated slightly (by setting them on the kiln roof) before being placed in the glowing kiln. The pieces are best handled with long tongs, and the operator should wear asbestos mittens, a jacket, cap, and goggles for protection from the heat and open flames.

Small raku pieces are removed from the kiln with tongs when the glaze melts. The pots are placed immediately in a metal can containing shavings, sawdust, or dry leaves to produce a smoky, reducing atmosphere. The body is usually blackened, and lusters and copper-reds appear on the decorated portions of the clay. Excessive reduction, however, may result in a gray and rather dirty glaze. After only a few minutes small raku forms are cooled in cold water. This creates a severe crackle in most glazes. If covered with carbon, the piece must be cleaned carefully—by brushing—to reveal the surface decoration. Too heavy a brushing may remove the delicate lusters.

Larger sculptural pieces often need a different firing and reducing technique. Since large pieces cannot be lifted easily with tongs, they are placed on a ramp mounted in front of the kiln and coated with silica sand. This allows the pots to slide in and out of the kiln. (You can also use a layer of sand for sliding large pieces.) In Figure 401 the raku pot is being pulled from the glowing kiln onto the ramp. Shavings placed on the ramp are soon

below left: 400. Temporary raku kiln made from two layers of dry-stacked insulating firebricks. The kiln has a corbel arch roof and is fired by two Alfred-type burners.

below right: 401. A large raku piece is pulled from the kiln with tongs and slid on sanded kiln shelves into a pile of wood shavings.

ignited by the red-hot form. To assist the reduction process and the development of lusters, the vertical form is covered with a metal can filled with shredded paper. Damp burlap placed over the form permits rapid cooling. The final result reveals the varied effects of luster, crackle glaze, and smoked areas possible in the raku technique.

Improved lightweight insulating materials have made possible new designs for raku kilns. A very light weight (about 12 pounds) means that at the end of a firing the kiln can be lifted easily off the ware; then the ware is replaced with a new batch, the kiln is lowered over it, and the next firing proceeds as usual.

above left: 402. A metal can filled with combustible material is placed over part of the form to promote the development of luster.

above right: 403. Damp burlap covering the form reduces the body and glaze.

404. Walter Hyleck, U.S.A. *Landscape in L Composition,* from the series *The Brink.* The completed raku form with engobes, crackle glaze, and luster; height 24″ (60 cm). The antenna-like segments were fired separately and epoxied into place.

Firing Lead Glazes

Lead glazes require extra care in formulation (see pp. 171–172) and also precautions in firing. Lead melts at a relatively low temperature, so a portion of the lead volatilizes into the kiln atmosphere. In cooling this free lead settles back onto the glaze surface. This unstable lead film easily breaks down under normal use, thus increasing the danger of lead poisoning. The problem is limited to electric kilns, because in a fuel kiln all gaseous impurities are drawn off by the chimney draft. Several small holes near the base and the top of the electric kiln will allow the lead particles to be drawn off by the natural movement of the heated air. This need be done only during the end of the firing cycle. A hood with an exhaust fan must be installed over the electric kiln, for otherwise the potter will inhale the lead-bearing air. The same is true of the gas kiln. There are always cracks that open up in the firing and allow gaseous impurities to escape into the studio, especially during reduction cycles.

Salt Glaze Firing

Salt glazes are unusual from several standpoints. Decorative pieces, or those glazed raw on the inside, can be fired in a single firing. Salt is not applied directly to the ware to form the glaze but is inserted in the kiln when the maturity of the clay body has been reached. This procedure causes the salt (sodium chloride) to volatilize and combine with the silica in the clay body to form the glaze. The clay body should have a high silica content. If silica is added to the body, it should be finely ground, because coarse silica particles will not unite with the vaporous sodium to form a glaze.

The interior of any kiln used for salt glazing must be lined with either a hard refractory firebrick or a castable, because insulating firebrick will soak up the sodium and deteriorate rapidly. Traditionally, salt kilns were made of hard firebrick. The salt was permitted to build up in a coating on the brick surface. During the first firings in a new kiln a great deal of salt was needed. In effect, the kiln was being glazed along with the ware. After a while, when the glaze coating had built up, much less salt was needed. The kiln used in this manner is unsuitable for normal glaze firings. And, in time, the interior surfaces deteriorate as the salt reacts with the silica contained in the refractory firebrick and literally eats into it.

Some potters try to prevent this corrosion by either coating the interior of the kiln with alumina compounds or using a high-alumina cement to cast the interior and the kiln roof. ALCOA's calcium-aluminate cement (#CA-25) and tabular-aluminate (grog) will produce a refractory wall that can withstand temperatures higher than 3000°F (1650°C). The usual mixture for this refractory is 15 parts cement, 85 parts tabular-aluminate, plus 10 percent water. Larger amounts of water will result in a weaker bond. Since the mixture sets up in an hour, all forms must be ready. It is possible to pour in sections if the joints are left rough. However, the roof arch must be completed at once.

Salting begins when the body has matured. (Cones are not completely accurate in determining the body maturation temperature, because the sodium vapor from the kiln walls will react on the cones.) Coarse rock salt is the preferred material, and you will need about $\frac{1}{3}$ pound per cubic foot of kiln space, less if you are using a well-coated salt kiln. The salt should be moistened with water and divided into 8 portions. You can place these portions in small paper condiment cups (purchased from a restaurant supply house). By forming a ring from a wire coat hanger, you can insert the salt packets through the salting ports into the firebox area. In a Rhineland downdraft salt kiln the ports are located in the arch of the roof; in an open-draft design, salting can be done through the burner ports. A closed, forced-draft kiln design will have to be modified to allow for special salting ports.

The draft must be cut back slightly when the salting begins to prevent the salt from being drawn out the stack. The coarse, damp rock salt will explode and scatter through the kiln. At this point deadly fumes of chlorine gas are given off, so the kiln room must be well ventilated. Many salt kilns are constructed in outside sheds that can be opened during salting to discharge the fumes harmlessly.

A recommended salting procedure requires 2 hours, with the 8 portions of salt introduced at 15-minute intervals. Because the draft is cut back, a slight reduction will occur. After about 5 minutes the draft can be adjusted to a neutral fire so that the heat lost during reduction can build up again. You may want to develop a slightly different salting procedure to account for variations in kiln design, materials, and clay body, but the 2-hour sequence is recommended as a starting point. Too short a salting sequence will not allow for a proper buildup of the glaze.

Instead of the cones normally used to gauge the firing, you should place several draw rings or clay doughnuts in the areas of the kiln where you would usually place cones. After about half the salt has been used, hook one or more test clay rings out of the kiln so that you can observe the glaze buildup. Be careful in placing and removing the clay rings, or you may knock them down into the kiln.

A characteristic of the salt glaze is its pebbly appearance. Potters who prefer a smoother glaze surface sometimes add about 5 percent borax. Feldspar and other semifluxes can be used in slip decoration to obtain sections of still glossier glaze. As in normal kiln firings, the body must be reduced, if desired, before any appreciable glaze buildup occurs.

Due to the toxic effects of chlorine gas given off by rock salt, many potters have experimented with sodium bicarbonate ($NaHCO_3$) instead of sodium chloride (NaCl). The bicarbonate form does not disperse so readily in the kiln as does the rock salt when inserted through the burner ports, so it is helpful to use a small, low-powered electric blower. The atmosphere can be neutral or slightly reducing. As in the customary salting procedure, the glaze buildup will take several hours.

Salt glazes generally fire in the cone 8 to 10 range and can be used on either a stoneware or a porcelain body. Lower-fire salt glazes (as low as cone 04) are possible with additions of borax.

Since the salt glaze alone is colorless, any color in the glaze must come from the body or from coloring oxides applied in engobes on the raw ware. Soluble forms of oxides, such as nitrates or chlorides, can also be brushed onto the ware. Deep forms must be glazed inside, for little vaporous salt will reach the interior. The kiln load must be uniform and not too tight, or else the glaze coating will be uneven. Incised or pressed designs will be accentuated by uneven amounts of glaze buildup, a factor that adds to the interest of the salt glaze.

Some potters fume their ware to produce an iridescent sheen on portions of the glaze. The general technique is to cool the salted kiln to a low red heat. Then, water-soluble colorants (such as chlorides or nitrates) are sprayed into the kiln in a thin mist. Often the sole chemical used is the chloride form of tin. This will react with the other colors in the clay and engobes to form varied iridescent hues. Dry colorants that volatilize under the heat can also be used.

Kiln Materials

Thanks to the industrial market, most kiln materials are available in any large city, but prices may vary. Even in a small town a building-supply dealer can generally provide firebrick and other basic supplies.

Firebrick Firebrick is made in a number of special compositions, but the common alumina-silica *hard refractory firebrick* is satisfactory for most purposes. Different grades are produced for operating temperatures of 1600°, 2000°, 2300°, 2600°, and 2800°F (870°, 1093°, 1260°, 1427°, and 1538°C), and some can be used at temperatures as high as 3000° and 3200°F (1650° and 1760°C).

The bricks used for higher operating temperatures are denser and lose much of their insulating ability. They are also more expensive. Therefore, you should not purchase a higher grade brick than you need. A 2600°F (1427°C) brick is generally used for kilns firing from cone 8 to 10. Special arch- and wedge-shape bricks can be ordered for the curve of the kiln roof. A kiln constructed entirely of hard firebrick will consume a great deal of fuel, since the bricks absorb and conduct a considerable amount of heat. Fortunately, porous insulating firebrick is also made, which has an insulating value from three to five times as great as the hard brick. Insulating firebricks are available in a temperature range similar to that of hard brick, but the cost is much higher. They are most often used as a backup layer next to the hard brick, although kilns made entirely of insulating bricks are common. Insulating firebricks require less fuel and can be cut easily with a coarse-tooth saw, such as an inexpensive pruning or bow-saw.

Ceramic-Fiber Insulation Research in new lightweight high-temperature insulating materials for the space program resulted in the development of ceramic-fiber insulation. These new materials are, for the most part, extruded, fine-dimension fibers of alumina and silica. They have a purer composition than the denser, heavier firebrick. Ceramic-fiber insulation comes in several forms: 3/4- and 1-inch rigid panels, 24 by 36 inches in size; 1-inch lightweight ceramic fiber blankets, in a roll 24 inches wide and 25 feet long; loose granular materials; and a lightweight ceramic-fiber castable mixture. These materials are compounded for operating temperatures between 2300° and 2600°F (1260°–1427°C). Ceramic-fiber cements are available for joining sections and filling cracks. Ceramic studs can be used to tie inner rigid panels to the outer kiln structure. When these products first appeared on the market, they had a number of flaws. Considerable shrinkage occurred in the rigid panels, and cracks appeared in the castable mixture when it was exposed to long firing cycles. However, improvements have been made in recent years.

The fiber insulation, athough costlier than firebrick, is much lighter, and the size of the panels speeds up construction time. The Peach Valley raku kiln (Fig. 472) could not have its convenient lift-up feature without the lightweight blanket insulation. The Westwood kiln (Fig. 475), made of lightweight ceramic-fiber material, is one-third the weight of similar size models using traditional construction. The new fibers can also serve as a sandwich layer or a backup layer to the conventional firebrick.

Castable Refractories Castable refractories of varying compositions for several operating temperatures are also available. These can be mixed and poured like concrete. Although more expensive than brick, castable refractories are useful for forming odd shapes, such as burner ports or small arches. They are dense and conduct heat much as hard brick does. A castable calcium-alumina refractory can serve as liner for a dual-purpose salt kiln, so that salt will not accumulate on the firebrick interior. With this arrangement a bisque or glaze kiln can safely be used for the occasional salt-glaze firing. Over a long period the door bricks will have to be replaced several times, and the combustion area near the burner ports will require chipping out and recasting due to the salt action, but the rest of the kiln will remain largely unaltered.

Other Insulating Materials   Insulating materials of a lower heat tolerance but with great insulating value can also be used for a backup layer. Even common soft red brick will serve this purpose. Kilns of more than 30 cubic feet are commonly built with a hard firebrick core, a middle portion of insulating firebrick, and an outer layer of red brick.

Asbestos sheets and blocks of various sizes provide good insulation, although the fibers are dangerous if inhaled and should be sealed if exposed. When the outer walls rise to a height of several courses, loose granular vermiculite poured to a depth of 6 to 8 inches will give further insulation to the roof crown, which in most cases tends to be rather cool. To further insulate a high curved brick roof, such as a catenary arch, vermiculite can be mixed with plaster of paris and troweled on. Chicken wire embedded in the mixture will provide additional support as expansions and cracks occur during firing. Commercial block insulation made of vermiculite, asbestos fibers, and cement is available in slabs 2 by 6 by 24 inches. This will serve as a backup insulation at temperatures below 1800°F (980°C).

Transite   A rigid cement asbestos sheet material, transite comes in 4-by-8-foot panels, in $\frac{1}{4}$ and $\frac{3}{8}$ inch thicknesses. It is useful for the outer wall of a small kiln having an angle iron frame, since it protects and dresses up the brickwork and serves as a retainer for loose insulation poured between the brick wall and the transite. Transite is also available in tubular form, and in this guise it makes a quite satisfactory chimney or flue duct, provided sufficient air space surrounds the pipe. A thickness of $\frac{1}{2}$ inch is usually sufficient; thicker sections tend to chip and flake off due to the great difference in the heats to which the inner and outer surfaces are exposed. Sometimes a bad mixture of materials or dampness in the flue will cause transite to explode. It is safer to use a fireclay-lined, steel-encased chimney section or a heavy sheet-metal chimney, provided it is kept a proper distance from any flammable material.

Kiln Furniture   The shelves, posts, and other props used in the kiln comprise the kiln furniture. Heavy fireclay shelves have been replaced by newer materials. Mullite shelves are suitable for earthenware temperatures, but the more expensive *silicon carbide* shelves give longer service and are compounded for higher temperatures. A $\frac{3}{4}$-inch thickness is adequate for standard loads. To avoid sagging and possible breakage in spans of 24 inches or more, a center post is necessary. Rectangular shelves are less subject to strain in cooling and heating, so they give longer service than square ones. A slow heating and cooling cycle not only minimizes damage to the pots but will prolong the life of the kiln furniture, especially the shelves. Salt glazes eat away the normal kiln shelves. Coating all surfaces with alumina hydrate mixed with a binder will help. The best solution is to use an especially compounded high-alumina shelf, but these are usually expensive.

Posts made of fireclay are available in various sizes. They often have a center opening to promote a more even expansion. High-temperature insulating bricks can be cut to make satisfactory posts. Dipping the ends of the fireclay posts into aluminum paint will lessen their tendency to stick to silicon carbide shelves. This problem does not arise with triangular slip-cast posts made of porcelainlike material. Triangular porcelain stilts having pointed contact areas and often a nickel-nichrome wire insert, can be used for some covers or for small pieces that must be glazed overall. The small contact blemishes are not noticeable. (See Chap. 9, pp. 282–284, for a description of saggers and industrial setting methods.)

left: 405. Paul Soldner, U.S.A.
Covered bowl.
Stenciled figures coated
with a 3 percent copper slip,
low-fired and smoked;
diameter 17″ (42.5 cm).

below: 406. Wayne Higby, U.S.A.
Tidesands Inlet.
Earthenware with white slip
and coloring oxides, raku-fired;
diameter 19″ (47.5 cm).

Kiln Construction

Twenty-five years ago few potters were building their own kilns, but with the burgeoning interest in ceramics and with increased knowledge this practice is now quite common. The beginner, who has little experience in the principles of kiln design, would be advised to duplicate a proven design, rather than to experiment. Not counting the value of labor, the potter may save 50 percent over the cost of a prefabricated model. Moreover, larger heavy-duty downdraft kilns are seldom available readymade.

The Electric Kiln

The electric kiln, which needs no chimney or gas lines, presents the least challenge to the novice (Fig. 407). Unless you are technically inclined, it is best to forego the problems of calculating length of element wire, size, resistance, and ohms necessary to obtain the desired heat in the kiln chamber. It is easier to purchase replacement elements for a standard kiln made by a reputable manufacturer. The electrical switches may be quite difficult to locate, for the best type is not commonly available. Kiln manufacturers carry replacements.

The angle-iron frame with supporting angles can be fabricated easily, but it must be square and accurate. Transite in $\frac{1}{4}$-inch thickness, cut a bit small to allow for heat expansion, can make the floor base and outer walls. Standard insulating firebrick straight ($9 \times 4\frac{1}{2} \times 2\frac{1}{2}$ inches), laid "on the flat," is used for the side walls—the 2300°F (1260°C) grade for a cone 04 kiln, 2600°F (1427°C) for a cone 6 to 8 kiln. No cutting of the bricks is required for an 18 by 18 inch interior. The bricks must be staggered as the courses are built up. You can prevent them from shifting by driving long finishing nails through the bricks or by applying a thin coat of fireclay and sodium silicate after first moistening with water. No cement should be used within $1\frac{1}{2}$ inches of the elements, in case the elements are placed in the joint between bricks.

The element recess can be cut with a coarse saw (a Swedish pruning saw, for example) and a round rasp, or with a simple cutting tool in a drill press. To retard possible contamination the recesses can be coated with aluminum paint or with a thin coat of kiln wash before inserting the elements. Low-fire nickel-nichrome replacement elements come in a coil like a screen-door spring. They can be stretched to fit the kiln by driving four nails into a section of plywood at a distance comparable to the size of the element recess and a fifth at the point where the element end enters the kiln from the control box. Most elements go twice around the kiln and need a diagonal slot to complete the circle. The coils must not touch at any point, or a hot spot will develop.

Unless you have some electrical experience, it is advisable to hire an electrician to hook up the wiring. Bolts in the transite to hold the control panel should be inserted before the bricks are laid in place. A piece of transite can serve as the base. Brass bolts should be used as connecting posts between the elements and the insulated switch wires (Fig. 408). The usual switch has three positions—low, medium, and high—hooked up on 110 volts, 210 volts in series, and 210 volts in parallel to give the needed current. After repeated firings the nickel-nichrome elements will contract, but they can be removed, carefully stretched again, and put back in place. A ventilated cover with adequate clearance must enclose the exposed connections.

The cover on a top-loading kiln presents little problem, for $\frac{1}{4}$-inch bolts—two in each brick, running through an angle iron on each side—will

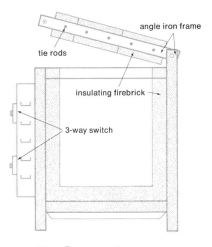

407. Cross section of an electric kiln.

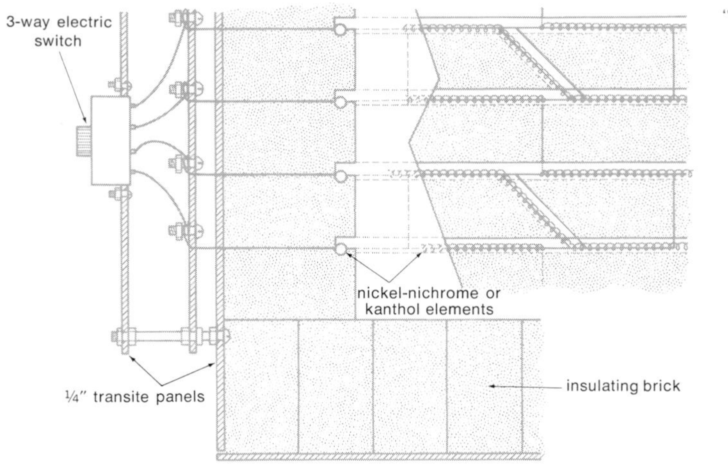
3-way electric switch
nickel-nichrome or kanthol elements
¼" transite panels
insulating brick

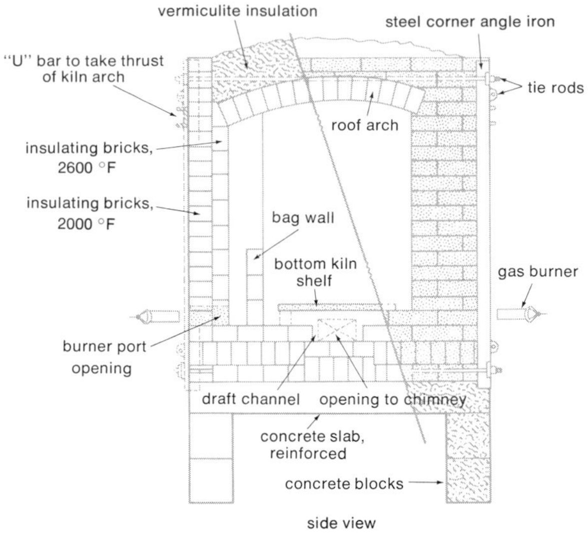
vermiculite insulation
steel corner angle iron
"U" bar to take thrust of kiln arch
tie rods
roof arch
insulating bricks, 2600 °F
insulating bricks, 2000 °F
bag wall
bottom kiln shelf
gas burner
burner port opening
draft channel
opening to chimney
concrete slab, reinforced
concrete blocks
side view

above left: 408. Detail of an electric kiln showing wiring and element placement.

above right: 409. Construction details of a gas kiln.

provide adequate support. If the angle is continued to the rear and the back frame angle is elevated 2 inches, a hinge can be contrived by drilling a hole and inserting a rod. Similarly, an extension in front and a rod inserted in a pipe will provide a lifting handle.

The high-fire (cone 8) electric kiln can also use bricks $4\frac{1}{2}$ inches thick. However, in this case, an extra 1-inch backing of asbestos or ceramic fiber would be desirable. Unless a porcelain insert channel is used, you must take greater care in selecting firebricks. Because of the higher heat, any iron impurities in the firebricks will melt and cause the element to flux and burn out. It is extremely important to obtain the proper bricks before attempting any construction. The hard kanthol elements become brittle after use, but their tendency to contract is diminished if they are first fired to cone 8, even though subsequent firings are lower.

The Gas Kiln

Thanks to the uniformity of insulating firebricks, you can build a small gas kiln with no cement (Fig. 409). This is particularly true of raku kilns, which are small and temporary in nature. A single burner can be placed in a simple box, with the pots set on a few bricks. A flat roof with a small hole for exhaust is sufficient. Either a bolted top or a similar side section can be used, since the ware is inserted and removed from the hot kiln with tongs.

A portable raku kiln can be constructed by cutting a 55-gallon steel drum about 3 inches from the top to make a cover. The remaining drum is too deep to load conveniently, so an additional 10 inches can be cut off and discarded. Cut a 4-inch hole in the cover section to serve as an exhaust; cut a 3-inch hole into the base section about 4 inches from the bottom to serve as the burner inlet.

Since raku kilns fire at a low heat, the usual high-temperature castables are not necessary and can be replaced by a calcium-aluminate cement, with vermiculite substituting for a large part of the grog. Pour a 3-inch layer in both cover and base, and, using a fiberboard drum as a mold, pour a 3-inch side wall. Use a portion of a plastic container as a mold for the firing and exhaust ports. Iron rods shaped and welded to the cover and base facilitate loading and make the kiln portable. A ceramic fiber blanket can be used in place of the castable, as in the kiln shown in Figure 472. A few firebrick posts and a small kiln shelf form the combustion chamber and loading floor.

Since the heat can be raised quickly, a small burner and fan unit works well, although a regular Bunsen burner can also be used.

For a small gas kiln a single $4\frac{1}{2}$-inch wall of insulating brick may be adequate, as in the single-bag-wall design illustrated in Figure 390. A 4- or 5-cubic-foot kiln can be fired easily with two atmospheric burners. The square kiln is most likely to have a uniform heat. Deep kilns are hard to load, and a tall chamber will often cause a temperature variation from top to bottom. Insulating bricks are not hard to cut, but it is easier to plan a design based on the uncut unit.

After the desired size has been established (as close to a cube form as possible), make a calculation to determine the burner capacity needed. Manufacturers supply information on the B.t.u. (British thermal units) of their various burners. Unless the kiln is quite small, several burners are preferable to one large unit, in order to avoid a concentration of heat. Generally about 6000 or 7000 B.t.u. are required in a stoneware kiln for each cubic foot of capacity, including the combustion area. For the average Bunsen or aspirating burner, a 3-inch opening is sufficient. The chimney size should be at least equal to the area of all burner ports, even slightly larger if possible, especially if there are angles in the flue connection or if the chimney is unusually high (both of which result in friction loss).

The opening through which the depressed floor flue exhausts into the chimney should be smaller than the chimney itself to prevent a too-rapid heat loss. However, it should be constructed in such a way as to allow easy enlargement, if necessary. Unless the kiln is unusually large, a bag wall constructed of firebrick laid on edge is sufficient. Only the first few courses of bricks need be permanent. The function of the bag wall is to force the flames and heat upward in the kiln. Its height will depend upon the kiln size, the chimney draft, and other factors. Additional bricks can be laid without cement if more heat is needed in the upper kiln area. Openings may be desirable in the upper wall. About 4 or 5 inches of combustion area between the kiln and the bag wall is sufficient in the average gas kiln. A slightly larger area is needed if oil is used for fuel.

Refractory mortar cements are available for bonding the bricks, in either dry or wet form. A cheaper and essentially similar material can be mixed from two parts fireclay and one part fine grog. An even stronger bond can be made by adding 1 gallon of sodium silicate to 100 pounds of the dry mix. Unless the bricks are first moistened, they will soak up too much mortar, so it is best to immerse them in water and then allow them to drain. Only the thinnest layer of mortar is needed, since the bricks are very uniform and do not require a thick layer of cement for leveling purposes. The best method is to dip the edges of the bricks in a soupy mortar and tap them into place immediately with a hammer on a wood block. Because of their porosity, insulating bricks expand very little in heating and can be placed very close together. The dense firebricks, however, expand considerably under heat; therefore, about $\frac{1}{4}$ inch of space with no mortar should be left in every third or fourth space between bricks, for otherwise the outside layer of cooler brick will be forced open in firing.

It is especially advisable to plan on a unit brick size when using hard bricks. They can be cut by tapping a groove on each side with a mason's hammer, then hitting a solid blow on a mason's chisel with a heavy hammer. No such procedure is possible with the wedge-shape bricks needed for the kiln arch. The usual arch rises at the rate of $1\frac{1}{2}$ inches per foot. Placing the bricks on edge for a $4\frac{1}{2}$-inch thickness provides sufficient strength for the average-size kiln. The #1 arch brick tapers from $2\frac{1}{2}$ to $2\frac{1}{8}$ inches. By drawing two curves $4\frac{1}{2}$ inches apart on a large board and using a

$1\frac{1}{2}$-inch rise per foot over the desired span, you can calculate the required number of #1 arch bricks. Some straight bricks will be needed, but they should be kept to a minimum, as should the mortar.

These calculations present no problem in an insulating brick arch, since the softer bricks can be trimmed to a wooden pattern using a coarse rasp. A sharply angled skewback brick is needed where the arch meets the side wall. The kiln will require a $2\frac{1}{2}$-inch angle-iron support at each corner, with $\frac{1}{2}$-inch take-up rods at top and bottom. While these give a slight rigidity to the kiln, their main purpose is to hold the heavy angle iron brace, which is needed on the outer wall to take up the thrust of the kiln arch. A very heavy spring (such as a valve lifter spring from a car motor) is sometimes used under the nut, since some expansion takes place while firing.

A supporting form to hold the arch can be made easily by cutting several boards to the arch curve and covering them with a Masonite sheet. It is wise to leave a bit of slack and to place wedges under the uprights so that the form can be removed easily after the steel angles and rods are in place. The catenary-arch kiln is self-supporting and needs no metal bracing for the arch, but angle irons across the front and rear secured with a tie rod are still desirable. Its curve can be established by suspending a chain from two nails at the desired floor width. The result will be a rather pointed curve. The structure will be most stable if the height approximates the width of the base. This design is perhaps best suited to an oil-burning kiln, since the flare at the base provides the extra combustion area needed for oil fuel.

The weight of a kiln is considerable, and it requires at least a 4-inch concrete base. In order to avoid leaning over and bumping your head in loading, it is a good idea to build the kiln on a reinforced concrete slab elevated to the necessary height with concrete blocks. Such a kiln can be moved later, if necessary, with little or no damage. In arranging the brick structure always plan to stagger the joints and occasionally have a tie brick to bind two courses together. Lay the corner bricks first, making certain the plan is perfectly square. A level and a guide line are essential, since the eye is not dependable. Common red bricks can be used as backup for that part of the floor area not depressed for the exhaust channel. The kind of brick to be used and the wall thickness are determined by the size and general use of the kiln. For the salt kiln or oil-fueled kiln an inner course of $4\frac{1}{2}$-inch hard firebrick is necessary, backed up by 2000°F (1090°C) insulating firebrick. If the size reaches 30 cubic feet, an outer layer of red brick is desirable.

A properly constructed kiln will give many years of service and require few repairs. A stoneware kiln with a 15- to 25-cubic-foot capacity can be built with 2600°F (1427°C) insulating brick on edge and 2000°F (1090°C) brick on the flat, thus creating a 7-inch wall. Although the initial cost is high, the construction is easier and the fuel cost lower. However, insulating bricks retain little heat and cool more rapidly; therefore you may wish to use a hard inner liner for a 30-cubic-foot or larger kiln. The kiln door jambs should be built of the same brick as the inner liner, whatever the type used. Kilns that are covered by only a simple roof are often used in summer schools and camps. These should be covered with plastic during the winter to keep out moisture that can freeze and cause severe damage.

It should be obvious from all these examples that there is no one way to build a kiln. The illustrations show a variety of burner placements. Most potters find the downdraft layout (Fig. 389) to be the most satisfactory for the 15- to 30-cubic-foot size. Although the updraft muffle (Fig. 388) is a common design for commercial kilns, neither this nor the open-flame updraft are recommended for construction by the potter, because the downdraft design usually fires more uniformly and reduces more efficiently.

The Oil Kiln

In locations where natural gas is not available or propane (L.P.G., liquid petroleum gas) is difficult to obtain, you should consider the use of #2 fuel oil. Oil is slightly cheaper than gas, and it produces a hotter flame. However, there are several disadvantages. Except with the most sophisticated and expensive burner types, fuel oil tends to be very smoky in the early stages of firing. This will be objectionable to your neighbors, unless you live in an isolated location. Some potters have solved this problem by preheating the kiln with portable gas burners before starting the oil fire. During the early stages of firing an oil burner, there is a greater chance of soot building up and causing a malfunction, so you must carefully supervise the firing.

Since fuel oil contains many impurities not found in natural or propane gas, the inner lining of the kiln must be made of hard refractory brick or a castable. The usual soft insulating firebrick will deteriorate under these conditions. There is also a greater volume expansion of volatilized oil gases, and this mandates a slightly larger combustion chamber such as found in the catenary-arch kiln illustrated in Figure 395. Otherwise, the basic design of the oil-burning kiln is little different from the gas kiln illustrated in Figure 409. Oil-burning units, especially those with forced air, are often placed in the front of the kiln, where the flame can run down the length of the combustion area without immediately impinging against the bag wall.

The Wood Kiln

The increasing cost of electricity, gas, and oil fuels has stimulated much interest in the wood-burning kiln. Many potters are especially attracted to the accidental effects that may result from ashes settling on the pots in a

410. Ken Ferguson, U.S.A.
Teapot. Porcelain
with opaque mat glaze,
green overglaze, and iron engobe
fired in a wood-burning kiln;
height 13″ (32.5 cm).

random fashion. Delicate glazes can also be fired in wood-burning kilns if the pots are placed in saggers.

There are several drawbacks to the wood kiln. For one thing, the actual process of stoking the kiln is a long and arduous affair. There is no such thing as taking a dinner break or trimming pots while the kiln automatically goes up to temperature. The usual firing cycle of the wood kiln takes about 24 hours. It begins with a small amount of split wood in the ash pit. The fire is deliberately kept at a low heat for several hours as moisture leaves the ware and the kiln gradually warms up. Then, wood is placed on the grate, and the actual firing begins. Relatively large pieces of wood are needed in this beginning stage, because they burn slowly.

Although hard woods—oak, maple, birch, or ash—have potentially more heat value, soft woods such as pine, fir, and hemlock burn faster. The resin in soft woods volatilizes and produces a long flame that extends throughout the kiln. It is essential that the wood be perfectly dry—cut, split, and placed under cover for a period of about two years. Damp wood will expend a large proportion of its heat value in the process of drying out. The firing progresses from a stoking of relatively large split pieces every hour or so, to a rate of several 1- or 2-inch by 2-foot sticks every 5 minutes. These thin pieces explode in the heat of the firebox and send a long flame through the kiln and up the chimney. The stoke and ash pit holes remain closed so that excessive drafts will not cool the chamber. Air vents in the ash pit and the grate area must be regulated carefully as the firing progresses. Avoid disturbing the ashes unless it is absolutely necessary to level them out, because this will also cause a heat loss. Usually, wood is added only when the previous load has burned down to a bed of coals. Do not overload, for if there is not enough oxygen to keep the wood burning brightly, there will be a drop in temperature. Normally, there is a slight reduction after stoking, which changes to oxidation as the fuel is consumed.

A somewhat remote location is also desirable for wood firing. The white smoke given off is largely water vapor, the black smoke carbon. Neither is as harmful as the sulphur fumes of the oil kiln, but they will disturb neighbors, as will the flames that shoot out of the chimney when higher temperatures are reached. A screen is necessary on the chimney to contain the larger wood sparks. An open, well-ventilated kiln shed set a safe distance from buildings or trees would be a good solution.

The average wood kiln of 30 to 60 cubic feet will use from 1 to 2 cords of wood for each firing (a cord is a stack of split wood 4 by 4 by 8 feet), so a good source of fuel is essential. Woodworking factories often have a quantity of kiln-dried wood scraps available. Slabs from a sawmill (bark-covered first cuts from a log) are another good prospect. The considerable labor of cutting timber with a chain saw, then hauling and splitting it into small sizes, may not be justified. To eliminate part of the arduous firing schedule, some potters fire their kilns overnight to a low red heat on portable gas burners and then complete the firing with wood during daylight hours.

The catenary-arch design is especially well suited to the wood kiln, because the expanded base can contain a large portion of the firebox (Fig. 411). For the typical well-insulated stoneware kiln about 1 square foot of grate space is needed for each 6 square feet of floor area. A firing chamber on each side of the kiln generally provides a more even heat, but successful designs have also utilized a single firebox opposite the chimney. The single firebox design saves space, because only one bag wall is needed and a single grate need not be as wide as the combined width of two grates.

The floor and firebox area must be of hard refractory firebrick, while the inner kiln lining is usually of 2800°F (1538°C) firebrick backed up by

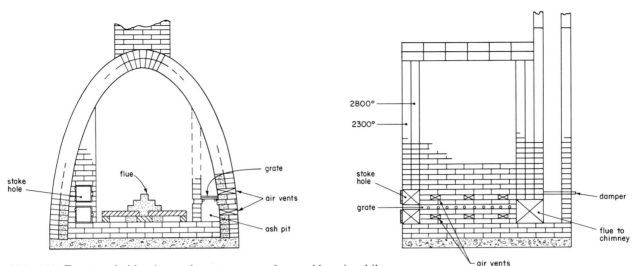

411, 412. Front and side views of a catenary-arch, wood-burning kiln.

2300°F (1260°C) insulating firebrick (Fig. 412). Wood ash does not do great damage to insulating brick, and the upper kiln area can be of such brick for greater insulating value. Plastic refractory coatings are available to coat the porous surface, if you want them.

Various materials have been used for the fire grates, ranging from old cast-iron sash weights to scrap iron rods. The most durable—although expensive—choice would be 1-inch stainless-steel rods. These can be placed at 1½- to 2-inch intervals. A greater width between rods is possible if you use a second grate of ½-inch rods below to catch the smaller embers. When laying up the brick, indent ½ inch at the grate level, to provide a supporting ledge. The grate rods should be cut ¼ inch shorter to allow for heat expansion. Two ½-inch rods welded to the heavier grates will prevent shifting. The ash pit should be 8 or 9 inches deep with three air intakes each 2½ by 4½ inches in the ash pit area and three more intakes immediately above the grate. Doors for the ash pit and stoke holes should be made of sheet steel on heavy hinges, because the chore of removing firebricks is too time-consuming.

As mentioned before, the curve of the catenary-arch kiln is determined by suspending a light chain between two points after the size of the floor has been decided. The height of the arch is normally chosen to equal its base width. The result is a somewhat pointed, completely self-supporting arch. Templates cut to this curve and faced with ⅛-inch Masonite will form a mold for the brick construction.

For convenience in loading, the reinforced slab foundation can be raised and cast on a foundation of concrete blocks. The outer 9 inches of slab floor should incline inward at a pitch of 1 inch to 10 inches. Otherwise, a #1 arch brick must be used for the base brick in order to obtain the proper angle between the foundation and the rising side wall. Afterward, the usual 2800°F (1538°C) hard firebrick straights can be used for the inner wall until you approach the crown of the arch, where several rows of #1 arch brick will be needed. A thin mortar of one-half fireclay and one-half grog can be used. Leave a ¼-inch space with no mortar between bricks at 3- or 4-brick intervals to allow for heat expansion. Because the brick courses must be staggered, a number of half bricks will also be necessary.

The large volume of hot gases in a wood kiln means that the opening from the chamber to the chimney must be about twice that for the usual gas kiln, and the chimney itself must be larger—about 12 by 12 inches for a 30-to 40-cubic-foot kiln. A rule of thumb is to have 1 foot of height for each inch in diameter, and more if there is any horizontal run from the kiln to the chimney. A kiln shelf that slides into a slot at the base makes a suitable damper. A firebrick and red brick combination is suitable for the lower chimney section with fireclay tile and red brick for the upper chimney.

The Chimney

Because of the extreme temperatures involved, a kiln cannot exhaust into an ordinary household chimney. For a shedlike studio a simple transite pipe may be sufficient to carry the exhaust. In the classroom, however, an insulated fireclay Van Packer unit may be necessary, especially for the portion within the building. The exterior section can have the usual fireclay liner and brick construction. Small kilns can exhaust into a metal hood above the kiln, thus sucking the cooler room air into the stack and eliminating some of the temperature problem.

A short, direct connection from kiln to chimney is just as important for a proper draft as is the height of the stack. If needed, overhead connections can be made with a metal fireclay-lined pipe. Undue length or angles in this connection will require a much higher and larger stack size than normal. Tall stacks with unusual connections will probably need a burner or a fan in the stack base to induce an initial draft. If there are no surrounding buildings to cause a downdraft, a 15- to 20-foot chimney should be sufficient. A 6-by-6-inch flue is usually adequate for a 10-cubic-foot kiln, and a 9-by-9-inch flue for a 20-cubic-foot gas kiln. However, an even larger size is recommended, especially in a taller stack, which has some friction loss. A slot must be left in the draft flue at the point where it leaves the kiln for a damper. The damper can be a small or broken kiln shelf.

Burners

The proper burner size and type are of critical importance to the success or failure of a kiln. In the past many potters were forced to construct their own burners, because the small sizes they needed were not always available. Increased interest in kilns has changed this situation. The manufacturers listed in the Appendix (p. 322) produce a wide variety of burners and will recommend the type most suitable to individual kilns. Although burners can be improvised to duplicate commercial designs, the anticipated savings are not worth the potentially unsatisfactory firings.

Gas Burners Natural draft gas burners are easy to install and quiet in operation. The Bunsen-type burner pictured in Figure 413 has a rating of 26,000 B.t.u. Six of these burners are needed for a downdraft gas kiln with a loading area of about 30 cubic feet. The burner ports should be about 3

413. Simple Bunsen-type burner, 26,000 B.t.u.; length 10$\frac{7}{16}$″ (33.75 cm). Johnson Gas Appliance Co.

414. Venturi-type gas burner, 75,000 B.t.u.; length 14$\frac{1}{4}$″ (35.5 cm). Johnson Gas Appliance Co.

415. Forced-draft gas burner,
$\frac{1}{3}$ horsepower blower motor,
200,000 to 800,000 B.t.u.;
length 30–34″ (75–85 cm).
Johnson Gas Appliance Co.

inches in diameter, with the burner installed about 1 inch behind the opening to allow additional air to be sucked into the kiln. The burner has a brass valve to control the flow of gas, as well as an adjustment on the tip to regulate the length of the flame during firing. An average kiln will need a 2-inch gas line direct from the natural gas main. If you use propane gas, a 500-gallon tank is recommended. Several smaller tanks can be hooked up together but will need frequent filling. The amount of gas generated by the liquid propane decreases in cold weather and when the tank is less than a quarter full. There should be 10 pounds of pressure from the tank to a regulator at the kiln that reduces the pressure to 6 to 8 ounces. A T-fitting at the rear of the kiln will distribute equal pressure to the burners on each side. A thermocouple unit and a solenoid safety valve should be installed on at least the first burner on each side. School safety regulations may require a solenoid valve on each burner.

Larger kilns, such as car kilns (Fig. 396), will need the larger burner unit pictured in Figure 414, which has a B.t.u. rating of 75,000. Large car kilns require 5 or 6 such burners for a uniform heat distribution. The units can be installed sideways with 90-degree elbows to conserve space.

The forced-draft gas burner illustrated in Figure 415 provides from 200,000 to 800,000 B.t.u. per hour. A large kiln will require two of these units. The burners can be located at either the front or the rear of the kiln; the blower will cause the flame to travel the length of the firing chamber. The blower unit can be fitted with a T-joint to service two units placed on the same side of the kiln.

Smaller forced-draft units, although expensive, provide a quick and portable means for a raku firing. Many potters have also used discarded vacuum cleaner fans in conjunction with a straight pipe containing a gas aperture. Such improvised units are satisfactory for the relatively short span of the raku firing but are not capable of standing up under longer firings at higher temperatures.

Oil Burners Oil burners range from simple to very complex devices. A rudimentary burner consists of a cast-iron pan placed beneath a 4-inch hole leading into a chamber below the kiln floor. A small metal pipe running from a 55-gallon drum to the pan should have a valve to control the flow of oil. To begin firing, an oily rag is placed in the pan and ignited. The valve is adjusted so that oil drips slowly into the pan, resulting in a very smoky flame. When a red heat is reached, the oil will volatilize sufficiently to produce an efficient use of the oil. A slightly more practical device consists of a square steel port with a series of ladderlike angled plates. The oil drips down these plates and is volatilized with a better air mixture. Both these methods produce a very sooty chimney exhaust until a red heat develops.

A forced-air unit that disperses the oil and provides a greater amount of oxygen for oil combustion is a more desirable solution. Many potters have used the simple arrangement pictured in Figure 416. The blower must be a heavy-duty type capable of continuous operation with a ⅓-horsepower motor. Two burners can be run from a single blower. The burner should be preheated before the blower is started. This can be done by igniting some oily rags as mentioned earlier. When a good blaze develops, allow a little oil to trickle in to maintain the fire. To eliminate this smoky period some potters preheat with a small portable gas unit or a gas line connected to the oil line. It is preferable to begin the firing with a light oil (such as kerosene), which has a lower flash point. Later, you can switch to #2 fuel oil or strained and filtered crank case oil.

Even more efficient are the commercial burners that inject oil under pressure into a mixing chamber and blow it into the kiln in a gaseous mixture. This provides a cleaner and more complete combustion. Some burners are even equipped with ignition and safety cutoff devices. In view of the increasing cost of all fuels, the expensive but efficient burner may be a bargain in the long run.

The operation of an oil burner is not automatic, since the oil and air supply must be monitored constantly. Too much air will cool the kiln, while excessive oil will result in incomplete combustion, reduction, and a lowering of temperature. Air and oil input both will be smaller in the early stages of firing and must be increased gradually as higher temperatures are reached.

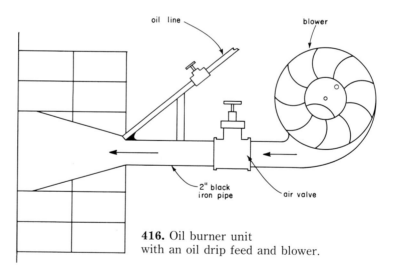

416. Oil burner unit with an oil drip feed and blower.

9
The Professional Potter

ottery making in school can be an exciting experience, and a relief from the routine of academic studies, but the life of a professional potter is one of hard work and long hours, with compensation often out of proportion to the training required. For most students the prospect is not encouraging, and ceramics fills the role of an interesting hobby, relaxation from an industrial or professional livelihood.

A few trained potters become teachers, which requires additional work at the graduate level. For the prospective teacher it is useful to have considerable background in other craft media or in sculpture, for beginning positions often include teaching assignments in more than one area. Situations vary widely in terms of facilities, class size, and administrative duties. Ideally, the college or university should provide a studio and sufficient free time to allow ceramics teachers to experiment with new techniques. Unfortunately, many institutions hire creative and productive potters, only to overwhelm them later with oversize classes and administrative red tape.

The Studio Potter

In view of the time and energy that must necessarily be expended in teaching, it is natural that many talented students are attracted to the prospect of opening their own studios, and the general affluence of large segments of society has made the idea much more feasible now than it was in years past. The hand-made pot is today truly a luxury item; it hardly qualifies as a necessity.

Perhaps the most difficult task for potters dreaming of their own studios is to develop a realistic dollars-and-cents approach. The few pots sold during student days seem to represent a great profit. However, you must calculate the cost of the kiln, fuel, and chemicals and clay. All these items, plus the rental of studio space, the expense of utilities, and such miscellaneous expenditures as advertising and mailing, add immeasurably to overhead.

Paradoxical as it may seem, the Internal Revenue Service, with its insistence upon accurate records, may well provide the prospective potter with the best means of judging a venture's chances of success. When sales are finally made and cash is in the till, the potter too often considers this to be profit. Many people starting out in business disregard items of overhead and incidental expenses, so they are unaware that they are working at less than a living wage. A glance at the tax laws governing self-employed persons will provide a checklist of deductible items—and thus a list of expenses to be calculated in determining profitability.

The first item to be considered is the studio and in some cases a sales room. Such quarters will involve a yearly rental or lease and the accompanying insurance. If, by good fortune, the potter owns the property, then a proper return on the investment must be allowed, plus any taxes, mortgage payments, and insurance. Depreciation should be calculated upon the building and major equipment items, such as kilns, pug mill, wheels, and fixtures. Additional costs may be incurred in installing gas lines, propane tanks, or heavy electrical wiring. After the initial outlay, there will be continual small maintenance expenses.

Too often the above items are disregarded and the potter only considers the costs of clay, glaze chemicals, and fuel. Beyond these are the usual overhead items such as light, heat, and the telephone. Under some circumstances, paid newspaper announcements, business cards, brochures, stationery, and postage may be necessary. Wrapping paper, twine, tape, packing material, and boxes will be needed to send pottery to customers. Mailing will involve shipping fees, insurance, breakage losses, and perhaps a bad

417. Erik Magnussen
for Bing & Gr∮ndahl
Copenhagen Porcelain, Ltd.
Teapot. Unglazed stoneware.

debt or two. Mileage costs should be determined in the transport of materials and merchandise. Travel and living expenses are usually involved in attending craft fairs. Membership in professional organizations, magazines, books, and attendance at meetings and exhibitions are also tax deductible.

Only when you keep an accurate record of such varied items can you determine how your operation is actually progressing. Unnecessary expenses should be eliminated and the more profitable items and outlets expanded. The workshop must be laid out for the greatest efficiency. Shortcuts made in the forming and decorating processes will enable you to create an interesting and pleasing product in less time.

The school environment is so unlike that of the producing studio that it would be a great advantage for you to apprentice yourself for a year or so to a professional potter or to find employment in a small pottery. If you plan to have a sales outlet in connection with a studio, location becomes very important. The expense and restrictions of a metropolitan area often make such a situation impractical, and, moreover, many potters prefer to live in the country. Setting up shop near a major highway is not really necessary. True pot lovers will seek out an excellent craftsman and bring their friends.

Some potters sell mainly through outside shops, but since the usual markup in these outlets is 100 percent, it is easy to price yourself out of sales, unless you can produce an attractive line that can be thrown and decorated quickly. Items placed on consignment traditionally have a 50 percent markup. Unfortunately, shops that carry consignment goods often have commercial lines as well and use the consignment pieces primarily as window dressing, without making much effort to sell them. For some years craft fairs have been popular in many parts of the country. Many potters have found these to be an important source of summer sales, with orders taken for winter. One potter operating in a rural location near a large city has had good results by holding a "kiln opening" periodically during the summer. Post cards sent to a list of interested customers ensure a good turnout over the weekend.

What to make is perhaps more important than the details of the selling procedure. It is usually a great shock for beginning potters to realize that the public does not always have the same preferences that they do. While the craftsman may like the mottled brown-glazed bowl, it could sell twice as fast if it were blue. It is not that treasured show pieces will not sell, for indeed they will. But new customers are more likely to buy, for example, a set of mugs. As they grow to enjoy the feel of the handle and the slight irregularity of form and glaze, they may become interested in something that is more exciting to the potter. Unlike the usual retail operation, a very personal relationship develops between studio potters and their customers. Buyers greet a kiln opening with the same degree of anticipation as does the potter.

While ceramics teachers to some degree are subsidized to allow freedom of design, the professional studio potter must sell consistently. This does not mean a lowering of standards, but rather an orientation toward salable items, because the market for the large show piece is limited. Although the average home may have room for a few decorative vases, its capacity for mugs, sugarbowls and creamers, casseroles, pitchers, planters, and so forth, is almost unlimited, and these objects will constitute the major area of sales. To idealistic beginners the ash-tray-and-candy-dish line may seem like the lowest form of ceramics, and most talented potters would agree. But upon opening a shop, you will discover that the customer who will pay $30 for a vase also wants a hand-made ash tray and will buy anything that could remotely serve this purpose.

In a callous and practically anti-aesthetic world, which often seems to pander to the lowest taste, the high standards of the craftsman are refreshing. However, to make what one pleases and insist that the public take it or leave it can be self-defeating. For example, it is not logical to have only one teapot on the shelf, no matter how attractive it may be. Rather, it is essential to have several styles, colors, and so forth in different price ranges. Some customers will want the most expensive, the best in the house! Others will be bargain hunters. It really makes no difference that all the teapots may represent the same amount of effort on the part of the craftsman. Just as the customer in a clothing store would be distressed to find that all the suits were brown and bore the same price, so the potential buyer of ceramics will hope to find a wide selection.

418. Nils Refsgaard for Dansk International Designs.
BLT dinnerware, intended for "breakfast, lunch, and tea."

above: **419. Sergio Asti.**
"Dada" ceramic tableware.
1972. Produced by Ceramica Revelli,
Laveno, Italy.

right: **420.** Drawings
for "Dada" tableware,
designed by Sergio Asti.

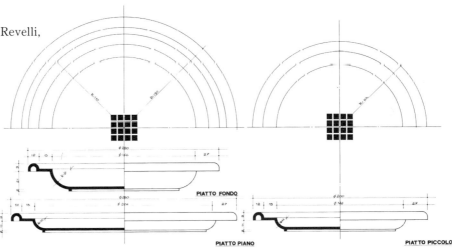

PIATTO FONDO

PIATTO PIANO

PIATTO PICCOLO

The Potter in Industry

If Greek or Chinese potters of two thousand years ago were suddenly
transported into the studio of today's hand potter, they would not find the
procedures unfamiliar. But the Industrial Revolution, which began in the
mid-18th century, changed drastically the methods in the large commercial
pottery. Today only the few universities that have associations with schools
of ceramic engineering offer the courses necessary to an understanding of
the problems of ceramic design in industry. In Europe, especially in Scandinavia, there is a much closer contact between industry and the art schools
than there is in the United States. For example, the dinner set illustrated in
Figure 419 was designed by an Italian architect who also creates furniture
and products in plastic and metal. The drawing (Fig. 420) reveals the
structure and proportional relationship of the plates, practical considera-

left: 421. Loading a double-shuttle car kiln at Bennington Potters.

below: 422. *Tema* teapot, coffee pot, cups and saucers. Stoneware.
Bing & Grøndahl
Copenhagen Porcelain, Ltd.

right: 423. Stig Lindberg
for Aktiebologet Gustavsbergs
Fabriker, Sweden.
Present flameware.
Stoneware with temmoku glaze.

below: 424. David Gil
for Bennington Potters, U.S.A.
Stacking dinnerware.
Press-molded stoneware.

tions that make the ware more convenient for stacking purposes and more
resistant to warpage in the manufacturing process.

Labor-saving devices were used by the ancients. The Etruscans worked
with bisque molds as early as the 5th century B.C., and slip casting was
practiced in a limited fashion in T'ang China (A.D. 618–906). But these
mechanized processes were limited, and pottery remained largely a handcraft industry. During the 18th century the use of steam power to process
clay and glaze chemicals and the new plaster of paris for molds made
extreme changes in the age-old techniques. Unfortunately, while these and
other technical advances made pottery and soon even porcelain both
cheaper and more accessible to the masses, the quality of design deterio-
rated rapidly. None of the small hand potteries had the capital, and often not
even the business skill, necessary to manage a large commercial enterprise.
Furthermore, the importation of Oriental porcelains had become very
profitable. Although the new porcelain factories were often not successful,
they were thought to be immensely profitable, and so were either held as the
property of the Crown or parceled out among close retainers.

The great tragedy in the industrialization of ceramics was not so much
the change in technique, but rather the fact that design decisions were no

left: 425. **David Gil** for Bennington Potters, U.S.A. *Gourmet Cookware:* pie plate and loaf pan. Stoneware with mat white glaze.

below: 426. *Korinth* dinnerware. Porcelain. Shapes by Martin Hunt; pattern by Erik Clemmesen and Carl-Henry Stålhane, for Bing & Grøndahl Copenhagen Porcelain, Ltd.

longer made by the potter, who could draw on centuries-old ceramic tradition. Instead, decisions were imposed by the new factory manager, an entrepreneur whose major desire was to show a profit by whatever means possible. The potter became merely a hired hand. European ceramics of the 18th and 19th centuries thus became a weird assemblage of borrowed Greek forms decorated in the Chinese or Italian fashion. The flexibility of plaster as a mold material made feasible the easy copying of forms and decoration conceived in metal, glass, and even basketry.

427. Craig Holmes
throwing bottles
on a constant-speed,
heavy-production wheel
at Pacific Stoneware, Inc.

Colonial American potters, for example, were overwhelmed by the mass-produced import, with the result that a native pottery tradition was never truly established in the United States. In time American potteries became as industrialized as those abroad. With few exceptions they have continued to reflect the influence of foreign wares. (The borrowing is, of course, reciprocal, for there are European cars with Detroit styling and Japanese versions of many Scandinavian designs.)

Today there are numerous stores abroad and an increasing number in the United States that consistently display an attractive line of excellently

428. Don McPherson
loading a car kiln
with the daily output of mugs
at Pacific Stoneware.

429. A selection of salt and pepper shakers from various dinnerware sets by Mikasa. Stoneware with shiny and mat glazes, average height 4″ (10 cm).

designed handcraft products. The widespread availability of quality merchandise in Scandinavia is made possible by the close cooperation of the schools, the government, and industry over a period of many years. In the United States only industry as a whole has the widespread resources and influence to promote a genuine improvement in design. It is encouraging to note that there are a few large and several small potteries that are "bucking the tide" and are attempting to furnish the public with ceramics designed with originality and with a true feeling for clay. When potteries have studios attached to their factories, designs can evolve from a clay prototype in a more natural manner, as distinguished from the drafting board industrial design concept.

Designing for Production

While the prototype for a mass-produced piece may evolve on the potter's wheel, it is essential that the ceramic designer have a working knowledge of the techniques of slip casting and jiggering. The long process that finally results in placing a pattern in production requires close cooperation among the designer, the mold maker, the glaze chemist, and the production engineer. The prototype is usually thrown on the wheel, but the mold maker most often works from a scale drawing.

The designer first works up a variety of designs and then gradually eliminates those that are obviously nonfunctional, too commonplace, or too difficult to reproduce. Since the cup is the most-used item in a dinner set, it is often the starting point. When its shape has been roughly determined, other pieces are designed to relate to it. It is essential that the designer have a feeling for the clay form and a knowledge of how it can deform in firing. Heavy dinnerware is not very popular. Therefore, the foot rim and wall thickness must be of a dimension only sufficient to support the form.

430–440. *Designing forms for production, from scale drawings through the mold-making process to the finished product. Courtesy Peter A. Slusarski.*

above: 430. Scale drawings are made from the thrown prototype.

left: 431. Cross sections are used to prepare the plaster model.

432. A metal template develops a solid plaster study.

433. The plaster model is refined with cutting tools.

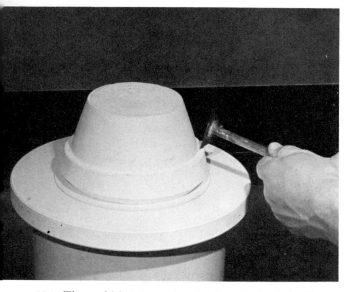

434. The mold is trimmed to fit the wheel of the jigger.

435. Top and bottom sections of the case mold.

After the cross sections are determined, a plaster model is made. A metal template made from the profile drawing is placed on the turning rig. Plaster is poured around the pin in small amounts until the form is completed. A circular movement of the template trims off the excess and develops a solid plaster study model.

Because of shrinkage that will occur in firing, the final model is oversize. Minor refinements in form can be made with cutting tools. After the plaster cup model is complete, it is coated with a plaster separator. A retaining collar is put in place, and fresh plaster is poured over the cup model to form the original jigger mold. Figure 434 shows the trimming of the mold to fit the wheel head of the jigger machine. It is necessary to have a mold for each cup to be made in the day's production, which may be thousands. Figure 435 illustrates the top and bottom sections of the case mold used to make the jigger block mold. The ball-and-socket projections allow for an accurate positioning of the sections prior to pouring the block mold. The case molds are made of a harder and denser plaster mix than that used for the jigger cup mold, which must readily absorb water from the clay after it is jiggered.

In jiggered ware, only one surface is shaped by the plaster form. The inner cup surface is formed by the jigger template. Figure 436 shows the steel template being checked for clearance. Figure 437 illustrates a half section of the cup handle on a plaster or marble base. After the retaining walls are in place and the surface has been shaped, a layer of plaster is poured in, forming one half of the mold. Keys are carved out of the fresh plaster, and the complete handle section is put in place. English Crown soap commonly serves as a mold separator. If the plaster mold is dry, it must be moistened before soaping and casting, for otherwise the soap would be drawn into the dry cast, causing the two sections to stick. After the cast is finished, it is a simple matter to carve pouring openings into the damp plaster. Before a clay handle is poured, however, the mold sections must be dry. For the pilot design project, a single handle mold is adequate; in production, a dozen handles normally are cast at one time.

436. Steel template inside plaster cup mold.

437. Half section of a cup handle on a plaster base.

438. Two halves of a plaster mold for a cup handle.

439. A steel template will shape the bottom surface of a saucer

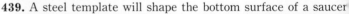

440. The completed place settings.

Designing a plate or saucer is a somewhat different operation from designing a cup. In this case, the plaster mold is shaped to form the inside, or upper contour, of the plate. The template is cut to form the bottom surface.

The process from the initial sketches to the finished product is long, and several years may elapse before marketing can begin.

Mixing Plaster

There are available a variety of plasters of different hardness and setting rates for use in model making, block molds, or case molds. Theoretically, 18.6 pounds of water will set up 100 pounds of plaster; in practice, at least 60 pounds of water will be needed to achieve the proper flow. The less water used, the stronger the cured plaster will be. Plaster normally sets in about 20 minutes, but it must be poured before it hardens. This time will depend upon the amount of mixing. The plaster must be sieved into the water (to avoid large lumps) until the water will absorb no more. It is then allowed to set from 3 to 4 minutes until it is thoroughly wet. Small batches can be mixed by hand or larger ones with a power mixer. After a few minutes of mixing, the plaster will begin to thicken. It must be poured at this point. Once it begins to set, it is useless and must be discarded. (It cannot be poured down the sink, for it will clog the drains.) Plaster manufacturers furnish tables giving strength and porosity for various mixtures. For production it is most important that all molds have a similar porosity.

Slip-Casting Techniques

Slip casting is a method of making ceramics in which liquid clay is poured into a hollow, absorbent mold. Within a few minutes after pouring, a film of firm clay appears on the inner surface of the mold. As water is absorbed into the plaster, the clay becomes thicker. When the desired thickness develops, the mold is upended and the excess clay, which is still liquid, is poured out. The remaining clay coating continues to harden and eventually shrinks away from the mold. Simple cup forms can be made in a single piece mold, while undercut and more complicated shapes require two, three, or occasionally more pieces in the mold.

441. Pouring liquid slip clay into hollow, plaster molds held together with heavy rubber bands.

442. Preparing molds for slip casting.

When multiple sections are used, they are keyed together with ball-and-socket projections and are held together during pouring with heavy rubber bands, such as one might cut from an automobile inner tube. As the water soaks into the plaster mold, the level of slip in the cavity falls, and a small amount must be added. To avoid frequent slip additions during casting, a collar is added to the top of the original model to serve both as a funnel for the slip and as a clay reservoir. The angle of the collar is used as a guide in trimming the top edge of the formed piece. This is done with a fettling knife when the cast piece has hardened sufficiently. At this stage the mold sections are carefully removed, and the casting seams on the piece are scraped off and sponged to create a smooth surface.

In order to avoid uneven shrinkage or air pockets, some pieces must be cast in sections and joined together with slip. This is particularly true of small handles, which are cast solid rather than drain cast. Depending upon

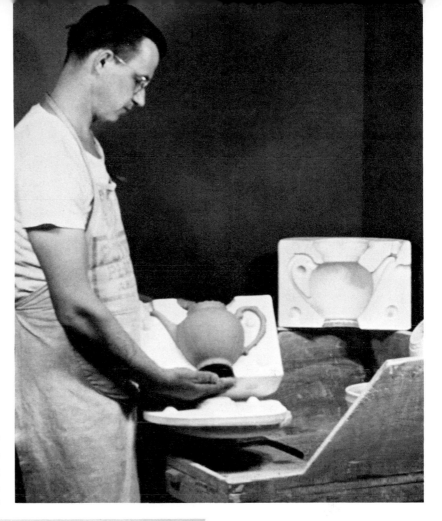

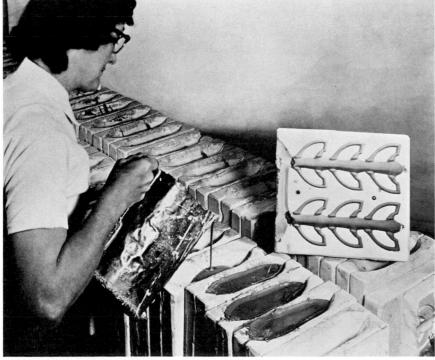

right: **443.** Removing a slip-cast creamer from a three-piece mold.

below: **444.** Cup handles cast twelve to a mold are removed, separated, and joined to the cup when leather hard.

445. Joining a spout to a coffee pot. The pieces have been cast separately.

the character of the clay, this type of joining can be done at either the leather-hard or the dry stage. The procedure is quite different from that used for thrown objects, in which sections should be joined as soon as they can be handled without distortion.

Casting Slips

Unlike a clay used in throwing, a clay body for jiggering and casting need not be very plastic. In fact, the plastic clays are often avoided, since their greater water absorption means more shrinkage, which is usually accompanied by warping. Various types of binders are used to impart greater green and dry strength to the ware. This more than compensates for the substitution of less-plastic ingredients.

Of great importance in a casting slip is the use of *deflocculants,* such as sodium silicate and soda ash. The addition of about 1 percent of either of these chemicals to the dry weight of the clay will reduce considerably the amount of water needed to make a fluid slip. A properly deflocculated casting slip is easily pourable but has a clinging, syrupy consistency that substantially retards the settling of the heavier slip particles. Georgia kaolin, which has a uniform particle size, is the major porcelain clay used in casting slips. One negative feature of the slip body is that its bland smoothness is relatively uninteresting when compared to the color and texture of a throwing clay. Some typical casting slips for various temperatures are listed in the Appendix.

A common name for sodium silicate is water glass. It is, in fact, a solution of sodium silicate in water. The sodium silicate is made by fusing a mixture of soda ash and silica sand. The term is a general one, since the proportion of sodium to silica may vary greatly. N-brand solution is the trade name given to the type commonly used as a deflocculant in ceramics. Soda ash (sodium carbonate), either alone or in combination with sodium silicate, is a more effective deflocculant than sodium silicate alone in casting slips containing organic matter, such as is found in ball clay. Slip should not be stored for long periods, especially in warm weather, because fermentation occurs, and this may cause pinholes in the cast ware.

A standard practice is to use about 3 parts N-brand sodium silicate by weight to 1 part soda ash. The proportions depend on the body formula. If it includes a large amount of clay, a 1-to-1 mixture of soda ash and N-brand silicate solution may prove more satisfactory. After weighing, the soda ash should be dissolved in hot water and then both deflocculants added to the water. As a beginning you might take 100 pounds of slip body and slowly add it to a large crock containing 50 pounds of water, which is about 6 gallons (8.3 pounds to the gallon). More or less of the slip body may be needed, depending upon the ingredients and the deflocculant action. The resulting slip should have a thick, syrupy consistency. A *blunger* is helpful in mixing the ingredients, although a large wire whisk can be used for test batches. Slip should always be screened before using, for any lumpy particles will settle and give a poor casting. You must take care in screening and filling the mold in order not to trap air bubbles in the slip.

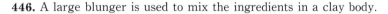

446. A large blunger is used to mix the ingredients in a clay body.

It is better to use not more than 1 percent deflocculant, even less if possible, in relation to the dry ingredients' weight, since an excess will sometimes cause the slip to become pasty and nonpourable. It will also gradually seal the pores of the plaster mold with an insoluble film of calcium silicate, making removal of the casting difficult and eventually spoiling the mold completely. Soda ash is more troublesome in this regard than silicate. Drying the molds from the outside by inverting them or covering the mouths will help to prevent this accumulation on the inner mold surface.

Jiggering Methods

As every novice potter soon learns, it is impractical to throw large, flat shapes on the potter's wheel. Countless generations of potters have used bisque molds to shape one surface of flat dishes and to support the soft clay in drying. With the use of plaster molds, the forming process is quite rapid and accurate. In addition, the plaster mold produces a smoother surface than would be possible with a bisque mold.

The composition of the clay used for jiggering is different from that of throwing clay. Since the ware is supported by the mold during the initial drying period, the clay need not be so plastic. In fact, since plastic clay shrinks more in drying, thus increasing the likelihood of warpage, it is used in limited amounts. To compensate for this loss in green and dry strength, various binders—such as lignin extract and methocel—are frequently added to the clay body.

Sections of clay can be extruded from the pug mill in different diameters, depending on the use to which they will be put. The size used for the plate shown in the jigger machine (Fig. 447) would be 6 to 8 inches. A slice about

447. A metal template trims off the excess clay from the bottom profile of a dinner plate while the plate revolves on the jigger machine.

118, 119. A rough cup shape is thrown on the wheel and later expanded and refined in a mold by the action of the template.

1 inch thick is cut off the pugged clay with a wire and placed over a square of canvas on the bench. The clay slice is then hit with a malletlike weight that compresses it to half this thickness. This clay bat is in turn slapped down over a plaster plate mold resting on the jigger head. The next step is to force out any air remaining between the clay and the plaster mold. This is usually done with the moistened hand as the jigger head revolves slowly. The operator then brings the steel template down toward the mold, further compressing the clay and cutting away the excess to form the bottom contours of the plate and the foot rim. The mold bat and plate are placed on a conveyor belt that carries them through a dryer. Finally, the plate is removed from the mold, and the seam created where the template and mold meet is trimmed away.

It is difficult to obtain a perfectly uniform thickness in slip casting. Heavy cups with attached handles are often slip cast, but thinner porcelain cups are jiggered, since even the slightest variation would be noticeable. The procedure in jiggering cups and bowls is slightly different: the mold is a hollow form, and the template is shaped to the inside surface of the piece. One method of jiggering cups is to throw a wad of clay into the mold and allow the template to force the clay downward and outward to form the walls of the cup. Another way begins with the throwing of a rough cup form on a potter's wheel. This form is placed into the mold and jiggered. The particular method used would depend largely upon the characteristics of the clay body and to some extent upon the shape desired. The latest machines are completely automatic and produce a fantastic hourly output.

Press Forming

Certain forms can be duplicated very economically by the use of molds in hydraulic presses. Most electrical insulators are made in this fashion, using a nearly dry body with wax as a forming lubricant. The process illustrated is more adaptable to pottery production, provided the shapes are simple and have no undercuts.

The body ingredients are weighed and mixed in a blunger as in the preparation of a casting slip. The resultant liquid is screened and pumped into a *filter press,* an accordionlike machine of metal and canvas that squeezes excess water from the slip, leaving plastic clay. Clay comes from the filter press in slabs about 1 to 1½ inches thick and 16 to 24 inches square. These slabs are then placed in the hopper of a *pug mill,* which operates much like a meat grinder. At one end is a vacuum attachment, which, combined with the compressing action of the screw blades, removes even the smallest air pockets from the clay. This feature not only eliminates possible body defects but also makes the clay more plastic. Though not as crucial as in throwing, the absence of air bubbles in clay used for jiggering and press forming is still important. Male and female (positive and negative) dies shape the form and, under great pressure, squeeze out the excess clay. An unusual feature is that the hard but porous gypsum plaster die has a tubular grid embedded in the plaster. Compressed air flowing from the tubes into the die allows the clay form to be released immediately after pressing. The pressing operation is very rapid. Compressed air released into the lower die breaks the clay suction, and the press rises.

450. Cutting off a section of clay after extrusion from the pug mill.

451–453. *Three steps in the press-forming of a plate.*

451. A disc of plastic clay is placed on the plate mold.

452. The disc is compressed between the two sections of the press mold to form the plate.

453. As the upper section of the mold is raised, the plate form revolves, and a trimming tool removes the excess clay.

right: 454. Press-molding cups.

455–459. *Various steps in the decorating and glazing process.*

455. Initially, the designer develops several patterns.

456. Even in commercial production, stripes are often applied by hand.

Decorating and Glazing

Most commercial potteries employ teams of designers to develop decorative patterns. These designers make scale drawings, which are later converted to decals or to a step-by-step process for the decorators to follow. Some designs consist of both decals for the more intricate patterns and hand-painted stripes or fields of background color. Once the design has been applied, the ware is glazed. The dip method used by studio potters is facilitated in commercial production by enormous vats of glaze. Spray booths—either automatic or hand-operated—are also used for glazing.

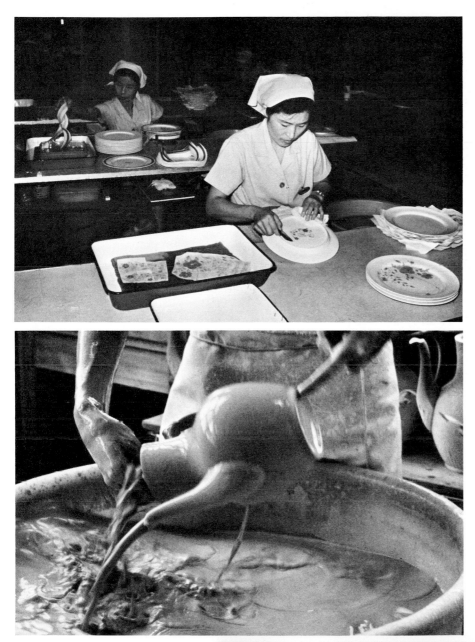

457. Intricate patterns
usually are applied with decals.

458. A coffee pot is glazed
by the traditional dip method.

459. Glaze also can be sprayed on
in a spray booth.

Production Kilns

The term *commercial production* covers a wide range of activities from the manufacture of huge tonnages of building bricks to the forming of minute electrical insulators. Special kilns have been developed to fire the ever-increasing volume of commercial ware. Industrial kilns are not merely larger versions of the small pottery kiln, since a larger kiln is difficult to fire uniformly and has a long cycle of firing, cooling, and loading. Instead, part of the kiln is made movable, as in the car kiln. The car kiln is easy to load and unload and does not lose as much heat in the process as do standard kilns. By placing a door at each end of the kiln, the loading cycle is speeded up even more. This type of construction is called a shuttle kiln.

As lightweight, high-temperature refractories became common, an envelope type of kiln was developed. In this design, two permanent kiln beds are built, and the kiln moves back and forth over them. Its advantages are the smaller floor area required and the fact that lighter kiln furniture can be used, since there is not even the vibration of a moving kiln car. These kilns are available in many sizes, but they are primarily intended for small-size pottery or special-order production.

The huge production of the larger potteries would not be possible without the tunnel kiln, which has continuous operation, with no stoppage for cooling or loading. Figure 461 shows a loaded kiln car entering the tunnel. The chamber is approximately 5 by 9 feet and 200 feet long. The cars, fitted tightly together, move through the kiln at a slow but constant speed, taking 70 to 90 hours to heat, fire, and cool. The entering temperature is 300°F (149°C), which gradually increases to 2300°F (1260°C) in the center section, and then tapers off as the cars move away from the burners. The kiln cars have a heavily insulated floor. A channel iron on the car side usually projects into a sand seal on the kiln wall, which protects the undercarriage from a direct flow of heat. Hot air escaping toward the end sections is piped back to preheat the burner-port air. This factor, plus the possibility of continuous operation for months on end, provides a most economical system.

As would be imagined, loading of this kiln is quite different from that of a small studio kiln. Because of the long firing cycle and the great number of duplicate shapes, a very tight load is possible. However, thin dinnerware pieces must be supported to prevent warpage. It is common practice in dinnerware manufacture to fire the bisque to the maturity of the body while it is well supported. Cups are loaded in pairs, lip to lip, with a weak cement to prevent accidental slippage. Dry refractory clay is shot into openings between stacked dinner plates for support. A coaster of high alumina content is placed under each stack to prevent its sticking to the shelves.

After glazing, the ware is fired at a lower temperature, so that there is no shrinkage and less chance of warping. A studio potter can keep a small kiln relatively clean and need not worry about dust and brick particles in an open glaze fire. However, this is not true of large kilns firing continuously for long periods. To protect the ware in the glaze fire, it is loaded into boxlike forms made of fireclay, called *saggers*.

Figure 463 shows a sagger load of cups after the glaze fire. A layer of coarse silica sand, which does not adhere easily to the thin glaze on the foot

461. A car entering a tunnel kiln with a load of cups stacked lip to lip for a bisque firing.

462. Removing bisqued plates from the kiln. Refractory clay has been shot into the openings between the plates to provide additional support.

463. A sagger load of cups after the glaze firing.

466. A car load of saggers is pushed slowly into the tunnel kiln.

rim, covers the sagger bottom. High-fire porcelains are always fired on the
foot rim in the individual sagger. The foot rims will be unglazed but
smoothly polished. High-fire china ware, such as the sagger load of saucers
shown in Figure 464, is completely glazed. The individual pieces rest on
dowels of porcelain that are inserted into the sagger wall as the pieces are
loaded. This porcelain spur will cause a tiny blemish in the glaze, but it does
provide a great economy in loading and firing. Figure 465 shows the loading
of saggers containing glazed cups and dinner plates.

10
Studio
Equipment

Because of the heightened interest in ceramics in recent years, there has been an increase in firms making kilns, wheels, and other items of studio equipment. Some are obviously more dependable than others. In addition to reading the sales literature, the prospective buyer should seek out local potters and college ceramics departments for their more experienced opinions. In this chapter some of the standard items are illustrated and discussed briefly. The Appendix (p. 322) lists a wide range of manufacturers and suppliers, along with their addresses. Kilns, wheels, and some of the heavier equipment are often available from local supply houses as well as directly from the manufacturer.

Ceramic Kilns

The prospective kiln buyer should first read Chapter 8, which discusses kiln designs in greater detail. After a careful comparison of costs the potter may well decide to build a kiln, especially if a larger size is needed, because these are expensive to ship and subject to damage.

The Electric Kiln

The electric kiln is undoubtedly the first choice for the beginning potter as well as for the public school program. Although it needs a heavy-duty 220-volt line, it avoids the problem of a fireclay-lined chimney or a large-diameter gas inlet. Top-loading units from 3 to 7 cubic feet are the most inexpensive. These come with a nickel-nichrome type element for temperatures below 2000°F (1090°C), or with the heavier kanthol alloy for temperatures to cone 8 (2300°F or 1260°C). For longer operating life the kanthol

167. Paragon top loading electric kiln
for temperatures to cone 8.
Chamber 17 × 17 × 18″ (43 × 43 × 45 cm).

above: 468. Paragon octagonal electric kiln, cone 8. Chamber 7 cubic feet (0.2 m³) with optional 4½″ (11.25 cm) extension.

right: 469. Skutt top-loading electric kiln, cones 6 or 8. Chamber 7 cubic feet (0.2 m³), blank ring available.

element is preferred. However, if this kiln is fired at lower temperatures, the elements will creep out of their recesses. A firing to 2300°F (1260°C) will tend to set them in place. Unlike the kanthol elements, which are hard and rigid, the nickel-nichrome wire remains soft and can be stretched back into place when it contracts.

Electric kilns hold up well if they are not overfired and if no accidents occur in firing. Should a glazed piece explode during firing, the glaze particles are likely to lodge in the element recesses and cause the elements to burn out. Replacements are costly. In addition to the conventional square models (Fig. 467), there are a number of octagonal models on the market (Figs. 468, 469). These have a lighter construction and separate rings that can be added for firing very tall pieces.

Front-loading electric kilns are also available. Because of the heavy frame and electrical connections needed for the door, they are more expensive per cubic foot than the top-loading units. Several sizes are offered, many

left: 470. Unique (Hed Industries)
front-loading electric kiln
for temperatures to cone 10.
Chamber 17 × 17 × 17″ (42.5 × 42.5 × 42.5 cm),
weight 600 pounds (270 kg).

below: 471. Alpine front-loading electric kiln
for temperatures to cone 10.
Chamber 60 cubic feet (27 m³),
shipping weight 8,500 pounds (3825 kg).

of which have commercial uses in the electronic insulator field and are capable of extremely high temperatures (Figs. 470, 471).

With the increased interest in decal and luster decoration potters often find a need in their studios for a small electric kiln. These smaller models are less expensive, because they need only reach temperatures between cones 020 and 010.

A *kiln sitter* is a device that employs a cone and sliding spring mechanism to turn off the power in an electric kiln. Because the metal parts can corrode over a period of time, it will eventually begin to malfunction and is not always a dependable control. Some manufacturers provide *limit timers* with their kilns. These are set to the average number of hours required for a firing (for example, 6 hours for a bisque and 8 or 9 for a glaze) and will automatically shut off the power to the kiln. When used in conjunction with the kiln sitter, the limit timer permits the potter to leave the studio during the later stages of a firing. However, the character of the glaze load may cause firing variations.

The Gas Kiln

The gas kiln, because of its ability to reduce and obtain unusual glaze and body effects, is preferred by most professional potters and college ceramics departments. Gas kilns are available in many sizes and for different purposes. Suitable for the low temperatures of raku firing is the small, lightweight model illustrated in Figure 472. For higher temperatures and a larger chamber, a more conventional design will be necessary (Fig. 473). This is an updraft kiln with a 24-cubic-foot chamber constructed of insulat-

472. Peach Valley Pottery raku kiln with ceramic fiber insulation. Chamber 16 × 24″ (40 × 60 cm), weight 12 pounds (5.4 kg).

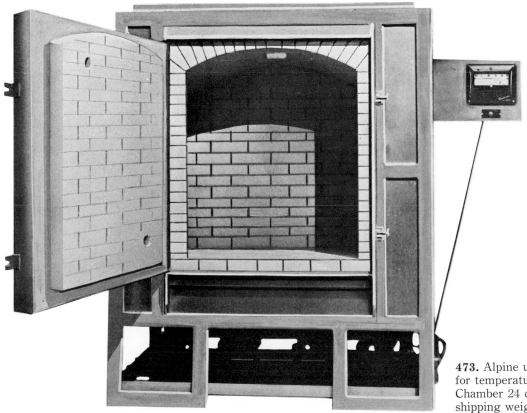

473. Alpine updraft gas kiln for temperatures to cone 14. Chamber 24 cubic feet (0.7 m³), shipping weight 4,000 pounds (1,800 kg).

474. Unique (Hed Industries) downdraft oil or gas kiln for temperatures to cones 8 through 12. Force draft with automatic cutoff controls, capacity 30 cubic feet (0.9 m³).

below left: 475. Westwood updraft gas kiln with ceramic fiber insulation for temperatures to cone 10. Chamber 12 cubic feet (0.36 m³), weight 725 pounds (326 kg).

below right: 476. Marathon shuttle car kiln of ceramic fiber insulation for temperatures to cone 15. Stacking chamber 20 cubic feet (0.6 m³).

ing firebrick with multiple gas burners. A downdraft oil-burning kiln is also suitable for temperatures between cones 8 and 12 (Fig. 474).

The updraft kiln shown in Figure 475 utilizes the newer ceramic fiber insulating materials. This kiln weighs approximately one-third as much as kilns of a similar size made with firebrick, which greatly reduces shipping costs. Fiber insulation kilns are proving to be efficient in terms of firing time and fuel. Catenary-arch and shuttle car models are now being manufactured (Fig. 476).

The professional potter often needs only a single 60-cubic-foot kiln, but a college ceramics department may find that several smaller kilns will better fit the instructional program. In the beginning of the term, when students need the experience of loading kilns and experimenting with glazes, the smaller kilns are useful. However, as the rush begins at the term end to get everything fired, a larger car kiln is a great advantage. Car kilns are convenient to load. They come in both portable updraft models (Fig. 477)

477. Alpine updraft gas car kiln for temperatures to cone 14. Chamber 60 cubic feet (1.8 m³).

478. Unique (Hed Industries) downdraft car kiln for temperatures to cone 12. Chamber 30 cubic feet (0.9 m³).

479. Alpine updraft shuttle-car gas kiln for temperatures to cone 6. Car area 24 × 60 × 25″ (60 × 150 × 63 cm), capacity 20 cubic feet (0.6 m³), shipping weight 7,000 pounds (3,150 kg).

and downdraft types constructed in place (Fig. 478). Both models are available with hard inner liners for use as salt kilns.

Commercial potteries often find that a shuttle car kiln is the most practical design for production (Fig. 479). Shuttle kilns have two sets of cars and two sets of rails. The potter can load one car as the kiln is firing and, as soon as the kiln is cool enough, open the doors and roll the new load in. For firing especially large, sculptural forms, a 90-cubic-foot car kiln will be needed (Fig. 480). The model shown here has a low kiln floor to facilitate loading with a fork lift.

All gas kilns should be equipped with a thermocouple and a solenoid cutoff valve in case of an interruption in gas service. The elaborate controls and regulating pyrometers found on industrial installations are unnecessary on smaller kilns. Final temperatures can be indicated accurately only by pyrometric cones. However, a pyrometer will help to gauge the draft, fuel, and air intake necessary to obtain a proper heat rise (Fig. 481). A permanent installation in a large kiln should be of a type that encases the thermocouple tips in a porcelain tube and protects the metal from corrosive elements in the kiln atmosphere.

480. Alpine updraft gas car kiln for temperatures to cone 14. Capacity 90 cubic feet (2.7 m³), shipping weight 14,000 pounds (6,300 kg).

481. Unique (Hed Industries) pyrometer with insulated leads and thermocouple.

left: **482.** Oak Hill kick wheel.
Waterproof plywood frame,
31″ (78 cm) flywheel,
with 80-pound (36 kg) iron weights;
14″ (35 cm) aluminum wheel head;
shipping weight 170 pounds (77 kg).

above: **483.** Soldner kick wheel.
Welded pipe frame;
reinforced-concrete flywheel, weight 90 pounds (40.5 kg);
aluminum wheel head,
20 × 38″ (50 × 95 cm) work table.
Available with ½-horsepower,
5 to 100 rpm motor attachment.

left: **484.** Denton-Vars side-treadle kick wheel
designed by Bernard Leach.
Hardwood frame, weighted flywheel,
fiberglass pan,
13″ (32.5 cm) aluminum wheel head.

Potters' Wheels

The selection of a suitable wheel is even more important for the beginner than for the experienced potter. Before making a purchase, you should try working on different wheels to find the most comfortable one for you. The cheap models advertised in hobby magazines should be avoided; a good piece of equipment will be costly but it will withstand many years of wear.

A well-designed kick wheel is the best choice for beginning students (Figs. 482–484). When the pot starts to go off center, the tendency is to stop kicking, and slower speeds make it easier to control the clay. It is essential that you be comfortable at the wheel without undue strain during long hours of work and concentration. Your posture should be erect, with your feet and hands braced to provide maximum control.

A number of kick wheels are available with power attachments, in both single- and variable-speed models (Figs. 485–487). The heavy fly wheel must be spinning before the power is turned on, for otherwise the motor is in danger of burning out.

below left: 485. Randall kick wheel. Welded steel frame, 9″ (22.5 cm) aluminum wheel head, splash pan, adjustable bucket seat; 28″ (70 cm) flywheel, standard weight 115 pounds (52 kg), adjustable if desired; shipping weight 200 pounds (90 kg). Available with ½-horsepower motor.

below right: 486. Brent (model J) kick wheel. Welded steel frame, 14″ (35 cm) aluminum wheel head, adjustable seat, 125-pound (56 kg) concrete flywheel; shipping weight 300 pounds (135 kg). Shown with optional ½-horsepower motor.

left: 487. Alpine kick wheel. Welded steel frame, 13″ (32.5 cm) aluminum wheel head, adjustable seat; 28″ (70 cm), 150-pound (68 kg) flywheel; shipping weight 275 pounds (124 kg). Pictured with optional ½-horsepower motor attachment.

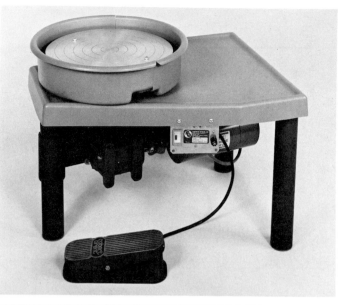

right: 488. Brent (model CX) electric wheel.
with 14″ (35 cm) aluminum wheel head,
plastic work table and splash pan,
1-horsepower motor, foot control;
height 20″ (50 cm),
shipping weight 140 pounds (63 kg).

below: 489. Randall direct-drive electric wheel,
with 18″ (45 cm) aluminum wheel head,
¾-horsepower motor with speeds from 0 to 175 rpm,
foot control; height 20″ (50 cm),
shipping weight 275 pounds (124 kg).
Styles with different wheel heads
and splash pans available.

490. Soldner (model 321) electric wheel, with 14″ (35 cm)
aluminum wheel head, ½-horsepower d.c. motor,
speeds from 0 to 250 rpm, foot control; height 18″ (45 cm).

Although the kick wheel is recommended for students, the production potter will probably need an electric wheel (Figs. 488–494). Motor sizes vary from ¼ to 1 horsepower; the greater the horsepower, the greater the torque. The torque rather than the speed of the motor determines the power of an electric wheel. In any case, the single-speed motor should be avoided, as should motors not capable of variable and quite slow speeds. Speeds in excess of 100 rpm are not necessary if the motor has adequate torque.

Many potters develop back problems from working long hours in a cramped position at their wheels. You should make adjustments to either the wheel or the seat to put as little strain on your back as possible.

above left: 491. Alpine electric wheel,
13″ (32.5 cm) aluminum wheel head,
½-horsepower motor, speeds from 0 to 160 rpm,
foot control; platform height 16″ (40 cm).

above right: 492. Craftool electric wheel,
with 10″ (25 cm) aluminum wheel head,
1-horsepower variable-speed motor
with gear drive.

left: 493. Skutt bench-type electric wheel,
with 12″ (30 cm) wheel head, cast-aluminum frame,
⅓-horsepower motor with variable speeds
of 35 to 125 rpm or 50 to 165 rpm.

below: 494. Shimpo (model RK-2) electric wheel,
with 12″ (30 cm) aluminum wheel head,
¼-horsepower motor, speeds from 20 to 220 rpm,
foot and hand control, switch to reverse wheel head;
height 20″ (50 cm), shipping weight 125 pounds (56 kg).

495. Soldner (model 310)
clay mixer with rotating tub
and 30 × 16″ (75 × 40 cm) steel frame,
3-horsepower motor, 115 or 220 volts,
safety top,
capacity 300 pounds (135 kg) wet clay;
weight 750 pounds (338 kg).

Clay Mixers

The development in recent years of smaller-scale clay processing equipment has been a great boon to the studio potter. The potter who uses from 5 to 20 tons of dry clay per year cannot afford to buy the more expensive bagged plastic clay. In addition, many pounds of clay trimmings and scrap pots must be reclaimed. The blunger and filter press method of preparing clay used by industries is too involved for the small studio. The three machines illustrated (Figs. 495–497) are not unlike commercial bakery dough mixers. In fact, dough mixers can be used for clay, and secondhand models are often available at a reasonable cost. Because of the abrasive nature of clay, the bearings may have to be replaced occasionally. If clay scraps are properly soaked, they can be mixed with dry clay to obtain a uniform body. The hopper-type mixers can be tipped for easy removal of the clay. The pug mills illustrated (Figs. 498, 499) may be more convenient for the small studio. The shearing action of the blades not only mixes the clay but compresses and discharges it in a stiffer consistency than the dough-type mixers.

496. Randall clay mixer.
Overall dimensions 56 × 36 × 34″
(140 × 90 × 85 cm),
capacity 100 pounds (45 kg) dry clay;
3-horsepower motor, 220 or 440 volts;
reduction gear, safety switch
and overload fuse;
shipping weight 600 pounds (270 kg).

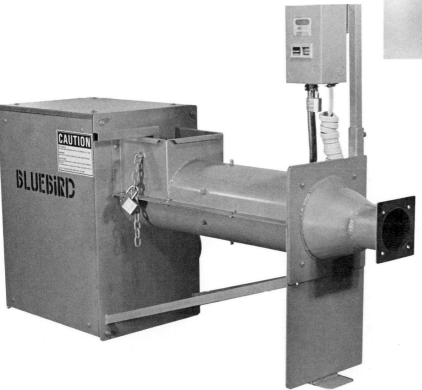

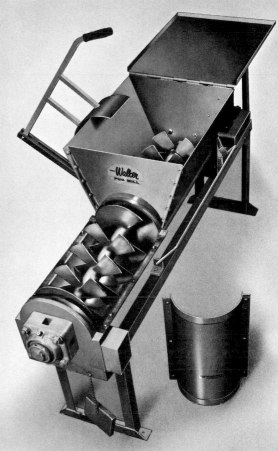

above: 497. Bluebird clay mixer.
Capacity 110 pounds (50 kg) dry clay;
1½-horsepower motor, 220 volts,
safety screen, stainless-steel barrel optional;
shipping weight 380 pounds (170 kg).

above: 498. Walker pug mill,
shown with mixing and
compression screw flight blades,
all operating parts stainless steel.
Overall dimensions 63 × 33 × 36″
(158 × 83 × 90 cm),
hopper size 16 × 20″ (40 × 50 cm);
¾-horsepower, 110-volt motor
with 150:1 reduction gear;
overload switch and knee cut-off bar,
safety lock; weight 270 pounds (122 kg).
A protective screen for school use
(not shown) is available.

left: 499. Bluebird pug mill,
steel or stainless steel,
overall dimensions 27 × 23 × 57″
(68 × 58 × 143 cm),
hopper size 8 × 8″ (20 × 20 cm);
1½-horsepower motor, 220 volts;
shipping weight 285 pounds (128 kg).

Slab Rollers and Extruders

Contemporary interest in large slab constructions and fanciful clay forms has led to the marketing of several new equipment items that save a great deal of labor in the studio. A slab roller, available in various sizes, will roll out a 25-pound mass of clay into a uniform thin slab (Fig. 500).

The clay extruder (Figs. 501, 502) is another time-saving device. Equipped with a die, it will produce strips or ribbons of clay. Metal dies can be used, but it is quicker to make the die shape from a stoneware clay slab. After firing, the die will last almost indefinitely, provided it is used with soft clay. Extruders can be improvised from a length of large-diameter pipe and an old hydraulic jack.

Glaze Room Equipment

Commercial chemicals today are so finely ground that a simple mixing with a wire whisk is usually sufficient. However, certain coarse materials, such as calcined ingredients or volcanic ash, may require the use of a mortar and pestle (Fig. 503) or, for larger amounts, a ball mill (Figs. 504, 505). The portable kitchen food mixer or a paint mixer in an electric drill are quite efficient for mixing moderate quantities of glaze. Brass sieves (Fig. 506) in mesh sizes of 80, 60, 30, 15, and 8 are useful. The finer sizes sift glazes, while the coarser work well for grog.

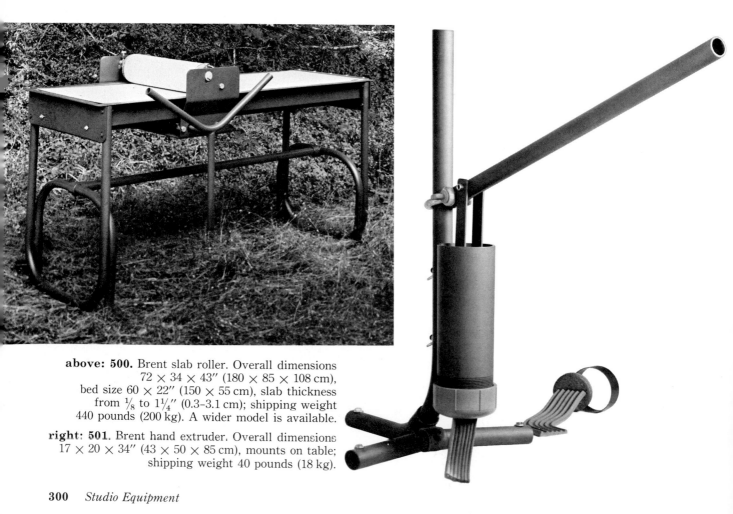

above: 500. Brent slab roller. Overall dimensions 72 × 34 × 43″ (180 × 85 × 108 cm), bed size 60 × 22″ (150 × 55 cm), slab thickness from ⅛ to 1¼″ (0.3–3.1 cm); shipping weight 440 pounds (200 kg). A wider model is available.

right: 501. Brent hand extruder. Overall dimensions 17 × 20 × 34″ (43 × 50 × 85 cm), mounts on table; shipping weight 40 pounds (18 kg).

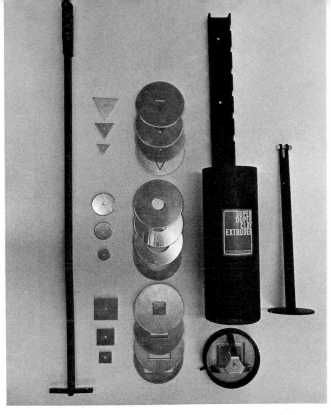

above left: 502. Scott Creek Pottery extruder, $2\frac{1}{2}''$ (6.25 cm) diameter, numerous die sets available, wall mounted.

above right: 503. Porcelain mortar and pestle. Available in 16-ounce (450 g) and 32-ounce (900 g) capacities.

right: 504. Porcelain ball mill jars. Available in gallon, half-gallon, and quart capacities.

below left: 505. Ball mill. Length 20'' (50 cm), $\frac{1}{4}$-horsepower motor.

below right: 506. Brass seive for glazes, available in 8- to 100-mesh sizes.

507. Bluebird hammermill.
Screen sizes $\frac{1}{8}$, $\frac{1}{4}$, and $\frac{1}{2}$ inch,
adjustable for 20-gallon (75 l)
to 55-gallon (200 l) barrel sizes,
$\frac{3}{4}$-horsepower electric or 5-horsepower gasoline motor;
shipping weight 155 pounds (70 kg).

508. Portable paint sprayer suitable for glazes,
with $\frac{1}{4}$-horsepower motor; comes with gun, hose, and nozzles.

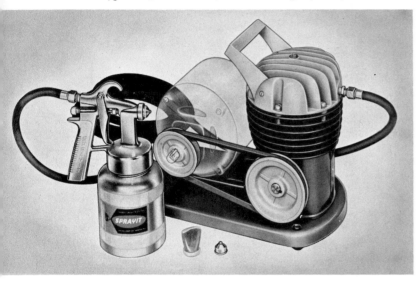

Certain areas of the United States abound with interesting rock formations. Students may be interested in experimenting with them as glaze materials. Pulverizing these materials to an adequate size is a laborious task without mechanical equipment. The hammermill (Fig. 507) operates with either a variable gas or 3-speed motor, is quite portable, and comes in 3 screen sizes. Although the finished product is quite fine, a further grinding in a ball mill might be desirable.

The hammermill is also useful for breaking up calcined mixtures and for producing grog. Heavy pots broken in the bisque fire can be ground down into grog. Glazed ware should be pulverized into very fine particle sizes, because the sharp glaze fragments will cut the fingers if used in a throwing body. Colored clays can also be fired and ground for special effects.

As a rule, glazes are most conveniently applied by pouring, dipping, or brushing. The sprayed glaze is very fragile and can be damaged easily in loading. Nevertheless, certain glaze and decorative effects are best achieved by spraying (Fig. 508). Since the amount of sprayed work is likely to be small, a booth with filters (Figs. 509, 510) rather than a permanent exhaust system will be less expensive and is usually adequate.

above: 509. Craftool portable spray booth, with exhaust fan and fiberglass filters, inside dimensions 30 × 24″ (75 × 60 cm).

right: 510. Craftool spray booth. Exhaust fan and turntable; available with air filter and pressure regulator.

Gram scales (Fig. 511), large pound scales, and banding wheels (Fig. 512) are necessary in every glaze room.

Other Equipment

The amount of heavy materials—bagged clay and chemicals, firebrick, and clay scraps—frequently moved about the ceramics studio necessitate some mechanical help. The common two-wheeled hand cart will aid in moving amounts of bagged clay and cans of wet clay scraps. Ideally, the pottery studio and especially the larger college studios should be located on the ground floor with ample storage space and a convenient loading entrance. Large and inexpensive storage space can be made by building a simple shed on a concrete slab adjacent to the studio. Bricks and clay are generally shipped strapped on wooden pallets and are loaded on both freight cars and motor trucks. Clay is usually loaded 3000 pounds to the pallet. You can save considerably by ordering a one- or two-year supply instead of more frequent smaller orders.

The shop lift (Fig. 513) is indispensible for the larger studio. Clay scrap cans and all clay bags should be placed on pallets in the studio and in the storage area. They can be moved to the clay mixing area on the shop lift. Potters working with large sculptural forms should consider an industrial-type fork lift. Figure 514 shows John Mason, an American sculptor, supervising the moving of one of his pieces.

A great deal of time and effort is expended in carrying individual pots about the studio. Ware racks (Fig. 515) are convenient for storing and moving ware from the throwing to the firing and glaze areas of the studio. Draped with plastic sheets they can serve as extra damp storage.

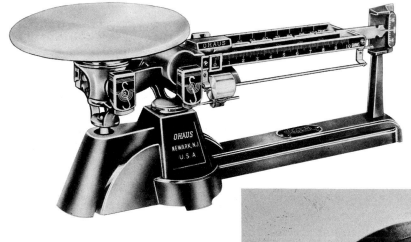

left: 511. Ohaus triple-beam gram scale. Several models with different capacities available.

below: 512. Craftool cast-iron banding wheel, with ball-bearing movement, available with 7″ (17.5 cm) or 10″ (25 cm) wheel head.

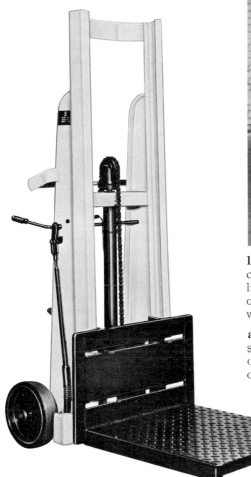

left: **513.** Big Joe hydraulic shop lift,
capacity 1000 pounds (450 kg),
lifting height 54″ (135 cm);
overall dimensions 45 × 29″ (112 × 72 cm),
weight 380 pounds (171 kg).

above: **514.** John Mason
supervising the loading
of a large ceramic sculptural form
on an industrial, electric-powered fork lift.

A plaster bat with a hollowed center section is convenient for drying small batches of clay. One or two large bats, which may hold up to 50 pounds of slip, are also helpful for drying special mixtures. While clay slabs can be rolled out on a sanded table, large flat plaster-of-paris slabs are useful, especially if the clay is a bit moist. In the classroom it is best to have wedging tables at two different heights to accommodate both shorter and taller students. Because of their constant use, a welded-steel base frame is recommended for plaster-faced wedging tables. The plaster must be scraped periodically to remove the colloidal clay particles that would otherwise seal the surface.

All ceramic supply houses offer a wide variety of hand tools—looping tools, scrapers, trimming and plaster tools (Fig. 516). The small elephant-ear sponges are preferable to the manufactured cellulose type for throwing and joining. Try to purchase one with a uniform thin section, because the thick lumpy ones are hard to manipulate. Potters always develop preferences for

515. Unique (Hed Industries)
welded-steel ware rack on casters;
65 × 22 × 28″ (163 × 55 × 70 cm).

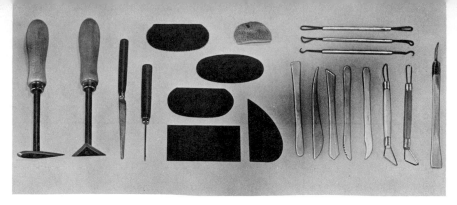

516. Craftool kit of common pottery tools.

particular tools. You may want to carve your own tools from hardwood or improvise hacksaw blades into special metal shapes.

The Ceramic Studio

The general layout of the studio is quite important for both the individual potter and the teacher. Work areas should be laid out in such a way that interference and unnecessary traffic are avoided. Raw materials and clay mixing should be concentrated near the delivery entrance, and this area needs adequate ventilation. A good arrangement is a rather open studio with drop panels from the ceiling to concentrate the kiln fumes and heat, which can then be exhausted from the studio. The throwing, modeling, and decorating areas should be spacious and well-lighted.

Ware racks have been mentioned before as an aid to moving thrown pots from the wheel area to the kilns, from the kilns to the glaze area, and finally back to the kilns for the glaze firing. Sinks should be conveniently located in the several work areas. Plaster work is best concentrated in a single area, and the sink used for this purpose should drain into a large open tank with several baffles to trap plaster particles, which stop up the drains.

A duplicate set of clearly labeled glaze chemicals is desirable in the glaze area. Odd lots of glaze, instead of being discarded, can be mixed together to form a shop (or slop) glaze. Large cans on rollers, some containing water, should be placed in the wheel area for clay trimmings and throwing water, as well as to provide a place to wash tools and hands. (This should not be done in the sinks, for eventually the drains will become clogged.) The aged clay can be reclaimed to serve as a base for new powdered clay in the pug mill or clay mixer.

The classroom-studio really is rather like a small commercial pottery. It should be an airy, clean, and enjoyable place to work. Unless the studio is organized efficiently, both student and teacher can suffer many frustrations. Students must develop the habit of cleaning up as they go along. All students should participate in the loading of the kilns, with the firing entrusted to the advanced students, for these skills are as important to master as throwing.

Clay preparation is a real problem in most studios, for it is laborious and time-consuming regardless of the equipment. Ideally, a rotating team of students can periodically make up clay as it is needed. In practice, some use more than their share, while others forget to reclaim discarded pots or thoughtlessly allow the clay to harden in the drying bats. As a solution many schools pay a few students to make up clay and place it in 25-pound plastic bags, which are sold at cost to the individual student. While this entails a bit of bookkeeping, it does help to eliminate careless studio practices.

Appendices

Reference Tables

Atomic Weights of Common Elements

Element	Symbol	Atomic number	Atomic weight
aluminum	Al	13	26.97
antimony	Sb	51	121.76
barium	Ba	56	137.36
bismuth	Bi	83	209.00
boron	B	5	10.82
cadmium	Cd	48	112.41
calcium	Ca	20	40.08
carbon	C	6	12.01
chlorine	Cl	17	35.457
chromium	Cr	24	52.01
cobalt	Co	27	58.94
copper	Cu	29	63.54
fluorine	F	9	19.00
gold	Au	79	197.20
hydrogen	H	1	1.008
iridium	Ir	77	193.10
iron	Fe	26	55.84
lead	Pb	82	207.21
lithium	Li	3	6.94
magnesium	Mg	12	24.32
manganese	Mn	25	54.93
molybdenum	Mo	42	95.98
neon	Ne	10	20.183
nickel	Ni	28	58.69
nitrogen	N	7	14.008
oxygen	O	8	16.00
palladium	Pd	46	106.70
phosphorus	P	15	30.98
platinum	Pt	78	195.23
potassium	K	19	39.096
silicon	Si	14	28.06
silver	Ag	47	107.88
sodium	Na	11	22.997
sulphur	S	16	32.066
tin	Sn	50	118.70
titanium	Ti	22	47.90
uranium	U	92	238.07
vanadium	V	23	50.95
zinc	Zn	30	65.38
zirconium	Zr	40	91.22

Common Ceramic Raw Materials

Material	Raw formula	Compound molecular weight	Equivalent weight	Fired formula
aluminum hydroxide	$Al_2(OH)_6$	156	156	Al_2O_3
antimony oxide	Sb_2O_3	292	292	Sb_2O_3
barium carbonate	$BaCO_3$	197	197	BaO
bone ash (calcium phosphate)	$Ca_3(PO_4)_2$	310	103	CaO
boric acid	$B_2O_3 \cdot 3\,H_2O$	124	124	B_2O_3
borax	$Na_2O \cdot 2\,B_2O_3 \cdot 10\,H_2O$	382	382	$Na_2O \cdot 2\,B_2O_3$
calcium borate (colemanite, gerstley borate)	$2\,CaO \cdot 3\,B_2O_3 \cdot 5\,H_2O$	412	206	$2\,CaO \cdot 3\,B_2O_3$
calcium carbonate (whiting)	$CaCO_3$	100	100	CaO
chromic oxide	Cr_2O_3	152	152	Cr_2O_3
cobalt carbonate	$CoCO_3$	119	119	CoO
cobalt oxide, black	Co_3O_4	241	80	CoO
copper carbonate	$CuCO_3$	124	124	CuO
copper oxide, green (cupric)	CuO	80	80	CuO
copper oxide, red (cuprous)	Cu_2O	143	80	CuO
Cornwall stone[a]	$(1\,RO \cdot 1.16\,Al_2O_3 \cdot 8.95\,SiO_2)$	652	652	same
cryolite	$Na_3 \cdot AlF_6$	210	420	$3\,Na_2O \cdot Al_2O_3$
dolomite	$CaCO_3 \cdot MgCO_3$	184	184	$CaO \cdot MgO$
feldspar, potash	$K_2O \cdot Al_2O_3 \cdot 6\,SiO_2$	557	557	same
feldspar, soda	$Na_2O \cdot Al_2O_3 \cdot 6\,SiO_2$	524	524	same
kaolin (china clay)	$Al_2O_3 \cdot 2\,SiO_2 \cdot 2\,H_2O$	258	258	$Al_2O_3 \cdot 2\,SiO_2$
kaolin (calcined)	$Al_2O_3 \cdot 2\,SiO_2$	222	222	$Al_2O_3 \cdot 2\,SiO_2$
iron chromate	$FeCrO_4$	172	172	$FeCrO_4$
iron oxide, red (ferric)	Fe_2O_3	160	160	Fe_2O_3
iron oxide, black (ferrous)	FeO	72	72	FeO
flint (quartz, silica)	SiO_2	60	60	SiO_2
fluorspar (calcium fluoride)	CaF_2	78	78	CaO
lead carbonate (white lead)	$2\,PbCO_3 \cdot Pb(OH)_2$	775	258	PbO
lead monosilicate	$3\,PbO \cdot 2\,SiO_2$	789	263	same
lead oxide (litharge)	PbO	223	223	PbO
lead oxide, red	Pb_3O_4	685	228	PbO
lepidolite	$LiF \cdot KF \cdot Al_2O_3 \cdot 3\,SiO_2$	356	356	same
lithium carbonate	Li_2CO_3	74	74	Li_2O
magnesium carbonate	$MgCO_3$	84	84	MgO
manganese carbonate	$MnCO_3$	115	115	MnO
manganese dioxide (black)	MnO_2	87	87	MnO
manganese oxide (greenish)	MnO	71	71	MnO
nepheline syenite[b]	$1\,RO \cdot 1.04\,Al_2O_3 \cdot 4.53\,SiO_2$	447	447	same
nickel oxide, green	NiO	75	75	NiO
nickel oxide, black	Ni_2O_3	166	83	NiO
petalite	$Li_2O \cdot Al_2O_3 \cdot 8\,SiO_2$	197	197	same
plastic vitrox[c]	$1\,RO \cdot 1.69\,Al_2O_3 \cdot 14.64\,SiO_2$	1139	1139	same
potassium carbonate (pearl ash)	K_2CO_3	138	138	K_2O
pyrophyllite	$Al_2O_3 \cdot 4\,SiO_2 \cdot H_2O$	360	360	$Al_2O_3 \cdot 4\,SiO_2$
sodium bicarbonate	$NaHCO_3$	84	168	Na_2O

Common Ceramic Raw Materials—*continued*

Material	Raw formula		Compound molecular weight		Equivalent weight		Fired formula
sodium carbonate (soda ash)	Na_2CO_3		106		106		Na_2O
spodumene	$Li_2O \cdot Al_2O_3 \cdot 4\,SiO_2$		372		372		same
talc (steatite)	$3\,MgO \cdot 4\,SiO_2 \cdot H_2O$		379		126		$3\,MgO \cdot 4\,SiO_2$
tin oxide (stannic oxide)	SnO_2		151		151		SnO_2
titanium dioxide (rutile impure TiO_2)	TiO_2		80		80		TiO_2
wollastonite	$Ca \cdot SiO_3$		116		116		same
zinc oxide	ZnO		81		81		ZnO
zirconium oxide	ZrO_2		123		123		ZrO_2
[a] formula for Cornwall stone	K_2O Na_2O CaO MgO CaF_2	0.4453 0.2427 0.1873 0.0821 0.0421	Al_2O_3 Fe_2O_3 *Mol. weight 652*	1.0847 0.0065	SiO_2	7.796	
[b] formula for nepheline syenite	Na_2O K_2O CaO MgO	0.713 0.220 0.056 0.011	Al_2O_3 *Mol. weight 447*	1.04	SiO_3	4.53	
[c] formula for plastic vitrox	CaO MgO Na_2O K_2O	0.045 0.058 0.054 0.842	Al_2O_3 Fe_2O_3 *Mol. weight 1139.40*	1.693 0.005	SiO_2	14.634	

Analysis of Common Clays and Chemicals

Material	SiO_2	Al_2O_3	Fe_2O_3	TiO_2	CaO	MgO	K_2O	Na_2O	Li_2O	Ignition loss
red Dalton clay	63.2	18.3	6.3	1.3	0.3	0.5	1.6	1.2		6.4
Barnard clay	41.4	6.7	29.9	0.2	0.5	0.6	1.0	0.5		8.4
Monmouth stoneware	56.8	28.5			0.3	0.3	0.3	1.3		12.2
Jordan stoneware	69.4	17.7	1.6	1.3	0.1	0.5	1.5	1.39		6.4
Albany slip	57.6	14.6	5.2	0.4	5.8	2.7	3.2	0.8		9.5
ball clay	51.9	31.7	0.8	1.5	0.2	0.2	0.9	0.4		12.3
sagger clay	59.4	27.2	0.7	1.6	0.6	0.2	0.7	0.3		9.4
fireclay	58.1	23.1	2.4	1.4	0.8	1.1	1.9	0.3		10.5
Georgia kaolin	44.9	38.9	0.4	1.3	0.1	0.1	0.2	0.2		14.21
English kaolin	47.25	37.29	0.84	0.05	0.03	0.28	1.8	0.04		12.21
petalite	77.0	17.5					(0.5)		4.3	0.7
pyrophyllite	73.5	20.0	0.5		0.1		1.4	1.2		3.3
bentonite	64.32	20.7	3.47	0.11	0.46	2.26	2.9			5.15
volcanic ash	72.51	11.55	1.21	0.54	0.68	0.07	7.87	1.79		3.81
plastic vitrox	75.56	14.87	0.09		0.22	0.20	6.81	0.29		2.04
feldspar, potash	68.3	17.9	0.08		0.4		10.1	3.1		0.32
feldspar, soda	66.8	19.6	0.04		1.7	trace	4.8	6.9		0.2
Cornwall stone	72.6	16.1	0.23	0.06	1.4	0.1	4.56	3.67		2.54
nepheline syenite	60.4	23.6	0.08		0.7	0.1	9.8	4.6		0.7
lepidolite	55.0	25.0	0.08				9.0	1.0	4.0	0.92[a]
spodumene	62.91	28.42	0.53		0.11	0.13	0.69	0.46	6.78	0.28

[a] plus 5 percent fluorine.

Analysis of Several Standard Feldspars[a]

Material	SiO_2	Al_2O_3	Fe_2O_3	CaO	MgO	K_2O	Na_2O	Ignition loss
Spruce Pine #4	67.9	19.01	0.05	1.54	trace	4.98	6.22	0.08
Bell	68.3	17.9	0.08	0.4	trace	10.1	3.1	0.32
Eureka	69.8	17.11	0.1	trace		9.4	3.5	0.2
Kingman	66.0	18.7	0.1	0.1		12.0	2.8	0.2
Oxford	69.4	17.04	0.09	0.38		7.92	3.22	0.3
Chesterfield	70.6	16.33	0.08	0.3		8.5	3.75	0.4
Buckingham	65.58	19.54	trace	0.16	0.2	12.44	2.56	0.32
Kona F-4	66.8	19.6	0.04	1.7	trace	4.8	6.9	0.2
Kona A-3	71.5	16.3	0.08	0.4	trace	7.5	4.0	0.2

[a] The variable quality of the feldspar fluxes is a major reason why glaze recipes may need alteration unless materials are identical.

Oxide Equivalents of Selected Commercial Frits[a]

Supplier	Supplier's Frit No.	K_2O	Na_2O	CaO	PbO	Al_2O_3	B_2O_3	SiO_2	Formula weight
Pemco	54		0.32	0.68			0.64	1.47	191
	67	0.12	0.19	0.69		0.37	1.16	2.17	311
	926	0.01	0.31	0.68		0.11	0.61	1.90	225
	83		0.28		0.72	0.20	0.26	2.43	276
	316				1.00	0.25		1.92	364
	349	0.09	0.09	0.58	0.24	0.19	0.36	2.80	313
Ferro	3124	0.02	0.28	0.70		0.27	0.55	2.56	279
	3134		0.32	0.68			0.63	1.47	210
	3211			1.00			1.11		133
	3223		1.00				2.00	5.00	502
	3419		0.28		0.72		0.57	0.89	276
	3386	0.02	0.08		0.90	0.13	1.77	4.42	499
	3396		0.50		0.50		1.00	2.00	332
Hommel	285	0.10	0.90			0.21	0.94	2.72	315
	267	0.13	0.31	0.56		0.29	1.24	2.05	301
	266		0.32	0.68		0.32	1.10	1.31	245
	22			0.47	0.53		0.98	2.88	385
	240		0.28		0.72		0.56	0.90	271
	13		0.30		0.70		0.39	0.41	227

[a] In most cases the above frits will constitute a complete glaze at cone 06.
[b] Cone deformation eutectic for $PbO \cdot Al_2O_3 \cdot SiO_2$ system.

Water of Plasticity of Various Clays

washed kaolin	44.48–47.50
white sedimentary kaolin	28.60–56.25
ball clays	25.00–53.30
plastic fireclays	12.90–37.40
flint fireclays	8.89–19.04
sagger clays	18.40–28.56
stoneware clays	19.16–34.80
brick clays	13.20–40.70

$$\text{water of plasticity} = \frac{\text{weight of plastic sample} - \text{weight of dry sample}}{\text{weight of dry sample}} \times 100$$

Average Temperatures to Which Various Ceramic Products Are Fired

Products	Degrees F
Heavy clay products	
common brick—surface clay	1600–1800
common brick—shale	1800–2000
face brick—fireclay	2100–2300
enamel brick	2100–2300
drain tile	1700–1900
sewer pipe	2030–2320
roofing tile	1960–2140
terra cotta	2070–2320
Pottery	
flowerpots	1580–1850
stoneware (chemical)	2650–2700
stoneware (once fired)	2318–2426
semivitreous ware	2282–2354
pottery decalcomanias	1400–1500
Refractories	
firebrick—clay	2300–2500
firebrick—silica	2650–2750
silicon carbide	3236–3992
White wares	
electrical porcelain	2390–2500
hotel china—bisque	2390–2436
hotel china—glaze	2210–2282
floor tile	2318–2498
wall tile—bisque	1886–2354
wall tile—glaze	1186–2246

Color Scale for Temperatures

Color	Degrees C	Degrees F
lowest visible red	475	885
lowest visible red to dark red	475–650	885–1200
dark red to cherry red	650–750	1200–1380
cherry red to bright cherry red	750–815	1380–1500
bright cherry red to orange	815–900	1500–1650
orange to yellow	900–1090	1650–2000
yellow to light yellow	1090–1315	2000–2400
light yellow to white	1315–1540	2400–2800
white to dazzling white	1540 and higher	2800 and higher

Melting Points of Selected Compounds and Minerals

	Degrees C	Degrees F
alumina	2050	3722
barium carbonate	1360	2480
bauxite	2035	3695
borax	741	1365
calcium oxide	2570	4658
cobaltic oxide	905	1661
copper oxide (CuO)	1064	1947
corundum	2035	3695
cryolite	998	1830
dolomite	2570–2800	4658–5072
ferric oxide	1548	2518
fireclay	1660–1720	3020–3128
fluorspar	1300	2372
kaolin	1740–1785	3164–3245
lead oxide (litharge)	880	1616
magnesium carbonate (dissociates)	350	662
magnesium oxide (approx.)	2800	5072
mullite	1810	3290
nepheline syenite	1223	2232
nickel oxide	400	752
orthoclase feldspar (potash)	1220	2228
potassium oxide	red heat	
rutile	1900	3452
silica	1715	3119
silicon carbide (decomposed)	2220	3992
sillimanite	1816	3301
sodium oxide	red heat	
tin oxide	1130	2066
titanium oxide	1900	3452
whiting (dissociates)	825	1517
zircon	2550	4622

Temperature Equivalents—Orton Standard Pyrometric Cones[a]

Cone number	Large cones		Small cones		Seger cones (used in Europe) Degrees C
	150°C[b]	270°F[b]	300°C[b]	540°F[b]	
020	635	1175	666	1231	670
019	683	1261	723	1333	690
018	717	1323	752	1386	710
017	747	1377	784	1443	730
016	792	1458	825	1517	750
015	804	1479	843	1549	790
014	838	1540			815
013	852	1566			835
012	884	1623			855
011	894	1641			880
010	894	1641	919	1686	900
09	923	1693	955	1751	920
08	955	1751	983	1801	940
07	984	1803	1008	1846	960
06	999	1830	1023	1873	980
05	1046	1915	1062	1944	1000
04	1060	1940	1098	2008	1020
03	1101	2014	1131	2068	1040
02	1120	2048	1148	2098	1060
01	1137	2079	1178	2152	1080
1	1154	2109	1179	2154	1100
2	1162	2124	1179	2154	1120
3	1168	2134	1196	2185	1140
4	1186	2167	1209	2208	1160
5	1196	2185	1221	2230	1180
6	1222	2232	1255	2291	1200
7	1240	2264	1264	2307	1230
8	1263	2305	1300	2372	1250
9	1280	2336	1317	2403	1280
10	1305	2381	1330	2426	1300
11	1315	2399	1336	2437	1320
12	1326	2419	1335	2471	1350
13	1346	2455			1380
14	1366	2491			1410
15	1431	2608			1430

[a] from the Edward Orton, Jr., Ceramic Foundation, Columbus, Ohio
[b] temperature rise per hour

Temperature Conversion Formula

Centigrade to Fahrenheit

example: $100°C \times \dfrac{9}{5} = 180 \quad 180 + 32 = 212°F$

Fahrenheit to Centigrade

example: $212°F - 32 = 180 \quad 180 \times \dfrac{5}{9} = 100°C$

Metric Conversion Tables

When dealing with foreign suppliers or consulting references printed abroad, the potter should be able to convert readily from the American system of weights and measures to the metric system, employed by virtually every country outside the United States. The following tables provide multipliers for converting from metric to U.S. and the reverse; the multipliers have been rounded to the third decimal place and thus yield an approximate equivalent.

Metric to U.S.

to convert from:	to:	multiply the metric unit by:
length:		
meters	yards	1.093
meters	feet	3.280
meters	inches	39.370
centimeters	inches	.394
millimeters	inches	.039
area and volume:		
square meters	square yards	1.196
square meters	square feet	10.764
square centimeters	square inches	.155
cubic centimeters	cubic inches	.061
liquid measure:		
liters	cubic inches	61.020
liters	cubic feet	.035
liters	*U.S. gallons	.264
liters	*U.S. quarts	1.057
weight and mass:		
kilograms	pounds	2.205
grams	ounces	.035
grams	grains	15.430
grams per meter	ounces per yard	.032
grams per square meter	ounces per square yard	.030

U.S. to Metric

to convert from:	to:	multiply the U.S. unit by:
yards	meters	.914
feet	meters	.305
inches	meters	.025
inches	centimeters	2.540
inches	millimeters	25.400
square yards	square meters	.836
square feet	square meters	.093
square inches	square centimeters	6.451
cubic inches	cubic centimeters	16.387
cubic inches	liters	.016
cubic feet	liters	28.339
*U.S. gallons	liters	3.785
*U.S. quarts	liters	.946
pounds	kilograms	.453
ounces	grams	28.349
grains	grams	.065
ounces per yard	grams per meter	31.250
ounces per square yard	grams per square meter	33.333

*The British imperial gallon equals approximately 1.2 U.S. gallons or 4.54 liters. Similarly, the British imperial quart equals 1.2 U.S. quarts, and so on.

Glaze and Stain Recipes

In the past ceramic glaze formulas were discussed with much secrecy. Fortunately, this attitude has changed. What is done with a glaze is much more important than how it is made. It is hoped that the reference tables in this text will allow more time to be spent on actual studio projects.

Regardless of the variety of glazes and decorative devices described, the student should not be too impressed by technique. Many of the finest potters use only a few standard glazes and stains and a minimum of decoration. Techniques are important and should be studied, but they should never overshadow the search for ideas.

The list of glazes in this section will supplement the general discussion of glaze types and the function of the various glaze chemicals (Chaps. 6 and 7). For convenience, the glazes are listed in the form of batch recipes. Because of variations in local chemicals, firing procedures, and so forth, adjustments may have to be made to some of these recipes. Temperatures given are for large-size cones.

Low-Fire Lead* and Alkaline Glazes, Cones 08–04

Cones 05–03, lithium blue

27.0	lithium carbonate
14.1	kaolin
55.9	flint
3.0	bentonite
4.0	copper carbonate

Cones 04–02, barium mat glaze

6.4	whiting
41.6	white lead
21.0	potash feldspar
12.5	barium carbonate
6.7	calcined kaolin
11.8	flint

Cones 08–09, chromium red

70.04	red lead
18.80	flint
2.13	soda ash
9.03	kaolin
5.00	potassium bichromate

Cones 04–02, alumina mat

48.0	white lead
12.0	whiting
21.8	potash feldspar
13.7	calcined kaolin
4.1	kaolin

Cone 04, lithium semiopaque
(from K. Green)

18.5	lithium carbonate
17.6	white lead
8.2	bone ash
6.0	soda feldspar
10.7	kaolin
37.1	flint
1.9	bentonite

Cone 06, lead glaze, resistant to food acids

14.80	white lead
38.17	soda feldspar
6.24	kaolin
16.16	gerstley borate
2.18	whiting
21.16	silica
1.27	zirconium oxide

Cone 04, semimat

5.8	barium carbonate
10.0	lithium carbonate
9.8	whiting
9.8	zinc oxide
22.4	kaolin
42.2	flint

Cone 04, volcanic-ash mat
(from A. Garzio)

22.7	colemanite
5.8	whiting
3.0	barium carbonate
7.0	white lead
5.0	borax
30.0	volcanic ash
20.0	kaolin
3.5	zinc oxide
6.8	tin oxide

Cone 04, semigloss rutile
(from K. Green)

66.00	white lead
5.03	plastic vitrox
15.68	kaolin
13.29	flint
5.70	rutile

Cone 04, lead-borax turquoise, fluid

12.0	whiting
26.0	borax
1.5	soda ash
19.5	white lead
27.5	potash feldspar
13.0	flint
0.5	kaolin
10.5	tin oxide
2.8	copper carbonate

Cone 04, burnt-red glaze

48.2	white lead
7.3	whiting
11.5	kaolin
3.0	zinc oxide

30.0   flint
6.0   tin oxide
4.0   red iron oxide

Cones 08–06, raku glaze

33.5   gerstley borate
50   kaolin
16.5   flint

* In substituting red for white lead, approximately 11½ percent less material is needed for the same PbO.

Medium-Fire Glazes
Cones 2–4

Cones 1–2, clear glaze

52.60   white lead
15.70   soda feldspar
3.36   whiting
2.84   zinc oxide
9.90   flint
15.60   Cornwall stone
0.2   gum tragacanth

Cone 2, plastic vitrox

29.0   white lead
16.7   potash feldspar
44.3   plastic vitrox
10.0   whiting

Cone 4, dinnerware glaze*

51.5   Ferro frit #3124
25.1   Pemco frit #316
4.0   whiting
4.7   kaolin
14.7   flint

Cone 2, colemanite

8.20   calcined zinc oxide
38.50   potash feldspar
17.55   colemanite
6.80   barium carbonate
6.45   talc
22.50   flint

* acid-resistant commercial glaze, containing 0.233 equivalents of PbO.

Medium-Fire Glazes,
Cones 5–6

Cone 5, thixotropic glaze
(this glaze crazes at cone 9)

16   kaolin (EPK)
24   nepheline syenite
60   ferro frit #3124

Cone 6, barium blue

55.5   potash feldspar
41.5   barium carbonate

3.0   zinc oxide
2.0   copper carbonate
1.0   methocel or gum

Cone 6, mat

63.6   potash feldspar
18.3   whiting
9.1   kaolin
4.5   talc
4.5   zinc oxide

Cone 6, ash

38   wood ashes
20   potash feldspar
20   whiting
13   talc
9   kaolin

Cone 6, mat

46.15   nepheline syenite
17.70   kaolin
10.60   talc
3.55   whiting
18.45   flint
3.55   zinc oxide

Cone 6, black mat, oxidization

40   Albany slip
25   kaolin
20   wollastonite
15   nepheline syenite

plus

2.0   red iron oxide
.75   cobalt oxide
0.25   chrome oxide

Cone 6, opaque semimat, oxidization

38   nepheline syenite
10   gerstley borate
15   wollastonite
15   barium carbonate
10   kaolin
5   flint
7   tin oxide

Cone 6, clear glaze

4.8   lithium carbonate
4.5   whiting
11.0   zinc oxide
49.2   potash feldspar
14.4   kaolin
16.1   flint

Cone 6, barium mat

31.0   barium carbonate
3.2   whiting
7.8   zinc oxide
26.8   potash feldspar
9.5   kaolin
21.7   flint

Porcelain
and Stoneware Glazes,
Cone 8

Cone 8, semimat

36.5   potash feldspar
25.7   kaolin
17.5   whiting
12.0   flint
8.2   rutile

Cone 8, lepidolite (crackle glaze)

18.8   lepidolite
43.4   potash feldspar
6.3   cryolite
6.3   bone ash
12.6   whiting
12.6   colemanite

Cone 8, mottled blue

27   barium carbonate
50   potash feldspar
4   dolomite
9   kaolin
9   flint
3.9   copper carbonate

Cone 8, feldspar

44.5   soda feldspar
12.0   whiting
7.3   kaolin
36.2   flint

Cones 7–8, semimat volcanic-ash glaze
(from A. Garzio)

26.7   volcanic ash
7.5   colemanite
19.7   nepheline syenite
6.1   whiting
7.5   magnesium carbonate
7.2   kaolin
5.3   flint

Cone 8, dolomite mat

35   potash feldspar
20   dolomite
10   whiting
5   kaolin
30   flint
3   bentonite

Porcelain
and Stoneware Glazes,
Cones 8–13

Cones 9–10, white mat
(from R. Eckels)

43.0   potash feldspar
18.3   whiting
11.2   flint
22.8   kaolin

4.7 zinc oxide
3.0 rutile
2.0 tin oxide

Cones 10–13 (from A. Garzio)

53.8 potash feldspar
19.2 whiting
19.2 ball clay
4.6 kaolin
3.2 zinc oxide

Cones 8–11, white opaque

45.35 potash feldspar
12.85 kaolin (Florida)
17.50 whiting
1.45 borax
20.50 flint
2.35 zinc oxide
30.20 zircopax

Cones 10–12, mat

40.0 potash feldspar
22.3 whiting
21.0 kaolin
16.7 silica
4.4 titanium oxide

Cone 9, oil spot temmoku

46.5 Albany slip
37.2 potash feldspar
9.3 Kentucky ball clay
4.7 red iron oxide
2.3 borax

Cone 9, opaque

10 gerstley borate
15 talc
5 dolomite
50 potash feldspar
5 kaolin
15 flint

Cone 9, red oxidization

11.5 bone ash
7.7 whiting
4.9 barium carbonate
6.0 talc
54.6 potash feldspar
15.3 flint
(plus 7–11% red iron oxide)

Cone 9, mottled blue-brown

18 whiting
42 potash feldspar
13 kaolin
27 flint
(plus 4% each of rutile and red iron oxide)

Reduction Glazes

Cone 04, celadon

20.5 white lead
1.6 whiting

52.5 soda feldspar
25.4 soda ash
1.5 red iron oxide
2.5 tin oxide
(Grind dry, use immediately if wet. Fire: reduction, cone 012–07; oxidizing, cone 07–04.)

Cone 2, local copper-red reduction (from Harder)

34.00 soda feldspar
28.40 borax
0.75 soda ash
6.60 fluorspar
12.45 kaolin
17.80 flint
2.00 tin oxide
0.50 copper carbonate [plus .5 percent silicon carbide (180 mesh carborundum)]

Cone 6, copper-red reduction (from Curtis)

11.8 white lead
11.8 red lead
5.9 whiting
2.9 kaolin
29.4 flint
29.4 borax
4.4 boric acid
4.4 soda ash
1.7 tin oxide
0.5 copper oxide

Cone 04, copper luster

66.3 white lead
24.5 Cornwall stone
9.2 flint
1.94 cobalt oxide
1.15 copper oxide
9.6 manganese oxide
(Black when thin, copper when thick. Fire: reduction cone 012–07; oxidizing cone 07–04.)

Cone 8, copper-red reduction

27.9 Cornwall stone
32.5 flint
4.0 zinc oxide
9.3 barium carbonate
4.3 soda ash
22.0 borax
2.0 copper carbonate
2.0 tin oxide

Cones 6–8, celadon reduction

62.2 potash feldspar
7.6 whiting
5.0 kaolin
25.2 flint
1.5 red iron oxide

Cones 8–10, celadon

79.5 potash feldspar
6.2 whiting
14.3 flint
2.0 red iron oxide

Cone 8, local copper reduction (from Baggs)

32.8 soda feldspar
1.9 soda ash
28.0 borax
7.3 whiting
12.3 kaolin
17.7 flint
1.8 tin oxide
0.3 copper carbonate
0.65 silicon carbide

Cones 9–11, celadon

26.55 whiting
25.50 Cornwall stone
25.50 kaolin (EPK)
20.40 flint
2.05 red iron oxide

Cones 9–10, copper red

13.0 Ferro frit #3191
44.0 soda feldspar
14.0 whiting
3.0 kaolin (EPK)
25.0 flint
1.0 tin oxide
0.2 copper carbonate
(Add .2 silicon carbide for local reduction.)

Cones 9–11, celadon

27.05 potash feldspar
19.45 whiting
19.80 kaolin
32.70 flint
1.00 red iron oxide

Ovenware and Flameware Glazes

Cones 9–10, flameware glaze (from Ron Propst)

32 lepidolite
25 dolomite
3 whiting
3 talc
2.5 gerstley borate
25 kaolin
9.5 flint

Cone 9, ovenware glaze

21.5 dolomite
18.0 spodumene
3.0 whiting
26.5 potash feldspar
22.0 kaolin
9.0 magnesium zirconium silicate

Crystalline Glazes

Cones 07–05, aventurine

45.7 borax
2.6 borium carbonate

3.3 boric acid
1.7 kaolin
46.7 flint
17.7 red iron oxide
(Grind and use immediately or frit without the clay.)

Cones 3–4, zinc crystal

13.4 soda ash
15.5 boric acid
22.2 zinc oxide
42.8 flint
6.1 ball clay
6.7 rutile
(Grind and use immediately or frit without the clay.)

Cone 11, zinc crystal

45.5 feldspar
15.9 whiting
15.9 flint
22.7 zinc oxide

Cones 03–04, aventurine

94 Ferro frit #3304
19 red iron oxide
6 kaolin (EPK)

Cone 8, zinc crystal (pale green)

11.6 sodium carbonate
6.6 whiting
18.2 kaolin (EPK)
42.2 silica
21.4 zinc oxide
3.1 copper carbonate
5.3 titanium (rutile)
(Grind and use immediately or frit without the clay.)

Cone 11, titanium crystal

25 soda ash
50 flint
25 zinc oxide
10 titanium oxide

Cones 9–10, zinc crystal
(from M. Hansen)

74 Pemco frit #283
21.5 zinc oxide
4.5 flint
1.0 bentonite

#1
plus MnO_2 5 percent
$CuCO_3$ 5 percent
rutile 4 percent

#2
$CuCO_3$ 3 percent
rutile 5 percent

#3
NiO 1 percent
$CuCO_3$ 3 percent

Ceramic Stains*
(For preparation, see Chap. 7)

#1 pink stain

50 tin oxide
25 whiting
18 flint
4 borax
3 potassium dichromate
(Calcine to cone 8; stain is lumpy and must first be broken up in iron mortar, then ground.)

#3 crimson stain

22.9 whiting
6.6 calcium sulfate
4.4 fluorspar
20.8 flint
43.7 tin oxide
1.6 potassium dichromate
(Calcine to cone 8 and grind.)

#5 blue-green stain

41.8 cobalt oxide
19.3 chromium oxide
39.0 aluminium oxide
(Calcine to cone 8 and grind.)

#7 black stain

43 chromium oxide
43 red iron oxide
10 manganese dioxide
4 cobalt oxide
(Calcine to cone 8 and grind.)

#9 red-brown stain

22 chromium oxide
23 red iron oxide

55 zinc oxide
(Calcine to cone 8 and grind.)

#11 yellow stain

33.3 antimony oxide
50.0 red lead
16.7 tin oxide
(Calcine to cone 6 and grind.)

#2 pink stain

50.5 tin oxide
19.0 whiting
7.5 fluorspar
20.5 flint
7.5 potassium dichromate
(Calcine to cone 8 and grind.)

#4 ultramarine stain

50 chromium oxide
12 flint
38 cobalt oxide
(Calcine to cone 8 and grind.)

#6 orange stain

29.8 antimony oxide
12.8 tin oxide
14.9 red iron oxide
42.5 red lead
(Calcine to cone 6 and grind.)

#8 turquoise stain

56 copper phosphate
44 tin oxide
(Calcine to cone 6 and grind.)

#10 brown stain

64.6 zinc oxide
9.7 chrome oxide
9.7 red iron oxide
8.0 red lead
8.0 boric acid
(Calcine to cone 8 and grind.)

#12 black stain

65 chromium oxide
35 red iron oxide
(Calcine to cone 8 and grind.)

* These stains must be finely ground to obtain the desired color.

Clay Bodies

The clay body preferred by the studio potter is quite different from that used by a commercial pottery. For slip casting or jiggering a uniformity of texture is necessary, for obvious technical reasons. Similarly, any impurities imparting color to the body are undesirable. Therefore, bodies used in commercial production are carefully selected, ground, and refined. Plasticity is of minor importance, and, since it is associated with high shrinkage rates, it is avoided.

Local supplies of earthenware and plastic fireclays are available in the United States, particularly in the Midwest. Since they are widely used in cement, plaster, and mortar mixtures, they are competitively priced and generally quite reasonable.

Because the volume of clay used in the school studio will normally be measured in tons per year, both the initial cost and the shipping charges are important. Thus, clay that can be bought locally has a decided advantage, even if it needs a certain amount of sieving or small additions. Occasionally, a truckload of raw clay can be purchased reasonably from a local brick or tile works.

Earthenware bodies present no real problem of supply in the Midwest, since there are many brick and tile factories which also sell bagged clay. Shale clays with coarse particles will cause trouble unless they are run through a sieve of from 15 to 20 meshes per inch. Some earthenware clays contain soluble sulfates, which will form a whitish scum on the fired ware; however, the addition of $\frac{1}{4}$ to 2 percent barium will eliminate this fault. Many such clays will not be very plastic unless they are aged. Adding about 5 percent bentonite, which is extremely plastic, will usually render a short clay workable. Often two clays that alone are not suitable can be mixed together to form a good body. Only experimentation will indicate the necessary changes.

Occasionally, the body will lack sufficient flint to fuse with the fluxes it contains. Cream-colored clays can be rendered more plastic by the addition of ball clays. Talc has some plasticity and is often used in low-fire white ware bodies as a source of both flux and silica. Feldspar, nepheline syenite, and plastic vitrox are also added to various bodies to contribute fluxing qualities.

Stoneware and porcelain bodies are usually compounded from several ingredients. In fact, it is quite rare for a single clay to satisfy all throwing and firing requirements. There is no clay that, by itself, will make a porcelain body. Oriental porcelain is made from one or two claylike minerals which are fairly plastic. Since nothing in the Western world compares with petuntze, porcelain bodies must be compounded from clay and various minerals.

Both stoneware and porcelain will form hard, vitrified bodies at cone 10. The major difference between the two is that stoneware contains some impurities, chiefly iron, which give it a gray or tan color. Both stoneware and porcelain bodies are compounded for varying temperatures and, in the case of porcelain, for different degrees of translucency. Greater translucency is usually obtained by increasing the feldspar ratio, which has the accompanying disadvantage of an increase in warpage when the ware is fired.

Fireclay and stoneware clays differ from pure clay (kaolin) chiefly in that they contain various fluxes and impurities which lower the fusion point and impart a gray, tan, or buff color. Fireclays, which have a more universal industrial use, can be substituted for stoneware. Some fireclays are very plastic and fine enough for throwing. They often contain some iron impurities, which give the body a flecked appearance. Depending upon the firing temperature and the effect desired, it may be necessary to blend in an earthenware or stoneware clay or ingredients such as feldspar, talc, or silica.

The following recipes for clay bodies are included merely as suggestions, since it usually will be necessary to vary these recipes depending upon the raw materials available locally.

Engobes are essentially clay slips, with the significant difference that some engobes are intended for use on either dry or bisque ware, thus necessitating additions of flint, feldspar, and occasionally a flux to the slip in order to adjust the varying shrinkage rates. The general purpose of an engobe is to provide a smoother surface and usually a different-colored base for glaze or brushed decoration.

If the engobe is to be used on a damp piece, a sieved slip of the throwing body can be used, provided the color is not objectionable. The usual colorants can be added, except for the chrome oxides, which react unfavorably with tin. One percent of a strong oxide, such as cobalt, is sufficient, although from 5 to 7 percent of iron or vanadium may be needed. Blistering will result if over 7 percent manganese is used. Five percent of an opacifier is often needed to lighten the color.

Engobes used on leather-hard ware must be adjusted to reduce shrinkage by calcining part of the clay and by additions of flint and feldspar. On dry ware the clay content of the engobe can rarely be more than 40 percent, with the balance composed of flint and feldspar. A 5-percent addition of borax will toughen the surface and aid adhesion.

When used on bisque ware, an engobe must have a clay content of less than 25 percent, or it will shrink excessively and flake off the pot. Furthermore, it must contain sufficient fluxes to fuse with the bisque surface. Its characteristics resemble those of an underfired glaze. In view of the low clay content, a binder may be necessary.

Too thick an application of an engobe on any surface, whether leather-hard clay or bisque ware, will crack or flake off. On the other hand, a thin coating will allow the body color to show through. In addition to the usual finely ground coloring oxides, you can add coarsely ground ores, ilmenite, rust chips, chopped copper scouring pads, and other materials to the engobe. Such additions melt out into the covering glaze with interesting effects limited to the area of the applied engobe.

Suggested Clay Bodies

Cone 08, Egyptian paste (self-glazing body)

40	Buckingham spar
20	flint
15	kaolin
6	bicarbonate of soda
6	soda ash
5	ball clay
5	dolomite
3	bentonite

Colorants for Egyptian paste

purple-blue	¾%	cobalt carbonate
light green	½%	copper carbonate
turquoise	2½%	copper carbonate
yellow	7%	vanadium stain

Cones 08-06, raku body

48	stoneware clay
12	Cedar Heights Redart clay
12	ball clay
20	grog

Cone 04, black basalt body

61	Kentucky ball clay
10	Pemco frit #25
5	nepheline syenite
2	bentonite
3	red iron oxide
2	cobalt oxide
2	manganese dioxide

Cone 6, black basalt body

40	red clay
18	kaolin
15	Kentucky ball clay
16	red iron oxide
6	manganese dioxide
3	bentonite
2	nepheline syenite

Cones 2-8, stoneware body

20	Jordan or Monmouth clay
25	ball clay
30	plastic fireclay
10	nepheline syenite
5	flint
12	grog (fine mesh for wheel work)

Cones 8-10, stoneware body

50	Cedar Heights clay (or Goldart, Jordan, Monmouth)
25	fireclay (APG)
10	Kentucky ball clay
5	flint
5	Cedar Heights Redart

Cone 9, white stoneware body

10	potash feldspar
25	kaolin (EPK)
30	sagger clay
20	Kentucky ball clay
15	flint

Cone 9, porcelain body

50	grolleg (English kaolin)
25	potash feldspar
25	flint (finely ground)

Cones 9-11, porcelain body

27	potash feldspar
45	grolleg (English kaolin)
6	bentonite
26	flint

Cones 8-12, porcelain body

27	ball clay
27	kaolin
27	potash feldspar
19	flint

Cones 10-15, porcelain body

25	ball clay
25	kaolin
25	potash feldspar
25	flint

Cones 9-10, flameware body
(from Ron Propst)

30	spodumene (Kings Mt., 200 mesh)
10	pyrophyllite (Pyrotrol, 200 mesh)
10	feldspar (Kings Mt., 200 mesh)
20	Kentucky ball clay
30	fireclay (A. P. Green)
2	bentonite
1	macaloid

Cone 9, ovenware body

40	spodumene
30	fireclay (A. P. Green)
20	Kentucky ball clay
10	Cedar Heights Redart

Cone 9, ovenware body

30	spodumene
30	sagger clay
20	fireclay (A. P. Green)
10	bonding clay (Cedar Heights)
10	grog (fine mesh)

Thixotropic Clay Bodies
(See medium-fire glaze recipes for a cone 5 glaze.)

cone 5	cone 9	
25	25	Kentucky ball clay
15	15	spodumene
15	15	Kona F-4
15	15	kaolin (EPK)
10	25	flint
20	5	Ferro frit #3110

Casting Slips

Cones 06-05, talc body

16	plastic vitrox
35	ball clay
49	talc

Cones 3-4, parian body

60	feldspar
30	kaolin
10	ball clay

Cones 8-9, porcelain body

20	flint
36	feldspar
30	kaolin
14	ball clay

Colorants for Clay Bodies

The oxides should be added to dry white stoneware or porcelain body ingredients, the mixture seived, and enough water added to make a muddy consistency. After the mixture has set up it should be wedged very well. As with other formulas, these should be tested in small batches.

pink	8% commercial pink stain
yellow	8% commercial yellow stain
yellow	8% rutile
black	½% cobalt oxide, 7% iron chromate
green	½% green chrome oxide
lavender	5% commercial pink stain, ½% cobalt carbonate
blue	½% to 1% cobalt carbonate
brown	3% red iron oxide

Sources of Equipment and Materials

The cost of kilns, wheels, clay, and glaze materials has increased at such a rapid rate in recent years that the potter and the teacher should develop a cost-efficient approach to purchasing. In the college program, a course in kiln building will be of benefit to both the department and the students, and the cost of materials will be much less than that of a manufactured kiln. Wheels, kilns, pug mills, and so forth available through local ceramic-supply houses, as well as from their manufacturers. Quite frequently a discount will be allowed by the dealers to schools. In case of damage or needed repairs, a local dealer will be of more assistance than a more distant source.

The price of clay, which seems so cheap by the pound, mounts alarmingly for the enormous quantities used in the classroom. The shipping costs often total as much as three times the actual cost of the clay at the mine. Considerable savings result from quantity purchases. Several potters or even nearby schools can share in a large shipment, since the relative shipping cost for a single ton is much more than for twenty tons. Fireclays have many industrial applications and are available at building supply houses. Plastic fireclay is a suitable base for a stoneware body. Earthenware clays are often used commercially to make concrete more dense and waterproof. They may be sold under a trade name, but they are essentially clays suitable for both earthenware and stoneware bodies. Many are of a shale origin and need sieving, but they are relatively inexpensive and therefore worth the bother.

The public school teacher, often limited by time, cannot arrange the usual studio procedures, especially complex glaze formulation. It is wasteful to buy the expensive little 1-pound glaze packets, when frits in 100-pound lots are much more economical. Most fire to cone 06, but the addition of 10 percent kaolin will increase adhesive properties and lower the maturing temperature to cone 04. Coloring oxides can be purchased in 1- to 10-pound lots. Since these are used in relatively small amounts, the total cost per pound of glaze will be small. Due to the dangers resulting from improper compounding of lead glazes, the borosilicate frits are recommended.

Manufacturers

Kilns

A-1 Kiln Manufactures (electric), 369 Main St., Ramona, Calif. 92065

American Art Clay Co. (electric), 4717 W. 16th St., Indianapolis, Ind. 46222

A. D. Alpine, Inc. (gas & electric), 3051 Fujita St., Torrance, Calif. 90505

California Kiln Co. (gas), 3036 Oak St., Santa Ana, Calif. 92707

Cress Mfg. Co. (electric), 1718 Floradale Ave. South, El Monte, Calif. 91733 or 201 Bradshaw Pike Ext., Hopkinsville, Ky. 44240

Crusader Industries, Inc. (electric), 937 S. Washington, Holland, Mich. 49423

Geil Kilns (gas), Box 504, Hermosa Beach, Calif. 90254

Hed Industries (Unique Kilns, gas, oil & electric), Box 176, Pennington, N.J. 08534

L & L Mfg. Co. (electric), Box 348, 144 Conchester Rd., Twin Oaks, Pa. 19104

Marathon Potter (gas), 2008½ Preuss Rd., Los Angeles, Calif. 90034

Olsen Kilns (gas), Pinyon Crest, Box 205, Mountain Center, Calif. 92361

Olympic Kilns (electric), 2222 N. Pacific St., Seattle, Wash. 98103

Paragon Industries (electric), Box 10133, Dallas, Tex. 75207

Peach Valley Pottery (raku), Rt. #1, Box 101, New Castle, Colo. 81647

Skutt Ceramic Products, Inc. (electric), 2618 S.E. Steele St., Portland, Ore. 97202

Warrington Engineering Co. (electric & gas), 2048 Bunnell Rd., Warrington, Pa. 18976

Westby Supply and Mfg. Co. (gas), 620 85th St., Seattle, Wash. 98103

Westwood Ceramic Supply Co. (gas), 14400 Lomitas Ave., City of Industry, Calif. 91744

Potter's Wheels

A. D. Alpine, Inc. (kick & electric), 3051 Fujita St., Torrance, Calif. 90505

Robert Brent Corp. (kick & electric), 128 Mill St., Healdsburg, Calif. 95448

Conway Wheels (kick & electric), P.O. Box 4032, Boulder, Colo. 80302

Craftool Co., Inc. (electric), 2323 Reach Rd., Williamsport, Pa. 17701.

Creative Industries (electric), P.O. Box 343, La Mesa, Calif. 92041

Earth Treasurers Mfg. (electric), P.O. Box 1267, Rt. 150, East Galesburg, Ill. 61401

Holmgren Corp. (kick), P.O. Box E-816, 102 Wamsutta, New Bedford, Me. 02742

Menco Engineers, Inc. (electric), 5520 Crebs Ave., Tarzana, Calif. 91356

Oak Hill Industries, Inc. (kick), 335 N. Utah Ave., Davenport, Iowa 52804

Oscar-Paul Corp. (electric), 522 W. 182nd St., Gardena, Calif. 90248

Pacifica Wheels (kick & electric), P.O. Box 1407, Ferndale, Wash. 98248

Randall Pottery, Inc. (kick & electric), Box 774, Alfred, N.Y. 14802

Shimpo-West (electric), P.O. Box 2305, Bassett, Calif. 91744

Skutt Ceramic Products (electric), 2618 S.E. Steele St., Portland, Ore. 97202

Soldner Pottery & Equipment, Inc. (kick & electric), P.O. Box 428, Silt, Colo. 81652

Denton M. Vars (kick), 825 W. Minnehaha Ave., St. Paul, Minn. 55104

Clay Mixers

A. D. Alpine, Inc., 3051 Fujita St., Torrance, Calif. 90505

Bluebird Mfg., 100 Gregory Rd., Fort Collins, Colo. 80521

Walker Jamar Co. Inc., 365 S. First Ave., E. Duluth, Minn. 55802

Peter Pugger, 1402 Palm St., San Luis Obispo, Calif. 93401

Randall Pottery, Inc., Box 774, Alfred, N.Y. 14802

Soldner Pottery Equipment, Inc., P.O. Box 428, Silt, Colo. 81652

Webco Supply Co., Inc., P.O. Box 6054, Tyler, Tex. 75711

Slab Rollers and Extruders

Bailey Pottery Equipment, Hemingway Rd., Brant Lake, N.Y. 12815

Robert Brent Corp., 128 Mill St., Healdsburg, Calif. 95448

Menco Engineers, Inc., 5520 Crebs Ave., Tarzana, Calif. 91356

North Star Equipment, Box 21, Auburn, Wash. 98002

Scott Creek Pottery, 482 Swanton Rd. Davenport, Calif. 95017

Miscellaneous Equipment

Bluebird Mfg. (hammermill), 100 Gregory Rd., Fort Collins, Colo. 80521

Big Joe Mfg. Co. (forklift), 7225 N. Koster Ave., Chicago, Ill. 60646

Kiln Burners

A. D. Alpine, Inc., 3051 Fujita St., Torrance, Calif. 90505

California Kiln Co., Inc., 3036 S. Oak St., Santa Ana, Calif. 92707

Eclipse Engineering, 1105 Buchanan, Rockford, Ill. 61101

Flynn Burner Corp., 432 Fifth Ave., New Rochelle, N.Y. 10802

Charles A. Hones (buzzer burners), 130 Grand Ave., Baldwin, N.Y. 11510

Johnson Gas & Appliance Co., 1940 O'Donnell St., Cedar Rapids, Iowa 52400

North American Mfg. Co., 4455 E. 71 St., Cleveland, Ohio 44105

Pyronics, Inc., 17700 Miles Ave., Cleveland, Ohio 44128

Surface Combustion Co. (Div. Midland Ross), 2389 Dorr St., Toledo, Ohio, 43601

Weldit Div. (Turner Co.), 821 Park Ave., Sycamore, Ill. 60178

L. B. White Co., 1825 Thomas Rd., Onalaska, Wis. 54650

A few U.S. and many Canadian potters are using a very efficient type of oil and gas burner manufactured by the Auto Combustion Ltd., 360 Wandsworth Rd., London SW8 4TF, England.

Refractory Materials

Most large building supply dealers carry firebrick, insulating brick and castables. The following manufacturers will supply addresses of regional sources.

Aluminum Co. of America, 1501 Alcoa Bldg., Pittsburg, Pa. 15219

Babcock & Wilcox (Refractories Div.), 1288 Merry St., Augusta, Ga. 30903

Chicago-Wellsville Firebrick Co., 1467 N. Elston Ave., Chicago, Ill. 60622

Johns-Manville Corp., 22 E. 40th St., New York, N.Y. 10016

A. P. Green Refractories Co., Mexico, Mo. 65265

Kaiser Refractories, Kaiser Center, Oakland, Calif. 94604

Kiln Shelves

A. D. Alpine, Inc., 3051 Fujita St., Torrance, Calif. 90505

Carborundum Co. (Refractories & Electronics Div.), Box 337, Niagara Falls, N.Y. 14302

New Castle Refractories, Box 471, New Castle, Pa. 16103

Westwood Ceramic Supply Co., 14400 Lomitas Ave., City of Industry, Calif. 91744

Clays

Bell Operations, 157 Virginia Ave., Chester, W. Va. 26034

L. H. Butcher Co., 15th & Vermont Sts., San Francisco, Calif. 94107

Cedar Heights Clay Co., 50 Portsmouth Rd., Oak Hill, Ohio 45656

Edgar Plastic Kaolin Co., Edgar, Fla. 32049

Georgia Kaolin Co., 433 N. Broad St., Elizabeth, N.J. 07207

Hammill & Gillespie, Inc., P.O. Box 104, 154 S. Livingston Ave., Livingston, N.J. 07039

J. M. Huber Corp., Huber, Ga. 31040

Industrial Minerals Co., 1057 Commercial St., San Carlos, Calif. 94070

Interpace Corp., 2901 Los Feliz Blvd., Los Angeles, Calif. 90039

Kentucky-Tennessee Clay Co., Box 477, Mayfield, Ky. 42066

H. C. Spinks Clay Co., Box 820, Paris, Tenn. 38242

Western Stoneware Co., Monmouth, Ill. 61462

Ceramic Chemicals & Colors

L. H. Butcher Co., 15th & Vermont Sts., San Francisco, Calif. 94107

Ceramic Color & Chemical Mfg. Co., P.O. Box 297, New Brighton, Pa. 15066

Hercules, Inc. (Drakenfeld Div.), Box 519, Washington, Pa. 15301

Ferro Corp (Color Div.), 4150 E. 56th St., Cleveland, Ohio 44105

General Color & Chemical Co., Inc., Box 7, Minerva, Ohio 44657

Harshaw Chemical Co., 1945 E. 97th St., Cleveland, Ohio 44106

O. Hommel Co., Box 475, Pittsburg, Pa. 15230

Kraft Chemical Co., 917 W. 18th St., Chicago, Ill. 60608

Mason Color & Chemical Works, Inc., Box 76, 206 Broadway, East Liverpool, Ohio 43920

Pfizer Minerals (Pigments & Metals Div.), 235 E. 42nd St., New York, N.Y. 10017

Trinity Ceramic Supply, Inc., 9016 Diplomacy Row, Dallas Tex. 75247

Whittaker, Clark & Daniels, 100 Church St., New York, N.Y. 10007

Local Supply Houses
Clay, Chemicals, Kilns, Wheels, Etc.

East Coast

Baldwin Pottery, 540 La Guardia Pl., New York, N.Y. 10012

Bennett Pottery Supply, Inc., 707 Nicolet Ave., Winter Park, Fla. 32789

Byrne Ceramic Supply Co., Inc., 95 Bartley Rd., Flanders, N.J. 07836

Ceramic Supplies, Inc., 369 Mill Rd., East Aurora, N.Y. 14052

Clay Art Center, 40 Beech St., Port Chester, N.Y. 10573 or 342 Western Ave., Brighton, Mass. 02135

Creek-Turn Ceramic Supply, Rt. 38, Hainesport, N.J. 08036

Delta Clay Co., 5272 Highway 42, Ellenwood, Ga. 30049

Eagle Ceramics, Inc., 12264 Wilkins Ave., Rockville, Md. 20852

Earthworks, 2309 W. Main St., Richmond, Va. 23220

Earthworks Studio Supply Ltd., 420 Merchants Rd., Rochester, N.Y. 14609

Arch T. Flower Co., Queen St. & Ivy Hill Rd., Philadelphia, Pa. 19118

Kickwheel Pottery & Supply, 802 Miami Circle N.E., Atlanta, Ga. 30324

Miller Ceramic, Inc., 8934 N. Seneca St., Weedsport, N.Y. 13166

New England Ceramic and Kiln Supply (Div. Cutter Firebrick Co.), P.O. Box 151, 54 Emerson Rd., Waltham, Mass. 02154 or corner of Lee Mac Ave. and Shelter Rock Rd., Danbury, Conn. 06810

Salem Craftsmen's Guild, 3 Alvin Pl., Upper Montclair, N.J. 07043

Stewart Clay Co., P.O. Box 18, 400 Jersey Ave., New Brunswick, N.J. 08902

Midwest & South

American Art Clay Co., Inc., 4717 W. 16th
St., Indianapolis, Ind. 46222

A. R. T. Studio, 921 Oakton St., Elk Grove,
Ill. 60007

Cecas Enterprises, Inc., 29 W. Batavia Road,
Warrensville, Ill. 60555

The Earthen Vessel, 7116 Miami Rd., Cincinnati, Ohio 45243

L. & R. Specialties, P.O. Box 309, 202
E. Mt. Vernon, Nixa, Mo. 65714

Medusa Pottery Supply, 608 Lafayette Ave.,
Grand Haven, Mich. 49417

Minnesota Clay Co., 8001 Grand Ave.,
S. Bloomington, Minn. 55420

Ohio Ceramic Supply, P.O. Box 630, Kent,
Ohio, 44240

Owl Creek Pottery, 11416 Shelbyville Rd.,
Louisville, Ky. 40243

Paramount Ceramics, 220 N. State St., Fairmount, Minn. 56031

Robbins Clay Co., 1021 W. Lill St., Chicago,
Ill. 60614

Rovin Ceramics, 6912 Schaefer Rd., Dearborn, Mich. 48126

Wilmars Ceramic Supply, 1121 Bolton St.,
Alexander, La. 71301

West & Pacific Coast

Anhowe Ceramic Supply Inc., 3825 Commercial N.E., Albuquerque, N.M. 87107

Capitol Ceramic, Inc., 2174 S. Main St., Salt
Lake City, Utah 84115

Ceramics, Hawaii Ltd., 543 South St., Honolulu, Hawaii 96813

Ceramic Store, Inc., 706 Richmond Ave.,
Houston, Tex. 77006

Good Earth Clays, Inc., 3054 S.W. Blvd.,
Kansas City, Mo. 64108

Seattle Pottery Supply, 400 E. Pine St., Seattle, Wash. 98122

Leslie Ceramics Supply Co., 1212 San Pablo
Ave., Berkeley, Calif. 94706

Montana Ceramic Supply, 2016 Alderson
Ave., Billings, Mont. 59101

Sherry's Ceramic Supply Co., 948 Washington St., San Carlos, Calif. 94070

Van Howe Ceramic Supply, 11975 E. 40th St.,
Denver, Colo. 80239

Way-Craft, 394 Delaware St., Imperial Beach,
Calif. 92032

Webco Supply Co., Inc., P.O. Box 6054, Tyler,
Tex. 75711

Western Ceramic Supply Co., 1601 Howard
St., San Francisco, Calif. 94103

Westwood Ceramic Supply Co., 14400 Lomitas Ave., City of Industry, Calif. 91744

Sources of Materials and Equipment in Canada

Clays

A. P. Green Firebrick Co., Rosemount Ave.,
Weston, Ont.

Baroid of Canada, Ltd., 5108 Eighth Ave.,
S.W., Calgary, Alta.

Jean Cartier, 1029 Bleury St., Montreal, P.Q.

Clayburn Harbison, Ltd., 1690 W. Broadway,
Vancouver, B.C.

Maycobac Mining Co., 510 Fifth St., S.W.,
Calgary, Alta.

Pembena Mountain Clay, 945 Logan, Winnipeg, Man.

Plainsman Clays, Box 1266, Medicine Hat,
Alta., T1A 7M9

Saskatchewan Clay Products, P.O. Box 970,
Estevan, Sask.

Glaze Materials

Barrett Co., Ltd., 1155 Dorchester Blvd.,
W. Montreal, P.Q.

Blyth Colors, Ltd., Toronto, Ont.

Ferro Enamels, P.O. Box 370, 26 Davis Rd.
Oakville, Ont.

E. Harris & Co. of Toronto Ltd., 73 King St.,
East Toronto, Ont.

Clay Mixers

Estrin Mfg. Ltd., 1916 Fir St., Vancouver,
B.C. V3J 3B3

Local Supply Houses
Clay, Chemicals, Wheels, Kilns, etc.

Alberta Ceramic Supplies, Ltd., 11565 149th
St., Edmonton, Alta.

Ceramic Supply Depot, 837B 50th St. E.,
Saskatoon, Sask.

Cobequid Ceramics, Ltd., 43 Forrester St.,
Truro, N.S.

Greater Toronto Ceramic Center, 167 Lakeshore Rd., Toronto, Ont.

Island Ceramic Supplies, Island Highway,
Nanaimo, B.C.

Jonasson Ceramic Supply Ltd., 267 Maryland
St., Winnipeg, Man.

Lewiscraft Supply House, 28 King St., West
Toronto, Ont.

Mercedes Ceramic Supply, 8 Wallace St.,
Woodbridge, Ont.

Pottery Supply House, 2070 Speers Rd., Oakville, Ont. L6J 5H2

Regina Ceramics, Ltd., 1733 McAra St., Regina, Sask.

Terra Ceramic Supplies, Ltd., 518 42nd Ave.
S.E., Calgary, Alta.

Tucker's Pottery Supplies, 30 Esna Park Dr.,
Unit #22, Markham, Ont.

Uniceram, Inc., 4070 St.-P.Q. Denis, Montreal

Sources of Materials and Equipment in England

Kilns and Burners

Auto Combustion Ltd., 360 Wandsworth Rd.,
London SW8 4TF _____

British Ceramic Service Co., Ltd., Bricesco
House, Wolstanton, Newcastle, Staffs.

Catterson-Smith Ltd., Tollesbury, nr. Moldon, Essex

Cromartie Kilns, Parkhall Rd., Stoke-on-Trent, Staffs. ST3 5AY

Kilns & Furnaces Ltd., Tunstall, Stoke-on-Trent, Staffs.

Potter's Wheels

Catterson-Smith Ltd., Tollesbury, nr.
Moldon, Essex

Ferro Ltd., Womborne, Wolverhampton WV5
8DA

Potters Equipment Co., 73 Britannia Rd.,
London

Robinson Ceramics, 3 Booth House, Holmfirth, Huddersfield

Woodley's Potters Wheel, Ltd., Newton Poppleford, Devon EX10 OBJ

Glaze Materials

Fulham Pottery, Ltd., 210 New Kings Rd.,
London SW6 4NY

Thomas E. Gray & Co., Ltd., 37 Headlands,
Kettering, Northants.

Harrison Mayer Ltd., Meir, Stoke-on-Trent,
Staffs. 5T3 7PX

Wengers, Ltd., Etruria, Stoke-on-Trent,
Staffs. ST4 7BQ

Clays

The Diamond Clay Co., Ltd., Hartshill,
Stoke-on-Trent, Staffs.

W. Doble & Sons, St. Agnes, Cornwall

English China Clay Sales Co., Ltd., John
Keary House, St. Austell, Cornwall

Fulham Pottery, Ltd., 210 New Kings Rd.,
London SW6 4NY

Thomas E. Gray & Co., Ltd., 37 Headlands,
Kettering, Northants.

Moria Pottery Co., Ltd., Burton-on-Trent,
Staffs. DE12 6DF

Podmore & Sons, Ltd., Shelton, Stoke-on-Trent, Staffs.

Potclays, Ltd., Brickkiln La., Etruria, Stoke-on-Trent, Staffs.

Watts, Blake, Bearne & Co., Ltd., Park
House, Courtency Park, Newton Abbot,
Devon. TQ12 4PS

General Supply Houses
Clay, Chemicals, Wheels, Kilns, etc.

Thomas E. Gray & Co., Ltd., 37 Headlands,
Kettering, Northants.

Fulham Pottery, Ltd., 210 New Kings Rd.,
London SW6 4NY

Harrison Mayer, Ltd., Stoke-on-Trent, Staffs.
ST3 7PX

Wengers, Ltd., Etruria, Stoke-on-Trent,
Staffs. ST4 7BQ

Bibliography

References

Leach, Bernard. *A Potter's Book.* Levittown, N.Y.: Transatlantic Arts, 1965. Now in its 18th edition, this text continues to be the "bible" of the potter interested in functional ware.

Rhodes, Daniel. *Clay and Glazes for the Potter.* Rev. ed. Radnor, Pa.: Chilton, 1973. A complete and well-illustrated treatment of clay, glazes, and calculations.

———. *Kilns: Design, Construction, and Operation.* Radnor, Pa.: Chilton, 1968. The historical development, design and materials, and operating procedures of kilns, with numerous illustrations.

———. *Stoneware and Porcelain: The Art of High-Fired Pottery.* Radnor, Pa.: Chilton, 1959. A companion book to *Clay and Glazes for the Potter* with an emphasis on high-fire glazes and bodies.

Sanders, Herbert H. *How to Make Pottery.* New York: Watson-Guptill, 1974. A short but complete and well-illustrated text on forming techniques.

Supplemental Texts

Billington, Dora M. *The Technique of Pottery.* London: B. T. Batsford, 1962. A good, basic text.

Berenson, Paulus. *Finding One's Way with Clay: Pinched Pottery and the Color of Clay.* New York: Simon & Schuster, 1972.

Chapell, James. *The Potter's Complete Book of Clay and Glazes.* New York: Watson-Guptill, 1977. Detailed material on a wide range of bodies and glazes.

Colson, Frank. *Kiln Building with Space Age Materials.* New York: Van Nostrand Reinhold, 1975.

Conrad, John W. *Ceramic Formulas: The Complete Compendium.* New York: Macmillan, 1973.

Fournier, Robert. *An Illustrated Dictionary of Practical Pottery.* Rev. ed. New York: Van Nostrand Reinhold, 1973.

Fraser, Harry. *Glazes for the Craft Potter.* New York: Watson-Guptill, 1974. A basic text on the formulation and testing of glazes.

Greabnier, Joseph. *Chinese Stoneware Glazes.* New York: Watson-Guptill, 1975. An excellent treatment of Chinese glazes with formulas.

Green, David. *Pottery: Materials and Techniques.* New York: Praeger, 1967. Although oriented toward materials available in England, this text will be of interest to all students.

Harvey, Roger, John Kolb, and Sylvia Kolb. *Building Pottery Equipment.* New York: Watson-Guptill, 1974.

Kenney, John. *Ceramic Sculpture.* Radnor, Pa.: Chilton, 1953.

Koenig, J. H., and W. H. Earhart. *Literature Abstracts of Ceramic Glazes.* Ellenton, Fla.: College Institute, 1951. Formulas from many technical sources, although somewhat dated at present.

Malmstrom, Margrit. *Terracotta: The Technique of Fired Clay Sculpture.* New York: Watson-Guptill, 1977.

Norton, F. D. *Ceramics for the Artist Potter.* Reading, Mass.: Addison-Wesley, 1956. A comprehensive treatment of techniques and glazes.

Parmalee, Cullen W., and Cameron G. Harman. *Ceramic Glazes.* Boston: Cahners, 1973. A revised edition of the standard text on chemicals and glazes.

Reigger, Hal. *Raku: Art and Technique.* New York: Van Nostrand Reinhold, 1970. A short but fairly complete treatment of raku procedures and kilns.

Rhodes, Daniel. *Pottery Form.* Radnor, Pa.: Chilton, 1977. Ceramic form as it evolves from imagination and tradition, as well as technique.

Sanders, Herbert H. *Glazes for Special Effects.* New York: Watson-Guptill, 1974. A beautifully illustrated text dealing primarily with iron and copper reduction, crystalline, luster, and raku glazes.

———. *The World of Japenese Ceramics.* Palo Alto, Calif.: Kodansha International, 1967. The many techniques shown will be of interest to all potters, as will the many illustrations.

Troy, Jack. *Salt-Glazed Ceramics.* New York: Watson-Guptill, 1977.

Winter, Thelma Frazier. *The Art and Craft of Ceramic Sculpture.* New York: Wiley, 1974.

Magazines

Ceramics Monthly, 1609 Northwest Blvd., P.O. Box 12448, Columbus,

Ohio 43212. Covers the North American ceramic scene, with many illustrations and useful articles for the student potter.

Craft Horizons, 16 East 52nd Street, New York, N.Y. 10022. Contemporary, historical, and related craft fields are featured in this publication of the American Crafts Council.

Studio Potter, Box 172, Warner, N.H. 03278. A well-illustrated semiannual publication with many practical articles on all aspects of ceramics. Especially recommended for the serious potter.

Foreign Publications

Dansk Kunstaandvaerk, Palaegade 4, Copenhagen, Denmark. Covers the entire Danish design field; well illustrated. Many sections are in English.

Designed in Finland, Finnish Foreign Trade Association, E. Esplanaadik 18, Helsinki. Illustrated booklet on Finnish design published each year with English text.

Domus, via Monte di Pieta 15, Milan, Italy. Covers the decorative arts fields, emphasizing architecture, beautifully illustrated.

Form, Svenska Slöjdföreningen, Nybrogatan 7, Stockholm, Sweden. This journal of the Swedish Design Society covers all design fields; well illustrated. Contains a short English section.

Kontur, Svenska Slöjdföreningen, Nybrogatan 7, Stockholm, Sweden. Beautifully illustrated booklet on Swedish design and crafts, published once a year. Text in English.

Kunst+Handwerk, Arnold-Heise Str. 23, Hamburg 20, Germany. Industrial design and handcrafts in Germany and Europe. Well illustrated, with German text.

La Ceramica, via F. Corridoni 3, Milan, Italy. Although an industrial publication, many articles concern studio potters and sculptors. English summary very short.

Pottery Quarterly, Northfields, Tring, Herts., England. A variety of articles, both historical and contemporary, as well as critiques. Well-illustrated.

Pottery in Australia, 30 Turramurra Avenue, Turramurra, N.S.W. Biannual journal of the Potters' Society, well illustrated.

Tactile, 100 Avenue Road, Toronto, Canada, M4V 2H3 Bimonthly publication of the Canadian Guild of Potters, with coverage of exhibitions, technical articles, and Guild news.

Selected Specialized and Survey Texts

General Texts and Contemporary Ceramics

Birks, Tony. *The Art of the Modern Potter.* New York: Van Nostrand Reinhold, 1977. Treats some of the experimental British potters.

Cardew, Michael. *Pioneer Pottery.* New York: St. Martin's Press, 1976.

Casson, Michael. *Pottery in Britain Today.* New York: Transatlantic Arts, 1967.

Charleston, Robert L. *World Ceramics.* New York: McGraw-Hill, 1968. A historical survey of the ceramics of the major world cultures.

Coyne, John, ed. *The Penland School of Crafts Book of Pottery.* New York: Bobbs-Merrill, 1975. Illustrates the step-by-step process of the handbuilding, throwing, and glazing techniques of eight of Penland's potters.

Cox, Warren E. *The Book of Pottery and Porcelain.* New York: Crown, 1953. A historical survey of world ceramics.

Hetts, Karel, and Rada Pravoslav. *Modern Ceramics.* London: Drury House, 1965.

Lewenstein, Eileen, and Emmanuel Cooper. *New Ceramics.* New York: Van Nostrand Reinhold, 1974.

Ramie, Georges. *Picasso's Ceramics.* New York: Viking, 1976.

Woodhouse, Charles P. *The World's Master Potters.* New York: Pitman, 1975. Discusses historical ceramics with an emphasis on the evolution of materials and techniques.

Ancient, Mediterranean, and Classical Ceramics

Alexion, Styliaros, Nicolaos Platon, and Hanni Gunanella. *Ancient Crete.* New York: Praeger, 1968.

Arias, P. E. *Greek Vase Painting.* New York: Abrams, 1961.

Boardman, John. *Pre-Classical, from Crete to Archaic Greek.* Baltimore: Penguin, 1967.

Chamoux, François. *Greek Art.* Greenwich, Conn.: New York Graphic Society, 1966.

Hambridge, Jay. *Dynamic Symmetry: The Greek Vase.* New York: Dover, 1967. Reprint of the 1920 edition.

Hutchinson, R. W. *Prehistoric Crete.* Baltimore: Penguin, 1962.

Martinatos, Spyridon. *Crete and Mycenae.* New York: Abrams, 1960.

Noble, Joseph Veach. *The Techniques of Painted Attic Pottery.* New York: Watson-Guptill, 1965.

Petrie, Flinders. *The Making of Egypt.* London: Sheldon Press, 1939.

Platon, Nicolaos. *Crete.* Cleveland, Ohio: World Publishing, 1966.

Raphael, Max. *Civilization in Egypt.* New York: Pantheon, 1947.

————. *Prehistoric Pottery.* New York: Pantheon, 1947.

Richardson, Emeline Hill. *The Etruscans.* Chicago: University of Chicago Press, 1964.

Richter, Gisela M., and Marjorie Milne. *Shapes and Names of Greek Vases.* New York: Metropolitan Museum of Art, 1935.

Swedish Institute in Rome. *Etruscan Culture.* New York: Columbia University Press, 1962.

Far Eastern Ceramics

Beurdeley, Michel. *Chinese Trade Porcelain.* Rutland, Vt.: Tuttle, 1966.

Chang, K.C. *The Archaeology of Ancient China.* New Haven: Yale University Press, 1977.

Egami, Namio. *The Beginnings of Japanese Art.* New York: Weatherhill/Heibonsha, 1973.

Griffing, Robert P. *The Art of the Korean Potter.* New York: Asia Society, 1968.

Hayashiya, Seizo, and Gakuji Hasebe. *Chinese Ceramics.* Rutland, Vt.: Tuttle, 1966.

Ho, Ping-Ti. *The Cradle of the East.* Chicago: University of Chicago Press, 1975.

Hobson, R.L. *Chinese Pottery and Porcelain.* New York: Dover, 1976 (reprint of 1915 edition).

Honey, William Bowyer. *The Ceramic Art of China.* London: Faber and Faber, 1944.

————. *Japanese Pottery.* New York: Praeger, 1970.

Jenyns, Soame. *Later Chinese Porcelain.* New York: Yoseloff, 1965.

Kidder, J. Edward. *Prehistoric Japanese Arts: Jomon Pottery*. New York: Kodansha International, 1969.

Kim, Chewon and Won-Yong Kim. *Treasures of Korean Art*. New York: Abrams, 1966.

Koyama, Fugio, and John Figgess. *Two Thousand Years of Oriental Ceramics*. New York: Abrams, 1960.

Leach, Bernard. *Hamada, Potter*. New York: Kodansha International, 1975.

———. *Kenzan and His Tradition*. London: Faber and Faber, 1966.

Medley, Margaret. *Yuan Porcelain and Stoneware*. London: Pitman, 1974.

Mikami, Tsugio. *The Art of Japanese Ceramics*. New York: Weatherhill/Heibonsha, 1972.

Miki, Fumio. *Haniwa*. New York: Weatherhill/Shibundo, 1974.

Munsterberg, Hugo. *The Ceramic Art of Japan*. Rutland, Vt.: Tuttle, 1964.

Peterson, Susan Harnly. *Shoji Hamada: His Way and Work*. New York: Kodansha International, 1974.

Prodan, Mario. *The Art of the T'ang Potter*. London: Thames and Hudson, 1960.

Islamic, Hispano-Moresque, and African Ceramics

Frothingham, Alice Wilson. *Lusterware of Spain*. New York: Hispanic Society of America, 1951.

Grube, Ernest J. *The World of Islam*. London: Hamlyn, 1966.

Lane, Arthur. *Early Islamic Pottery*. New York: Van Nostrand, 1948.

———. *Later Islamic Pottery*. London: Faber and Faber, 1957.

Meauzé, Pierre. *African Art*. Cleveland: World Publishing, 1967.

Mellaart, James. *The Neolithic of the Near East*. New York: Scribner, 1976.

Newman, Thelma. *Contemporary Afri-can Arts and Crafts: On-Site Working with Forms and Processes*. New York: Crown, 1974.

Wassing, René S. *African Art*. New York: Abrams, 1968.

Wilkinson, Charles K. *Iranian Ceramics*. New York: Abrams, 1963.

Wilson, Ralph Pinder. *Islamic Art*. New York: Macmillan, 1957.

Yoshida, Mitsukuni. *In Search of Persian Pottery*. New York: Weatherhill, 1972.

Medieval through 19th-Century European Ceramics

Berendson, Anne. *Tiles, A General History*. New York: Viking, 1967.

Hiller, Bevis. *Pottery and Porcelain, 1700–1914*. New York: Meredith, 1968.

Honey, William B. *European Ceramic Art*. London: Faber and Faber, 1949.

Lane, Arthur. *Italian Porcelain*. London: Faber and Faber, 1954.

Liverani, Giuseppe. *Five Centuries of Italian Majolica*. New York: McGraw-Hill, 1960.

Mountford, Arnold R. *Staffordshire Salt-Glazed Stoneware*. London: Barrie & Jenkins, 1971.

Rackham, Bernard. *Medieval English Pottery*. New York: Van Nostrand, 1949.

Savage, George. *Eighteenth Century German Porcelain*. New York: Tudor, 1968.

Pre-Columbian and Colonial American Ceramics

Anton, Ferdinand, and Frederick J. Dockstader. *Pre-Columbian Art*. New York: Abrams, 1968.

Barrett, Richard Carter. *Bennington Pottery and Porcelain*. New York: Bonanza, 1958.

Bushnell, G. H. S. *Ancient American Pottery*. New York: Pitman, 1955.

Disselhoff, H.D., and S. Linne. *The Art of Ancient America*. New York: Crown, 1960.

Dockstader, Frederick J. *Indian Art in South America*. Greenwich, Conn.: New York Graphic, 1967.

Evans, Paul. *Art and Pottery of the United States*. New York: Scribner, 1974.

Guilland, Harold. *Early American Folk Pottery*. Radnor, Pa.: Chilton, 1971.

Haberland, Wolfgang. *The Art of North America*. New York: Crown, 1964.

Ketchum, William C., Jr. *Early Potters and Potteries of New York State*. New York: Funk and Wagnalls, 1970.

Kubler, George. *The Art and Architecture of Ancient America*. Baltimore: Penguin, 1962.

Lehmann, Henri. *Pre-Columbian Ceramics*. New York: Viking, 1962.

Litto, Gergrude. *South American Folk Pottery*. New York: Watson-Guptill, 1976.

Peterson, Susan. *The Living Tradition of Maria Martinez*. New York: Kodansha International, 1977.

Ramsay, John. *American Potters and Pottery*. New York: Tudor, 1947.

Spargo, John. *Early American Pottery and China*. New York: Century Library of American Antiques, 1926.

von Hagen, Victor W. *The Desert Kingdoms of Peru*. Greenwich, Conn.: New York Graphic, 1964.

Watkins, Jura W. *Early New England Potters and Their Wares*. Hamden, Conn.: Anchron, 1968.

Webster, Donald Blake. *Decorated Stoneware Pottery of North America*. Rutland, Vt.: Tuttle, 1970.

Willey, Gordon R. *An Introduction to American Archaeology*. Englewood Cliffs, N.J.: Prentice-Hall, 1966.

Glossary

absorbency The ability of a material (clay, plaster of paris, and so forth) to soak up water.

acid One of three types of chemicals that constitute a glaze, the other two being the bases and the intermediates or neutrals. The acid group is symbolized by the radical RO_2. The most important acid is silica (SiO_2).

Albany slip A natural clay containing sufficient fluxes to melt and function as a glaze. It develops a dark brown-black glaze at cones 8 to 10 without any additions. Since it is mined in several localities in the vicinity of Albany, N. Y., its composition may vary slightly from time to time. Similar clays, found in various sections of the United States, were much used by early American stoneware potteries.

alkali Generally, the base compounds of sodium and potassium but also the alkaline earth compounds lime and magnesia. They function as fluxes, combining easily with silica at relatively low temperatures.

alumina (Al_2O_3) A major ingredient found in all clays and glazes. It is the chief oxide in the neutral group (R_2O_3) and imparts greater strength and higher firing temperatures to the body and glaze. When added to a glaze, it will assist in the formation of mat textures, inhibit devitrification, and increase the viscosity of the glaze during firing.

ash Generally, the ashes of trees, straw, leaves, and so forth. It is commonly used to provide from 40 to 60 percent of high-temperature glaze ingredients. Depending upon the type, ash will contain from 40 to 75 percent silica, from 5 to 15 percent alumina, and smaller amounts of iron, phosphorus, lime, potash, and magnesia.

aventurine A type of glaze in which single, often small, crystals are suspended in the glaze surface. The glaze usually contains soda, lead, or boric oxide flux often with an excess of iron oxide (more than 6 percent).

bag wall A baffle wall in a kiln, separating the chamber from the combustion area.

ball clay An extremely fine-grained, plastic, sedimentary clay. Although ball clay contains much organic matter, it fires white or near white in color. It is usually added to porcelain and white ware bodies to increase plasticity.

ball mill A porcelain jar filled with flint pebbles and rotated with either a wet or dry charge of chemicals. It is used to blend and to grind glaze and body ingredients.

barium carbonate ($BaCO_3$) A chemical used in combination with other fluxes to form mats in the low-temperature range. A very small percentage ($\frac{1}{4}$ to 2) added to a clay body will prevent discoloration caused by soluble sulphates, such as the whitish blotches often seen on red bricks and earthenware bodies.

basalt ware A hard, black, unglazed stoneware body developed about 1775 by the Wedgwood pottery in England in an effort to imitate classical wares.

bat A disk or slab of plaster of paris on which pottery is formed or dried. It is also used to remove excess moisture from plastic clay.

batch Raw chemicals comprising a ceramic glaze that have been weighed out in a specific proportion designed to melt at a predetermined temperature.

bentonite An extremely plastic clay, formed by decomposed volcanic ash and glaze, which is used to render short clays workable and to aid glaze suspensions.

binders Various materials gums, polyvinyl alcohol, and methylcellulose—that increase glaze adherence or impart strength to a cast or pressed clay body.

bisque or biscuit Unglazed ware fired to a temperature sufficient to harden but not mature the body.

bisque fire Preliminary firing to harden the body, usually at about cone 010, prior to glazing and subsequent glaze firing.

bistone Coarse crushed quartz used in saggers to support thin porcelain in the bisque.

blowing (bloating) The bursting or warping of pots in a kiln caused by a too-rapid temperature rise. The water content of the clay turns into steam and forces the body to distort or expand and explode.

blunger A mixing machine with revolving paddles used to prepare large quantities of clay slip or glaze.

bone china A hard, translucent white

ware produced chiefly in England. The body contains a large amount of bone ash (calcium phosphate), which allows it to mature at cone 6. It is not very plastic and is therefore difficult to form; it also tends to warp.

calcine To heat a ceramic material or mixture to the temperature necessary to drive off the chemical water, carbon dioxide, and other volatile gases. Some fusion may occur, in which case the material must be ground. This is the process used in the production of plaster of paris, Portland cement, and ceramic stains.

casting (or slip casting) A reproductive process of forming clay objects by pouring a clay slip into a hollow plaster mold and allowing it to remain long enough for a layer of clay to thicken on the mold wall. After hardening, the clay object is removed.

celadon A glaze characterized by a soft gray-green color that results from firing iron oxide in a reduction atmosphere. Because of the likeness to jade, celadon glazes were much favored by the ancient Chinese.

chemical water Water (H_2O) chemically combined in the glaze and body compounds. At approximately 842°F (450°C) during the firing cycle this water will begin to leave the body and glaze as water vapor. Little shrinkage occurs at this point, although there is a loss in weight.

china A loosely applied term referring to white ware bodies fired at low porcelain temperatures. They are generally vitreous, with an absorbency of less than 2 percent, and may be translucent.

china clay See kaolin.

clay A decomposed granite-type rock. To be classed as a clay the decomposed rock must have fine particles so that it will be plastic. Clays should be free of vegetable matter but will often contain other impurities, which affect their color and firing temperatures. They are classified into various types, such as ball clays, fireclays, and slip clays. Pure clay is expressed chemically as $Al_2O_3 \cdot 2SiO_2 \cdot 2H_2O$.

coefficient of expansion The ratio of change between the length of a material mass and the temperature to which it is subjected.

coiling A hand method of forming

pottery by building up the walls with ropelike rolls of clay and then smoothing over the joints.

combing A method of decoration developed by dragging a coarse comb or tip of a feather over two contrasting layers of wet clay slip or glaze.

Cornwall stone (also Cornish stone) A feldspathic material found in England and widely used there for porcelain-like bodies and glazes. Compared to American feldspar, it contains more silica and a small amount, though a greater variety, of fluxes. It comes closest to approximating the Chinese *petuntze,* which is a major ingredient of Oriental porcelain bodies and glazes.

crackle glaze A glaze containing minute cracks in the surface. The cracks are decorative and are often accentuated by coloring matter that is rubbed in. They are caused in cooling by the different rates at which the body and the glaze contract after firing.

crawling Separation of a glaze coating from the clay body during firing, caused by too heavy application, resulting in exposed areas of unglazed clay.

crazing An undesirable and excessive crackle in the glaze, which penetrates through the glaze to the clay body. It should be remedied by adjusting the glaze or body composition to obtain a more uniform contraction ratio.

crocus martis Purple red oxide of iron, used as a red-brown glaze colorant.

crystal glazes Glazes characterized by crystalline clusters of various shapes and colors embedded in a more uniform and opaque glaze. Macrocrystals are larger than aventurine and may on occasion cover the entire surface. The glaze ingredients generally used are iron, lime, zinc, or rutile with an alkaline flux, high silica, and low alumina ratio. A slow cooling cycle is necessary for the development of the crystals.

cupric and cuprous oxides Copper oxides (CuO, Cu_2O), the major green colorants. They will also produce red under reducing conditions, with an alkaline flux.

damp box A lined metal cabinet in which unfinished clay objects are stored to prevent them from drying.

decals Designs produced on thin sheets of paper and transferred to a glazed surface after being soaked in water. When fired to cones 020 to 018, the designs become permanent.

deflocculant Sodium carbonate or sodium silicate used in a casting slip to reduce the amount of water necessary and to maintain a better suspension.

Delft ware A light-colored pottery body covered with a lead-tin glaze, with overglaze decoration in cobalt on the unfired glaze. Delft was first made in Holland in imitation of Chinese blue-and-white porcelain.

della Robbia ware Ceramic sculpture of glazed terra cotta, generally in relief, produced in Florence by Lucca della Robbia or his family during the 15th century. The glaze used was the lead-tin majolica type developed in Spain.

dipping Glazing pottery by immersing it in a large pan or vat of glaze.

dryfoot To clean the bottom of a glazed piece before firing.

dunting Cracking of fired ware in a cooling kiln, the result of opening the flues and cooling too rapidly.

earthenware Low-fire pottery (below cone 03), usually red or tan in color with an absorbency of from 5 to 20 percent.

eggshell porcelain Translucent, thin-walled porcelain.

Egyptian paste A clay body that has glaze-forming ingredients and colorants incorporated into the body in a soluble form. The body is nonplastic and fires to between cones 08 and 05. First developed by the Egyptians before 5000 B.C., this paste was the earliest form of glaze known.

empirical formula A glaze formula expressed in molecular proportions.

engobe A prepared slip that is halfway between a glaze and a clay; contains clay, feldspar, flint, a flux, plus colorants. Usually applied to damp ware although may be used on bisque ware.

equivalent weight A weight that will yield one unit of a component (RO or R_2O_3or RO_2) in a compound. This is usually the same as the molecular weight of the chemical compound in question. In ceramic calculations, equivalent weights are also assigned to the RO, R_2O_3, and RO_2

oxide groups that make up the compound. If one of these oxide groups contains more than one unit of the oxide, its equivalent weight would be found by dividing the compound molecular weight by this unit number. (*See* Chap. 7.)

eutectic The lowest melting point of the mixture of materials composing a glaze. This is always lower than the melting points of the individual materials.

faience Earthenware covered with a lead-tin glaze; a French term for earthenware derived from the Italian pottery center at Faenza, which, during the Renaissance, produced this ware partially in imitation of Spanish majolica. (*See* also majolica and Delft ware.)

fat clay A plastic clay such as ball clay.

ferric and ferrous oxides (Fe_2O_3 and FeO) Red and black iron oxide. As impurities in clay, they lower the firing temperature. They are the chief source of tan and brown ceramic colors and, under reducing conditions, the various celadon greens.

fire box Combustion chamber of a gas, oil, or wood-fired kiln, usually directly below the kiln chamber.

fireclay A clay having a slightly higher percentage of fluxes than pure clay (kaolin). It fires tan or gray in color and is used in the manufacture of refractory materials, such as bricks and muffles for industrial glass and steel furnaces. It is often quite plastic and may be used by the studio potter as an ingredient of stoneware bodies.

flint *See* silica.

flocculation Thickening or settling of a glaze or slip.

flues Passageways around the kiln chamber through which the heating gases pass from the firebox to the chimney.

flux Lowest-melting compound in a glaze, such as lead, borax, soda ash, or lime, and including the potash or soda contained in the feldspar. The flux combines easily with silica and thereby helps higher-melting alumina-silica compounds to form a glass.

foot The ringlike base of a ceramic piece, usually formed by tooling the excess clay.

frit A partial or complete glaze that is melted and then reground for the purpose of eliminating the toxic effects of lead or the solubility of such compounds as borax or soda ash.

frit china A glossy, partly translucent chinaware produced by adding a glass frit to the body.

galena Lead sulphide, used as a flux for earthenware glazes; more common in Europe than in the United States.

glaze A liquid suspension of finely ground minerals that is applied by brushing, pouring, or spraying on the surface of bisque-fired ceramic ware. After drying the ware is fired to the temperature at which the glaze ingredients will melt together to form a glassy surface coating.

glaze fire A firing cycle to the temperature at which the glaze materials will melt to form a glasslike surface coating. This is usually at the point of maximum body maturity, and it is considerably higher than the bisque fire.

glost fire Another term for a glaze firing.

greenware Pottery that has not been bisque fired.

grog Hard fired clay that has been crushed or ground to various particle sizes. It is used to open up a raku body or to reduce shrinkage in such ceramic products as sculpture and architectural terra cotta tiles, which, because of their thickness, have drying and shrinkage problems. From 20 to 40 percent grog may be used, depending upon the amount of detail desired and whether the pieces are free standing or pressed in molds. Finely crushed grog is also used in throwing bodies to help the clay stand up.

grolleg A refined English kaolin that is relatively plastic.

gum arabic or gum tragacanth Natural gums used in glazes as binders to promote better glaze adhesion to the body. Binders are necessary for fritted glazes containing little or no raw clay. They are also useful when a bisque fire accidentally goes too high, or in reglazing. The gum, of course, burns out completely during the fire.

hard paste True porcelain that is fired to cone 12 or above; also called *hard porcelain.*

ilmenite ($TiO_2 \cdot FeO$) An important source of titanium. In the granular form it is used to give dark flecks to the glaze. It is often sprinkled upon the wet glaze without previous mixing.

iron oxide *See* ferric oxide.

jiggering, jollying An industrial method of producing pottery. A slab of soft clay is placed upon a revolving plaster mold of the object to be formed. As the wheel head turns, a metal template on a moving arm trims off the excess clay and forms the reverse side of the piece.

kanthol A special metal alloy produced in Sweden for wire or strip elements in electric kilns firing from cones 03 to 12.

kaolin ($Al_2O_3 \cdot 2SiO_2 \cdot 2H_2O$) Pure clay, also known as china clay. It is used in glaze and porcelain bodies and fires to a pure white. Sedimentary kaolins found in Florida are more plastic than the residual types found in the Carolinas and Georgia.

kiln A furnace made of refractory clay materials for firing ceramic products.

kiln furniture Refractory shelves and posts upon which ceramic ware is placed while being fired in the kiln.

kiln wash A protective coating of refractory materials applied to the surface of the shelves and the kiln floor to prevent excess glaze from fusing the ware to the shelves. An inexpensive and effective wash can be made from equal parts of flint and kaolin.

lead White lead [basic lead carbonates $2PbCO_3 \cdot Pb(OH)_2$], red lead (Pb_3O_4), and galena (lead sulphide, PbS) are among the most common low-fire fluxes.

leather hard The condition of the raw ware when most of the moisture has left the body but when it is still plastic enough to be carved or joined.

limestone A major flux in the medium- and high-fire temperature ranges when it is powdered in the form of whiting (calcium carbonate). If a coarse sand is used as a grog, it should not contain limestone particles.

luster A type of metallic decoration thought to have been discovered in Egypt and further developed in Persia during the 9th and 14th centuries.

A mixture of a metallic salt, resin, and bismuth nitrate is applied to a glazed piece and then refired at a lower temperature. The temperature, however, must be sufficient to melt the metal and leave a thin layer on the decorated portions.

luting A method of joining together two pieces of dry or leather-hard clay with a slip.

macaloid A refined magnesium montmorillonite clay. Used as a flocculating agent in glazes or a plasticizer in clay bodies.

majolica Earthenware covered with a soft tin-lead glaze, often with a luster decoration. The ware originally came from Spain and derived its name from the island of Majorca, which lay on the trade route to Italy. Faenza ware was greatly influenced by these Spanish imports. All Renaissance pottery of this type is now generally called majolica ware.

mat glaze A dull-surfaced glaze with no gloss but pleasant to the touch, not to be confused with an incompletely fired glaze. Mat surfaces can be developed by the addition of barium carbonate or alumina, and a slow cooling cycle.

maturity The temperature or time at which a clay or clay body develops the desirable characteristics of maximum nonporosity and hardness; or the point at which the glaze ingredients enter into complete fusion, developing a strong bond with the body, a stable structure, maximum resistance to abrasion, and a pleasant surface texture.

mold A form or box, usually made of plaster of paris, containing a hollow negative shape. The positive form is made by pouring either wet plaster or slip into this hollow. (*See* casting.)

muffle A lining, made of refractory materials, forming the kiln chamber, around which the hot gases pass from the firebox to the chimney. The purpose is to protect the ware from the direct flames of the fire and the resulting combustion impurities. Some of these panels may be removed for a reduction fire.

muffle kiln A kiln with muffle features as opposed to a kiln using saggers. (*See* saggers.)

mullite A mineral with interlocking needlelike crystals of aluminum silicate $(3Al_2O_3 \cdot 2SiO_2)$ which begin to form in high-temperature bodies between cones 06 and 6. This formation is responsible for much of the greater toughness and hardness of stoneware and porcelain, and in particular for the closer union developed between the glaze and the body.

neutral fire A fire that is neither oxidizing nor reducing. Actually, this can be obtained only in practice by a slight alternation between oxidation and reduction.

opacifier A chemical whose crystals are relatively insoluble in the glaze, thereby preventing light from penetrating the glass formation. Tin oxide is by far the best opacifier. Zirconium and titanium oxides are also used. Many other oxides are effective in certain combinations and within limited firing ranges. These are commercially available in frit forms under trade names, such as Zircopax, Opax, and Ultrox.

overglaze Decoration applied with overglaze colors on glazed and fired ware. The firing of the overglaze decoration is at a lower temperature than the glaze fire.

overglaze colors Colors applied on top of other glazes and containing coloring oxides or ceramic stains, a flux, and some type of binder. The fluxes are necessary to allow the colors to melt into the harder glaze beneath. The lower temperatures at which most overglazes are fired (about cones 016–013) allow the use of colorants that are unstable at higher temperatures.

oxidizing fire A fire during which the kiln chamber retains an ample supply of oxygen. This means that the combustion in the firebox must be perfectly adjusted. An electric kiln always gives an oxidizing fire.

paste The compounded bodies of European-type porcelains.

peach bloom A Chinese copper-red reduction glaze with a peachlike pink color.

peeling Separation of the glaze or slip from the body. Peeling may be caused when slip is applied to a body that is too dry, or when a glaze is applied too thickly or to a dusty surface.

peephole A hole placed in the firebox, kiln chamber, or muffle flues of a kiln, through which one can observe the cones or the process of combustion.

petuntze A partially decomposed feldspathic rock found in China, roughly similar in composition to Cornwall stone. With kaolin it forms the body of Oriental porcelains.

plaster of paris Hydrate of calcium sulphate, made by calcining gypsum. It hardens after being mixed with water. Because it absorbs moisture and it can be cut and shaped easily, it is used in ceramics for drying and throwing bats, as well as for molds and casting work.

plasticity The quality of clay that allows it to be manipulated and still maintain its shape without cracking or sagging.

porcelain (Chinese) A hard, nonabsorbent clay body, white or gray in color, that rings when struck.

porcelain (hard) A hard, nonabsorbent clay body that is white and translucent. In both types of porcelain the bisque is low-fired and the glaze is very high-fired (generally cones 14–16).

press-forming A commercial production method for forming clay objects by pressing soft clay between two plaster molds.

pug mill A machine for mixing plastic clay.

pyrometer An instrument for measuring heat at high temperatures. It consists of a calibrated dial connected to wires made of two different alloys, the welded tips of which protrude into the kiln chamber. When heated, this welded junction sets up a minute electrical current, which registers on the indicating dial.

pyrometric cones Small triangular cones ($1\frac{1}{8}$ and $2\frac{5}{8}$ inches in height) made of ceramic materials that are compounded to bend and melt at specific temperatures, thus enabling the potter to determine when the firing is complete.

quartz Flint or silica (SiO_2).

quartz inversion The changing of the crystalline structure of quartz (silica) during firing. The resultant expansion and contraction necessitates a slow cycle of heating and cooling.

raku Glazed, groggy earthenware originated in Japan and associated with the tea ceremony. Raku ware is unique in that the glazed preheated bisque is placed in the red-hot kiln with long-handled tongs. The glaze matures in 15 to 30 minutes, and the ware is then withdrawn and cooled immediately.

reducing agent Glaze or body material such as silicon carbide, which combines with oxygen to form carbon monoxide during the firing.

reduction fire A firing using insufficient oxygen; carbon monoxide thus formed unites with oxygen from the body and glaze to form carbon dioxide, producing color changes in coloring oxides.

refractory The quality of resisting the effects of high temperatures; also materials, high in alumina and silica, that are used for making kiln insulation, muffles, and kiln furniture.

rib A tool of wood, bone, or metal that is held in the hand while throwing to assist in shaping the pot or to compact the clay.

RO, R_2O_3, RO_2 The symbols or radicals for the three major groups of chemicals that make up a ceramic glaze. The RO radical refers to the base chemicals, such as the oxides of sodium, potassium, calcium, and lead which function in the glaze as fluxing agents. The R_2O_3 radical refers to the neutral or amphoteric oxides, some of which may on occasion function either as bases or acids. The chief oxide in this group is alumina (Al_2O_3), which always reacts as a refractory element. The third radical, RO_2, stands for the acid group, the glass formers, such as silica (SiO_2).

rouge flambé A type of Chinese copper-red reduction glaze (*sang de boeuf*) which is a mottled deep red with green and blue hues, also called a transmutation glaze.

rutile An impure form of titanium dioxide (TiO_2) containing much iron. It will give a light yellow or tan color to the glaze, with a streaked and runny effect. Used in large amounts, it will raise the maturing temperature.

sagger Round boxlike container of fireclay used in kilns lacking muffles. The glazed ware is placed in a sagger to protect the glaze from the combustion gases.

sagger clay A refractory clay able to withstand the thermal shock of the repeated firings of saggers. Often plastic and suitable for inclusion in a stoneware body.

salt glaze A glaze developed by throwing salt (NaCl) into a hot kiln. The salt vaporizes and combines with the silica in the body to form sodium silicate, a hard glassy glaze. A salt kiln is of a slightly different construction and is limited in use to the salt glaze.

sang de boeuf The French term for oxblood, which describes the rich, deep-red hues produced by the Chinese in their copper-red reduction glazes.

sgraffito Decoration achieved by scratching through a colored slip or a glaze to show the contrasting body color beneath.

shard A broken fragment of pottery.

short Descriptive of a body or clay lacking in plasticity.

shrinkage Contraction of the clay in either drying or firing. In the firing cycle the major body shrinkage for stoneware clays begins at approximately cone 09. Earthenware clays will begin to fuse and shrink at slightly lower temperatures.

silica Flint (SiO_2) produced in the United States by grinding almost pure flint sand.

silicate of soda A deflocculant. A standard solution of sodium silicate (commercial **N** brand) has the ratio of 1 part soda to 3.3 parts silica. Specific gravity 1.395.

single fire A firing cycle in which the normal bisque and glaze firings are combined. The advantages are a great saving of fuel and labor and development of a stronger bond between the body and the glaze. These are partially offset by the need for greater care in handling the ware, plus the danger of cracking if in glazing the raw pieces absorb too much moisture. In a salt glaze, however, these disadvantages do not occur.

sintering A firing process in which ceramic compounds fuse sufficiently to form a solid mass upon cooling but are not vitrified. An example is low-fire earthenware.

slab construction A handbuilding method in which forms are created by joining flat pieces of clay. The pieces are thinned and flattened with a rolling pin or slab roller.

slip A clay in liquid suspension.

slip casting *See* casting.

slip clay A clay such as Albany or Michigan containing sufficient fluxes to function as a glaze with little or no additions.

spinel Chemically, magnesium aluminate ($MgO \cdot Al_2O_3$), an extremely hard crystal arranged in an octahedron atomic structure. In ceramics, a spinel is a crystal used as a colorant in place of the metallic oxides because of its greater resistance to change by either the fluxing action of the glaze or the effects of higher temperatures.

spray booth A boxlike booth equipped with a ventilating fan to remove spray dust, which, whether toxic or not, is harmful when inhaled.

spraying Applying glazes with a compressed-air spray machine, the chief commercial method.

sprigging Applying clay in a plastic state to form a relief decoration.

stain Sometimes a single coloring oxide, but usually a combination of oxides, plus alumina, flint, and a fluxing compound. This mixture is calcined and then finely ground and washed. The purpose is to form a stable coloring agent not likely to be altered by the action of the glaze or heat. While stains are employed as glaze colorants, their chief use is as overglaze and underglaze decorations and body colorants.

stilt A ceramic tripod upon which glazed ware is placed in the kiln. Tripods with nickel-nichrome wire points are often used to minimize blemishes in the glaze.

stoneware A high-fire ware (above cone 6) with slight or no absorbency. It is usually gray in color but may be tan or slightly reddish. Stoneware is similar in many respects to porcelain, the chief difference being increased plasticity and the color, which is the result of iron and other impurities in the clay.

talc ($3MgO \cdot 4SiO_2 \cdot H_2O$) A compound used in most white ware bodies in the low to moderate firing ranges as a source of silica and flux. It is slightly plastic and can be used to lower the firing range, if need be, of a stoneware or fireclay body.

temmoku A Japanese term for a stoneware glaze high in iron that creates a streaked surface (*hare's fur*) or a mottled appearance (*oil spot*).

terra cotta An earthenware body, generally red in color and containing grog. It is the common body type used for ceramic sculpture.

terra sigillata The red slip glaze used by the Romans, similar to the Etruscan *bucchero* and Greek *black varnish* ware and made of fine decanted particles of red clay.

thixotropic clay A body containing alkaline electrolytes, which permit it to change to a fluid state when shaken. When allowed to rest, it returns to a plastic gel form.

throwing Forming plastic clay on a potter's wheel.

tin enamel A term used incorrectly to describe the tin-lead majolica type glaze. An enamel is a very low-fire glaze used as an overglaze decoration. It was extensively used by the Turks and the late Ming and Ch'ing potters.

tin-vanadium stain A major yellow colorant produced by a calcined mixture of tin and vanadium oxides.

trailing A method of decorating by applying slip with a rubber syringe.

translucency The ability of a thin porcelain or white ware body to transmit a diffused light.

turning or tooling Trimming the walls and foot of a pot on the wheel while the clay is leather-hard.

underglaze Colored decoration applied to the bisque ware before the glaze coating.

Veegum T Trade name for a refined magnesium silicate used as a flocculant in glazes and plasticizer in clay bodies.

viscosity The nonrunning quality of a glaze, caused by glaze chemicals that resist the flowing action of the glaze flux.

vitreous Pertaining to the hard, glassy, and nonabsorbent quality of a body or glaze.

volatilization Action under influence of extreme heat of the kiln in which some glaze elements turn successively from a solid to a liquid, and finally into a gaseous state.

ware Pottery or porcelain in the raw, bisque, or glazed state.

warping Distortion of a pot in drying because of uneven wall thickness or a warm draft of air, or in firing when a kiln does not heat uniformly.

water glass Another term for a liquid solution of sodium silicate that is used as a deflocculant.

water smoking The initial phase of the firing cycle up to a dull red heat (1000°–1100°F, 537°–594°C). Depending upon the thickness of the ware, this may take from two or three hours for thin pottery, up to twelve hours for sculpture. The heat rise must be gradual to allow atmospheric and chemical water to escape. In some cases there will be organic impurities which will also burn out, releasing carbon monoxide.

wax resist A method of decorating pottery by brushing on a design with a hot melted wax solution or a wax emulsion. This will prevent an applied stain or glaze from adhering to the decorated portions. The wax may be applied to either the raw or bisque ware, over or between two layers of glaze.

weathering The exposure of raw clay to the action of rain, sun, and freezing weather, which breaks down the particle size and renders the clay more plastic.

wedging Kneading plastic clay with the fingers and heels of the hands in a rocking spiral motion, which forces out trapped air pockets and develops a uniform texture.

white ware Pottery or china ware with a white or light cream-colored body.

whiting Calcium carbonate ($CaCO_3$), similar chemically to limestone and marble; a major high-fire flux.

zircopax Trade name of a commercial frit used as an opacifier. It is composed primarily of zirconium oxide and silica. It is about half as strong as tin oxide, but its price is much lower regardless of the quantity used.

Index

Photographic Sources